The Last Cow in the Chute

& other stories

[Second Edition]

Memoirs of a Country Vet
- 1 -

David E. Larsen, DVM

Wiley Creek
Publishers

The Last Cow in the Chute & other stories
[Second Edition]
Wiley Creek Publishers
Corvallis, Oregon

David E. Larsen, DVM
4859 SW Aster St.
Corvallis, Oregon 97333
email: d.e.larsen.dvm@peak.org
blog: docsmemoirs.com

Print ISBN: 979-8-9865226-4-7
eISBN: 979-8-9865226-5-4

Book design, editing & production:
David E. Larsen, DVM/Wiley Creek Publishers

Cover design by Eva Long/Long on Books
www.longonbooks.com

Printed in the USA

~

*To my wife, Sandy,
and the kids, Brenda, Amy, DeLaine, and Derek,
all of whom put up with a country vet's lifestyle
where a single ring of the telephone
could dash the best weekend plans.*

Contents

Author's Note

In this second edition, the stories I have added to the originals are stories that are gleaned mostly from my memory, as few early records survive. They are presented in a rough chronological order. But in a small town mixed veterinary practice in the 1970s and 1980s, there was little control in what came through the door. And to some degree, these memoirs try to reflect that chaos.

The Last Cow in the Chute is the first book in my *Memoirs of a Country Vet* series and are snapshots in my life. Stories of my early life, my Army experience, and my college days are told in my fifth book, *The Making of a Country Veterinarian* and reflect the challenges and opportunities I encountered on the path I chose to become a small town country vet.

David E. Fors

The *Memoirs of a Country Vet* Series

1

The Needle in the Brier Patch

The phone had shocked me awake from a sound sleep, the clock said 3:00 a.m. It was Ayers on the phone. Ayers was an old logger with a small farm on Scott Mountain. He had lost an eye in the woods, and I always had trouble making eye contact with his good eye rather than his glass eye.

"Doc, I have a cow down up on the hill, she is in bad shape. Glenn Hill and I have been looking for her all night." I hung up the phone and pulled myself out of bed and quickly dressed. The truck was cold at first but started to warm as I headed down the hill to the highway through Sweet Home.

The rain seemed heavier as I turned up Scott Mountain Road. Ayers had reminded me not to come to the house. "They would meet me at the upper corner of his place. The cow was close to that corner." I slowed the truck as I turned the corner, straining through the night and heavy rain to get a glimpse of Ayers. There they were, a couple of shadowy figures moving out from under a large tree. Dressed in rain gear and both wearing wide brim hats, they looked like something out of a Jesse James movie.

I waved as I stepped around the back of the truck. Ayers and Glenn Hill, a neighbor, both waved back. "Bring your stuff, and we will spread the wire so you can get through the fence."

Spreading the fence wire for me was quite an honor. My grandfather would have tanned our hides if he had seen any of us kids stretching the fence wire when we were growing up.

"This is that half Holstein cow. I raised her from a calf. She is about five or six years old. Calved yesterday, we have been looking for her all night. She rolled down the hill into a big old patch of Himalayan berry vines. One hell of a fix, she is flat out, Doc."

I grabbed the bucket filled with supplies and headed across the ditch full of runoff and ducked through the barbed wire that Ayers and Glenn were holding apart for me. I peered into the tunnel in the brier patch. Ayers shined his flashlight down into the tunnel, maybe thirty feet down the hill; you could see the cow. She was lucky her head was uphill, probably why she was still alive.

"How the hell did you find her?" I asked.

"Let me tell you, it wasn't easy. We looked all night in this damn rain, almost gave up but finally worked our way up to this corner. Glenn is the one who noticed this hole in the brush. I was surprised to see her down there."

With a deep breath, I squatted down, and sort of duck walked down the tunnel of briers to the cow. Her head was up, allowing the rumen gas to escape.

The rain clothes provided protection from more than constant rain. There was minimal room, and every stray movement was met with a tangle of berry vines. My exam was very cursory. I had already made my diagnosis of milk fever, I just wanted to make sure I wasn't going to miss something obvious.

The temperature was low, 98°, her udder normal, no vaginal discharge, rectal exam shows firm dry stool. All this was consistent with the diagnosis. Response to treatment will be the last confirmation.

I grasped the nostrils with the nose tongs and pulled her head back, tying the tongs to the hock with a quick release knot. I opened a bottle of Cal Dextro #2 and secured the IV set to the top. Everything was sterile, but that was sort of joke at this point. The rain was still heavy, but the vines caught the downpour and converted it to large heavy drops. Mud and rain, couldn't keep things clean. I took the needle out of the autoclaved pouch and leaned against her neck to further stabilize her. Holding the jugular vein with my left hand, needle in my right hand, held by thumb and forefinger, I struck the jugular with the heel of my right hand twice in a rapid motion and then turned my hand and seated the needle into the vein on the third stroke. Releasing my grip on the needle as it passed through the skin kept it from piercing through the vein. Then I quickly threaded it down the vein. I learned this technique when I worked in the feedlots while in school.

Hooking the IV set to the needle, I started the infusion at a rapid rate for the first bottle. Giving it too fast could cause a cardiac arrest (dead cow). Seldom happened to a cow this far advanced, her blood calcium could be below 4.0.

I leaned back and rested a little, looked at Ayers. He was concerned, hadn't said a word, just held the flashlight and watched.

"Milk fever!" I said. "Not an uncommon condition in older dairy cows. She would have been dead in the morning, good thing you found her."

"Is she going be okay?"

"I think you will be surprised. Might take a couple of bottles here and a little time but there is a good chance she will walk out of here."

When the first bottle was done, she was a little more alert but not struggling against the restraint. I started the second bottle a little slower. I couldn't decide what was worse, the torrential downpour or the constant large drops.

By the time the second bottle was done, she was struggling against the nose tongs. I pulled the needle out and put everything back into the bucket. I moved around to her side and pulled the free end of the rope, this released her nose. Her head swung around and almost knocked me down. I was able to pull the nose tongs out of her nose. She kicked and righted herself to her sternum, then in one motion, sprang to her feet and raced up the hill and out the tunnel. Glenn who was watching from the entrance had to jump out of her way. Ayers went flying one direction, and I went the other. The bucket and its contents were scattered.

When I got off my back, Ayers was still unhooking himself from the briers.

"Damn glad I was dressed for the rain," he said as he gathered the light and started to give me a hand.

I grabbed the bucket, a little bent now, and started putting things back into it. Everything was there, except the needle. Before me was a mire of mud, cow tracks, and footprints. I swept my hands across the wet ground.

"What are you looking for?"

"I lost the needle. Should be here somewhere."

Ayers helped me look for a minute or so then looked at me with his one good eye and asked, "Is it valuable?" His eyebrow over his good eye raised up a little for emphasis.

"No, not valuable, just not the kind of thing you don't want to leave behind."

"Look Doc, it's three o'clock in the damn morning, raining like hell. Here we are in the middle of large brier patch at the far corner of my place. There isn't going to be anybody in here for the next hundred years. Just leave it."

Made sense to me, besides I had a full day ahead of me. So I left the needle. We crawled up the tunnel and into the drenching rain. It felt good to stand up straight again.

Glenn was still standing there, looking somewhat like a drowned rat. "That was some show. What did you give her Doc? I might need some of that stuff."

I crawled back through the fence and stuffed things into the truck. I will have a chore cleaning things up in the morning. I peeled my raincoat off, just about as wet inside as outside.

I pulled myself into the truck and shut the door. Dry at last. Will be a short night tonight, I thought as I started up the hill looking for a spot to turn around.

***

The sun was hot, dust stuck to the back of your throat. It was one of those August days in the Willamette. Valley that made one wish fall would come early. I leaned over the low gate to get a better look at the horn on the old ram, trying not to disrupt his interest in the alfalfa in the feed rack.

Every movement stirred up more dust.

Flies were gathered around an ugly spot on the side of his head where the tip of his horn was buried into the skin.

A full curl plus some, this old ram would be a trophy in the wild. Ayers had called, worried about his ram.

Arthritic enough that he probably had problems getting around to service the ewes. It was late in the day before we had been able to work him in. The good part was I could go home after this, the sad part was it was the hottest time of the day.

Ayers had been a little embarrassed about having me look at the old guy.

"He probably ain't worth the cost of the call, poor old guy, probably should just put him out of his misery," Ayers had said when called.

Ayers was an old logger who ran a few sheep and cows on a forty-acre ranch out in Liberty.

He had lost one eye when a broken cable had recoiled and struck him on the right side of his head.

Probably lucky that it didn't take his head off.

Ayers was a big raw-bone Scotsman, well over six feet with broad shoulders and a sturdy frame.

His calloused hands and coarse complexion told of many years of hard work and exposure to the elements.

He was tough as nails but had a soft heart when it came to his animals.

"Sure enough, the tip of that horn is buried in the skin. We probably don't want to take the whole horn off, that would be pretty hard on a ram this old. I should be able just to trim the end and solve the problem for a couple of years."

"Couple of years? This guy will be lucky to survive the winter."

We put a halter on the ram with a little struggle and snubbed his chin to the upper corner of the stall. I retrieved a short piece of OB wire from my bag and threaded it around the tip of the horn. Then I clamped a handle on each end. Positioned the wire saw about one inch from the skin. Leaning back to apply my weight to the wire I started long slow strokes to get the wire embedded. At that point, I quickened the pace. Smoke rose from the horn. Makes the smell on the old dentist drill seem like nothing. Only took a few seconds and the tip of the horn flew over my left shoulder as I fought to regain my balance. Checking the horn where the tip had been, and there was no blood. A good thing about the wire saw, the heat generated usually cauterized any vessels.

I used a prep blade to shave the wool away from the wound. A few maggots had already hatched and were scurrying to avoid the Betadine. The horn had left a hole almost to the bone. It would do well after I cleaned the wound and applied Betadine ointment and screw worm spray. Long-acting Penicillin injection completed the treatment. I released his head, removed the halter and opened the gate. The ram looked at us like we were crazy, he returned to the alfalfa in the feed rack.

"This must be your last call?" Ayers asked, knowing full well that I wouldn't have anything scheduled after five-thirty on a Friday afternoon. He had asked me to have a drink with him on each visit for the last six months. I had always had the excuse of having more to do.

"Yes, this is my last call today."

"I have a new bottle of Pinch, best scotch that I know. Come on up the house and have a drink. You can wash up there."

"Sure, I'll put things away and pull the truck up there." Ayers was holding the door for me when I got there.

"New bar of soap right there at the sink, a clean towel is hanging on the hook."

After washing Ayers led me to the dining room table. His wife was sitting at the kitchen table and did not respond to us. I knew that she was suffering from Alzheimer's. Her care had really confined Ayers in recent months. Ayers grabbed a couple of large drinking glasses as we entered the dining room. New bottle of Pinch was on the table. I think he had planned this visit.

"Just a moment, I have a new bottle of soda, don't want to ruin good scotch with an old bottle of soda."

Ayers returned from the kitchen with ice and a new bottle of Schweppes Club Soda. He added a few ice cubes to each glass. Opened the Pinch and poured first two fingers then three into each glass. Filled the glasses with soda and sat down with a noticeable sigh.

"Love this stuff, about the only thing I have anymore. She doesn't remember anything now," nodding his head toward his wife, "makes things pretty tough."

I wasn't quite ready for a counseling session and never was very good at small talk. Taking a sip of the drink, I was a little surprised that it was pretty good. I hadn't drunk scotch since early in my army days at Fort Devens. This was maybe going to be easier than I thought.

"Must be difficult, do you have anybody to help?"

"Lady comes in the mornings, helps to get her up and through the bathroom and shower. Fixes breakfast and cleans the house a little. When she leaves she just sits there in the kitchen until bedtime." We continued to talk, mostly about Ayers' early days in the woods before he lost his eye, then about the developing cataract in his only remaining eye. Cataract surgery was advanced enough that most people went through it without a thought or worry. It would be different if you had only one eye. That low complication rate doesn't mean much if you are the one with the complication. "Do you remember that night that you lost that needle up in that brier patch four or five years ago?"

"Do I remember? That was quite a night, pretty hard to forget."

"Well, a couple of months ago I decided to clear some brush up in that corner. Don't know why, sure don't need any more and I can't do as
much as I used to do. I was working along, and damned if I didn't step right on that needle! It went through the sole of my boot, through my foot and poked out the top of my boot. Damn, that hurt! I sat down and pulled it out, that hurt like hell too.

"I was a real mess for a while. Limped around for better than a week. I was going to go to the doctor and get a tetanus shot but started to feel better, so I forgot about that. Must have been okay, I'm still alive. Maybe because that was a sterile needle?'

"I don't know, Ayers, that needle couldn't have been too sterile, lying in the mud and dirt for the last few years."

"Well, no matter now. I was the one who wanted you to leave it so I could get back to bed." ~

Ernie's Pig

I stood in the barnyard facing a long metal barn. Not a soul in sight. The barn is about ninety feet long, maybe thirty feet wide with ten foot walls. The light breeze coming off the Calapooia River stirs a little dust. Still, it feels cool in the midday heat of July in the Willamette Valley.

Ernie had called, saying he needed emergency help with a pig. There was no other explanation. I pondered my next step. The house looked empty, nobody ran to meet me. My guess was they must be in the barn.

Then I heard a very faint, "Help!" Where did that come from? It was too weak for me to get a bearing. Then it happened again. "Help!" A little louder this time, or maybe I was expecting it. It came from the barn, probably the left end.

I entered the barn and started threading my way toward the far corner. Now I could see them. Ernie's son-in-law, a stout young man with glasses and a crew cut, was lying across this hundred-and-fifty-pound pig, holding him down. Ernie, a thin, wiry old guy, was lying behind the pig holding a pile of intestines protruding from the rear end of the pig. The floor was loose dirt, and every movement produced a cloud of dust the settled on the men, the pig, and the pile of intestines.

"Thank God you made it, Doc," Ernie said. "I can't hold this much longer."

I walked over to them, trying not to not stir up too much dust. They were castrating this pig, and they had a big hernia with a pile of intestines that would fill a gallon bucket protruding from the scrotal incision. I looked close, the other testicle remained, that was a good thing. That would allow me to quickly sedate this pig and see if I could clean things up and replace all the gut.

"Hang on just a little longer, Ernie," I said. "I have to get a few things from the truck, and then I think we have a shot at fixing this guy up."

I slowly moved away from the group and then ran to the truck to gather things:—a drop cloth to put everything on, a plastic bag to put under the guts, an emasculator, surgery pack, scalpel blade, bucket of water with Betadine scrub and solution, suture material, fly spray and antibiotics. One bucket with water, the other full of everything else. I almost forgot the Pentothal. I mixed a five-gram bottle and drew up three grams into a 60-cc syringe, attaching a sixteen-gauge, one and one-half-inch needle to the syringe.

The office was too busy for me to bring anybody to help, and I could have used an extra hand right now. I knew that I would probably forget something, so I went over the list in my mind one more time before heading back into the barn.

"Just another couple of minutes and I will let you relax, Ernie," I said as I started laying out the drop cloth, moving Ernie a little to the side. Then I slid the plastic under the intestines.

"Now you can let them go, Ernie, we'll just let them lie here for a few minutes," I said. Ernie let them go, and he just rolled away, laying on his back in the dust with his bloody hands in the air.

I washed my hands and swabbed the scrotum over the intact testicle. This testicle was several inches in diameter and over four inches long. I popped the 16-gauge needle into the testicle up to the hub. The pig was about as tired as Ernie and only slightly flinched. I injected the three grams of Pentothal into the testicle. "This guy will be asleep in a minute, and you can also rest," I

said to Bill. He had been quiet throughout the whole time.

I opened the surgery pack quickly and attached the scalpel blade. The pig was pretty sleepy now. I incised the scrotum over the testicle and through the tunic. I squeezed the testicle out of the scrotum and clamped the cord with large Oschner forceps.

"You can relax now," I said to Bill. "I have him under control.

Just stay close in case I need you."

The beauty of this anesthesia in castration is the clamp on the cord. If the pig starts to stir, I release the clamp and let a little more anesthetic into his circulation. When I get the hernia repaired, I will remove this testicle and he will wake up pretty quickly.

Now I turn my attention to the gut pile. Covered with dust, but there does not appear to be any tears or other injuries. They are a little purple, but the time frame is such that they should be okay if I can replace them. I rinse the dust off with a good splash of water. Then Betadine Surgical Scrub, a little more water, and a good scrub.

"If you could take this other bucket and fill it with water from the hose in the back of the truck, I would appreciate it," I say to Bill. He jumps up and grabs the bucket. I think he wanted to have a little break.

"Doc, is he a goner?" Ernie asked as he sat up, mostly recovered from his ordeal.

"I think things look pretty good, Ernie," I replied. "I get these guts back where they belong and close up this hernia, he should be good to go."

"I'll be damned if I'm going to try to save a farm call again," Ernie said. "I'm done with castrating pigs."

"It is a lot easier if you do it when they're small," I said. "However, you could still have this problem even on the little ones."

Bill got back with the water. I made a solution with the Betadine solution in the bucket. Port wine color, they always said in school. I don't think I ever saw port wine. I flushed the guts with a large splash, then holding the mass up level with the inguinal canal, I began to feed them back into the abdomen. When the guts were mostly back into the abdomen, I freed the tunic from the scrotal tissues. Twisting the tunic like I was closing a plastic bag, the last of the exposed intestines squirted back into the abdomen. Then I placed a clamp across the tunic to hold everything in place while I got the suture ready.

I released the clamp on the testicle for a couple of minutes and watched as the pig made a big sigh. Then I reapplied the clamp.

I placed a transfixing suture of #2 Dexon on the tunic. Then I palpated the external inguinal ring. I could put three fingers into the ring. I placed one mattress suture in the posterior half of the ring and tightened it to close the ring's size. This done, I emasculated the other testicle. Again on this side, I freed the tunic and closed it up and sutured it closed. The external ring on this side felt normal. I don't remember ever seeing a bilateral hernia in pigs.

I squirted both incisions with Betadine solution and sprayed the whole area with fly spray. Then I gave a large dose of Amoxicillin SQ in the front quarter. The pig was starting to stir a little.

"He'll be on his feet before I have everything back in the truck," I said as I started gathering things up.

"Boy, was ever glad to see you, Doc," Ernie said with a still-bloody hand on my shoulder. "I don't know what we would have done without you, just would have had to butcher him, I guess."

"Just remember, Ernie, next time do it when they're little," I replied.

"I'm thankful you could come so quickly, I guess I wasn't even thinking of how much it was going to cost. Just remember, Doc, when you're filling out the bill, he's just a pig, can't be worth much," Ernie said.

"Well, Ernie, I'll tell you one thing: He's worth a damn site more today than he was yesterday," I replied. ~

A Saturday Afternoon Outbreak

Back in 1976, I remember an almost a perfect Saturday afternoon. Late August in the Willamette Valley provides a short stretch of weather that acts as an interlude between the summer heat and fall's rains.

Sandy and I were still getting settled into our newly purchased house. The kids were outside working in the garden and playing in the grass. I started to consider setting up the garage to see patients for a couple of months while waiting for the clinic construction to be completed.

The afternoon's calm was broken when the phone rang. "Doc, I know this is Saturday evening," Dave said while trying to catch his breath. "But Doc, I was just out in the pasture and I have seven dead calves, all about two months old. They were healthy as could be yesterday. I have about thirty more out there. What do you think I have going on?"

"It sounds like we need to get a necropsy on one or two of those dead calves," I said. "The Diagnostic Lab at OSU is closed for the weekend. I can do a necropsy, but any lab work would need to wait until Monday."

"If seven of them died overnight, they might be all dead by Monday," Dave said.

"I agree, Dave," I said. "I have a pretty good background in pathology. I worked in the necropsy room at Colorado State University the summer following my sophomore year in vet school. I can likely get a good diagnosis with a gross necropsy. I'll collect samples, just in case we need them for Monday."

Seven dead calves amounted to about fifteen percent of his herd. That was probably the profit for the year, at least a good chunk of it. A dead animal usually was not an absolute emergency, unless it was a herd animal. Unless it was a bunch of animals that died in a short time.

Dave had all seven dead calves lined up at the pasture gate when I pulled in the driveway.

What a waste. All seven calves were in good shape, looked good for a couple of months old. I surveyed the herd out in the pasture. Good pasture for August, and the herd looked like nothing was wrong.

"Where do they get their water?" I asked.

"There is a pond, just over the rise, at the far end. You can't see it from here."

I pulled on a pair of gloves and looked over all the calves. Jaundice was evident in each one.

"Let's take the smallest one and pull him over here out of the pasture," I said. "We don't want to contaminate things any more than they are already."

I laid the calf on his left side and quickly reflected his skin and right legs, stretching them out over his back. I took a moment to remember Dr. Norrdin's words, "Work with your mouth closed." Then I opened the chest and abdomen. The chest was fine, but the liver was swollen and dark in color. The urine in his bladder colored with bile. This was an acute outbreak of leptospirosis.

Lepto was known to cause abortion "storms" in pregnant cow herds. Acute outbreaks in young calves occurred only rarely. It always amazed me how I always seemed to see all the rare events in my first couple of years out of school.

I collected samples for the lab on Monday if we needed them, liver, kidney, spleen, gall bladder, urine, and blood. Then I roughly closed the animal up.

15

"Dave, I think you have an unusual outbreak of Lepto in these young calves."

"Is there anything we can do to stop it?" Dave asked. "Have you had any cows abort this year?" I asked.

"We had one cow abort about a week ago. I never thought much about it. It's not unusual for us to have an abortion or two every year."

"There's an antibiotic treatment that will stop an abortion storm in cows. The entire herd is treated with a single dose of streptomycin. I don't think anything is written about controlling an outbreak in young calves. But my guess is if it stops abortions in a herd, it will stop an outbreak in calves."

"So where am I going to get enough streptomycin to treat a herd at this hour on Saturday evening?" Dave asked.

"You're lucky enough that I ordered it on my initial stocking order. I didn't think I would ever use it, but I wanted to have it on hand. So, I think I have you covered in that regard."

"There are a couple of other items we need to cover," I said. "Number one, this is contagious to people. And it can do the same thing to people that it does to these calves. I was just talking with Dr. Craig the other day. He worked a herd with another veterinarian, and they both got sick. Dr. Craig went to the doctor as soon as he noted some blood in his urine and he got well. The other veterinarian waited till the next morning, he died."

"Number two is the pond. Lepto is usually spread via contaminated water sources. If you had a cow with a Lepto abortion, she sheds organisms in her urine for several weeks. If she pees in or near that pond, calves that drink out of the pond can end up here," I said as I pointed to the dead calves.

"You need to fence that pond and put a water tank in the pasture," I said.

"Do you think I should inject these calves tonight?" Dave asked. "If you're up to it, that's what I would recommend," I said. "You might wake up in the morning with another batch of dead calves." "I'll get you enough streptomycin and vaccine," I said. "I would give both. Lepto vaccines have some limitations in that there are many strains of Lepto. The vaccine protects against three of the most common strains, but there are others, and there is not a lotof cross-protection. It's the best we can do at the moment." "What should I do with these calves?" Dave asked.

"Move them out of the pasture. If you have the rendering truck pick them up, that's okay. Otherwise, bury them deep. And don't let the dogs get into this calf that we opened. They can get this also."

I fixed up Dave with the necessary antibiotic and dosages and left him enough vaccine for the entire herd. He had a crew coming to help him. When I left that evening, I left him with one last piece of advice.

"Dave, you make sure everyone works with their mouth closed tonight," I said. "And make sure they shower before going to bed."

"Thanks, Doc, wish me luck," Dave said.

"There's very little luck in this business. That's why it's important to do things the best we can at all times," I said. "I'll give you a call in the morning."

***

I spent a long time drinking my coffee in the morning, and Sandy noticed.

"What's wrong with you this morning?" she asked.

"I'm dreading calling Dave," I said, picking up the phone. "I'm hopeful that I solved his immediate problem last night, but if I didn't, he might have a bigger problem this morning."

"Dave, this is Doc. I was just checking in with you on how things went last night and how things look this morning," I said. "We got the herd done, had to get out some floodlights for the tail end of it, but they're done. Things look good so far this morn-

ing. I have a couple of guys stringing an electric fence around the pond this morning, and I have a small water tank in the pasture. I'm getting ready to run to Albany and see if I can pick up a large tank. Can't thank you enough, Doc. I'll keep you posted."

Dave never had another problem, and the lab confirmed the Lepto diagnosis on Monday. In the next forty years, I never saw another outbreak like this one. Go figure the odds. ~

A Summer Evening on Strychnine

B ill was brief and to the point on the phone. "I have a dog here who seems to be having a short seizure every few minutes,"

Bill said. "We were wondering if you could get a look at him?" "I've only been in town a couple of days, and I don't have all my stuff," I replied. "Does he have a history of seizures, or is this a new thing?"

"There are a bunch of kids here today," Bill said. "They've been running all over the hills. One of the girls thinks he's been poisoned." The sun was down, and the twilight was fading when I pulled into Bill's driveway. It looked like a large group had gathered on the front lawn of the farmhouse—guys and gals all about high school age or a little older. A young liver and white springer spaniel was in the middle of the group. He was quiet, but immediately went into seizures when I closed the car door.

Dixie, a young blond, hovered over Max. The others showed little concern.

"He's been getting worse, almost by the minute," Dixie said. "He got into something down by the road, along the fence line. I think it must have been poison."

"Was there an old deer carcass down there, or anything like that?" I said. "Sometimes, dogs can get pretty toxic from a belly full of rotten meat."

"No, we stopped and looked," Dixie said. "We couldn't find anything."

The guys were throwing a football, and it bounced past us. Max's legs stiffened, and he stood like a sawhorse for a moment before falling onto his right side. All four of his legs were extended and shaking, and his head pulled back over his shoulders. His entire body was stiff, with every muscle contracted. His respiration was only is short, rapid, inefficient little puffs of air.

"This looks like strychnine," I said. "Try not to stimulate him, I'll get an injection for him."

The bag that I carried was limited at this point. My pharmacy supplies were still arriving daily. I did have some Pentothal, which I mixed rapidly, with sterile water.

Max relaxed when the first few millimeters were in his vein. I continued the injection until he was completely relaxed and breathing comfortably. Then I placed an IV catheter in his front leg, capped it, and taped in securely in place.

"Strychnine kills when these convulsive seizures eventually cause respiratory paralysis," I explained. "At this point, we need to keep Max quiet, in a darkened room and sedated."

"How long does this injection last?" Dixie asked.

"Not long enough," I said. "It's best to use some pentobarbital. It's longer lasting, but it's no longer available to veterinarians. This stuff is about the same, but shorter duration. It does accumulate, so with each dose, the duration is longer."

Bill was standing over us now. "What are we going to do with him now?" Bill asked. "I'm not going to sit up with him all night. And I wouldn't know how much of that stuff to give him."

"I'm without a clinic," I said. "Right now, we're house hunting, and we're in a two-bedroom apartment with a baby and three other kids. And no pets are allowed. But I guess Max is a patient, not a pet. I can take him home with me and keep him sedated tonight. If I give you a call in the morning, can you come by and pick him up?"

"I'm an early riser," Bill said. "You give me a call, and I'll run right in and get him. You sound like you're pretty sure he's going to be alright."

"You want me to be honest?" I said. "The only time I've seen strychnine toxicity was in a lab in school. There's not much to do unless you get to them early. At this stage, there's no way I can give oral medication. It's just a matter of keeping him sedated until things wear off. He'll look a little hungover in the morning, but other than that, he should be good to go."

"When I talked with Stan at the feed store, he said you seemed to be a straight shooter," Bill said. "I like it when a guy is honest, even if it's not to his benefit."

I gave Max a small second dose of Pentothal before loading him in the back of our station wagon. He was still asleep when I carried him into the apartment.

"Where are you going to put him?" Sandy asked.

We were bursting at the seams. The three girls were in one bedroom, and Derek, who was a couple of months old, was in our bedroom in a small crib. I bedded Max down in the bathtub. I would be up hourly for the first half of the night. Then I could probably stretch out the checks a little. With the darkened room and quiet environment, he probably won't need too much more Pentothal tonight.

***

In the morning, Max was awake. Like I had told Bill, he looked like he had been out drinking all night. I offered him a small bowl of water from Sandy's best dishes. He lapped it up and was looking for more. I gave him another bowl before I called Bill.

"Bill, Max is awake and doing well," I said into the phone. "You can pick him up at any time. We probably aren't going anywhere this morning, but the girls will be up shortly, and they'll want to keep him if he stays around too long."

"I'll be right in," Bill said. "His kennel mate is sort of acting lost this morning."

The girls were up, and they squealed when they found a dog in the bathtub.

"No, he is not ours, and you can't keep him," I explained.

Max was licking hands and faces, I think he enjoyed the attention but was looking for a bite to eat also.

"Can I give him some cereal for breakfast?" Brenda asked. "You can just give him a small handful," I said. "His stomach is probably a little upset right now."

***

Bill's knock at the door was a welcome sound.

"Good morning," I said as I opened the door. "Max is going to be happy to see you, I think. He hasn't quite figured out where all these little girls have come from yet."

"He likes kids, always has," Bill said. "Is he walking, or do I need to carry him?"

"I haven't had him up, but when the girls got up, he really perked up," I said. "I'm pretty sure he'll walk out of here. Did you bring a leash?"

"He wouldn't know what a leash was," Bill said. "He'll just follow me."

We walked to the bathroom door, and Max looked up and jumped out of the tub in an instant.

"Come on, Max," Bill said as he handed me a check. "Thanks a lot, we're happy to see you in town. Let's go home, Max."

Max's tail stump was going a hundred miles an hour as he crowded to get through the door ahead of Bill. Bill smiled and chuckled, something I would learn was characteristic for him.

In the following year, Dixie would come to work with us. She was our most stable employee, working on and off for over thirty years. ~

It's Only a Bump, Doc

C huck was waiting patiently in the reception area. He was preoccupied with keeping his old dog, Hank, calm. Hank was sitting beside Chuck's chair, and Chuck had his hand on his back.

Hank was a Mastiff and an old one at that. I have been seeing Hank several times a since I came to town. He was over ten years old, ancient for a giant breed dog.

"Ruth, let's get Chuck and Hank into an exam room," I said. "Chuck looks pretty worried."

Ruth showed them into an exam room, and I gave her a few minutes to set things up before going into the room.

"How are things going, Chuck," I said as I shook hands.

"I'm doing okay, but Hank here has bumped his leg," Chuck said. "I debated about having you look at it. I didn't want to waste your time on a little bump."

"You don't have to worry about wasting my time, Chuck," I said. "And Hank is no spring chicken. Sometimes it is important to look at those little bumps."

Hank was sitting, trying to ignore my presence. I guess he figured if I was talking with Chuck, he was safe.

"Let's get a look at this bump," I said as I knelt down to look Hank in the eye. A long drool of saliva fell from the side of his mouth, almost reaching the floor before it broke free from his mouth. "Where is this bump?"

"It's right there on the inside of his left front leg, Doc," Chuck said. "Low on the leg, just above that lower joint."

My heart sank as I picked up Hank's left front leg. There was this boney swelling on the inside of the lower leg. All the odds, and all my experience, said this was a bone tumor.

"What's wrong, Doc?" Chuck asked as he noticed my change of expression.

Chuck's wife had passed away five years ago. Since that time, Hank has been his sole companion. How am I going to tell him that Hank is on borrowed time?

"Chuck, I think we should get an x-ray of this bump," I said.

"It's only a bump, Doc. Right?" Chuck asked.

"That's what an x-ray will tell us," I said.

"Doc, this isn't like you. You are always straightforward, almost to matter of fact, most of the time," Chuck said. "What are you thinking?"

"Chuck, I'm thinking this might be a bad bump," I said. "This is where a lot of bone cancers develop in old giant breed dogs."

"Bone cancer doesn't sound good," Chuck said. "Is there anything that can be done?"

"Let's not get ahead of ourselves, Chuck," I said. "Let's see what the x-ray looks like, and then we can talk about what needs to be done. This will take us a little time to get this film. We have several people to take care of first. Maybe if you go over to Mollie's, have a cup of coffee, and check back in about an hour."

"All you're going to do is take an x-ray, right?" Chuck asked as he patted Hank on the head.

"That's all we are going to do," I said. "You go relax for a bit, and we will have a set of films to look at when you get back over here."

We worked through the other patients and managed to get an x-ray of Hank.

"I want to make sure those films are dry when Chuck gets back," I said as Ruth hung the films on the drying rack in the dark room.

When I got a chance to look at films on the viewer, my fears were confirmed. On the distal end of the radius, there was a boney swelling with a star-burst eruption starting at the surface.

"Is that a bone cancer?" Ruth asked.

"Yes, when I was in school, this film would confirm the diagnosis," I said. "Today, I probably can't find a radiologist that would make that diagnosis without a biopsy, or at least cytolog."

"Chuck isn't going to want to hear this," Ruth said. "This old dog has been his whole world since Marilyn died."

I could see Chuck walking across the street, coming from Mollie's. I met him at the door with Hank on a leash.

"Let's step back to the surgery room, Chuck," I said. "We have a better viewer back there."

I placed the two x-rays on the viewer.

"So, here is the bump," I said as I pointed to the lesion on the bone. "Chuck, I don't have any good news here. In my mind, this is a bone cancer until I prove otherwise."

"What does that mean for Hank, Doc?" Chuck asked.

"If I'm right, Hank's days are numbered," I said. "There are a couple of things we can do to confirm the diagnosis. The radiologist is going to say we need to do a bone biopsy. We might be able to get a pathologist to confirm the diagnosis with cytology on a needle aspirate. But most of the time, they will also want a biopsy."

Chuck looked at Hank, sitting at Chuck's side, sort of pressed up against his leg.

"I don't want to put this old guy through a bunch of surgery or other stuff," Chuck said. "You sound like you're pretty confident in your diagnosis."

"When I was in school, not too awful long ago, these x-rays would be considered diagnostic," I said. "Time changes things for the experts."

"You're about the only expert Hank is going to see," Chuck said. "If this is a bone tumor, is there any treatment that will cure it?"

"Cure is a big word," I said. "No, Chuck, nothing is going to cure this. We can talk about buying some time, but that comes with some expense for Hank."

"Hank doesn't have many dollars," Chuck said with a wry smile.

"I'm not talking about dollars. I'm talking about the quality of life for his final days," I said. "There is good evidence that if we amputate this leg, we can buy some time by removing this primary tumor."

"Doc, it's just a little bump," Chuck said. "You can't mean you want to take his leg for that little bump, can you?"

"Chuck, this little bump is going to grow," I said. "In a couple of months, give or take some, this bump will be much larger. Then it will do one or two things. It will break open and drain, and/or the bone will fracture. Taking the leg removes all of that and allows Hank to live a little longer. The problem is Hank is a big old dog. He isn't going to be able to handle an amputation like a young dog. And this amputation only removes the primary tumor. Most of the time, these tumors have gone elsewhere in the body by this point, so the amputation is not curative."

"Doc, we aren't going to take his leg off," Chuck said. "Let's just make him comfortable and give the old guy whatever time he has left."

"I can agree with that, Chuck," I said. "The only problem is that most people go too long. If this tumor ruptures, that is not a big thing, but it will be very painful for Hank if the bone fractures."

Chuck was quiet for a couple of minutes while he looked at Hank and petted his head.

"Doc, I think we will go camp on one of the high lakes for a couple of weeks," Chuck said. "Hank used to love going camping up there and going fishing. I haven't done that since

Marilyn has been gone. Hank and I have just sat around and grown old. We will go fishing for a couple of weeks, and then we'll come to see you again."

"That will be good for both of you," I said. "I will fix you up with some pain medication. And by then, there will be enough change in this little bump, so we will know for sure what's going on with it."

***

It was close to a month when Chuck returned with Hank. The little bump had grown into a large swelling, and Hank was in obvious pain.

"We had a great time," Chuck said. "It wasn't like old times, but we still had fun. We even caught a few fish. But Doc, I'm afraid that you were right on all counts. I noticed this swelling was draining a little last night. Hank and I think that it's time for him to go sit by the fire with Marilyn in that great living room in the sky."

"How do you want to do this, Chuck?" I asked.

"We talked about that a lot last night," Chuck said. "Doc, I just can't stay. Hank and I decided that we want you to take Hank and send him on his way, and then if I could come back in a week or two and pick up his ashes, that would be great."

And that was the way it was done. With tears streaming down his face, Chuck said goodbye to Hank, stood up, did a military about-face, and marched out the clinic door.

Hank looked at me, and I imagined a tear from him as he lifted his sore leg and waited.

Dinner with Roy

We moved to Sweet Home in June of 1976. Or at least Sandy and the kids moved in June, I still had some contract obligations in Enumclaw, Washington, so I came and went for a few weeks. The clinic was scheduled to be finished in August, but there was one delay after the other, and it was evident that it was going to be months after August before it was completed.

When I finally moved to Sweet Home, we were going to have to have a plan B while we waited for the clinic to be completed. Clinic equipment was arriving daily, and the small apartment we had rented was bursting at the seams. We had finally put earnest money down on a house, so there was light at the end of the tunnel. I had enough equipment to start a house call practice. The phone had been ringing with the growing community awareness that we had moved to town. I was not swamped, but I was generating some income, so we were not going to starve just yet.

In late July, I took the time to visit all the other veterinarians in the county. Most were surprised that I chose to start a practice in Sweet Home. They were cordial but not extremely excited. There is an old saying in the profession, "The difference between a colleague and a competitor is fifty miles." That was probably reflected in their responses.

Dr. Roy Craig was utterly different. He had started a practice on Golden Valley Road out of Lebanon just the year before, having moved from Nebraska. He was a large man, amiable, and had a firm handshake. Roy was a generation older than I, both in age and in education. The profession was beginning to change, and Roy and I reflected the fulcrum in that change. Roy was a WWII veteran and had been older when he graduated from vet school. My age and military experience gave us some common ground outside of the profession.

We discussed my situation, and Roy expressed concern. He was going on vacation for two weeks and would not be around to lend a hand if I needed help.

"You're going to need a clinic to fall back on sooner or later," he said with genuine concern.

"House calls are okay for routine stuff, but sooner or later you're going to need a clinic. Here, you take a key to this place. Use it like it is yours if you need it, and we'll see you when we get back." Roy handed me a key to his clinic after a half an hour of conversation. He really didn't know me from Adam. Try to find a man today who would do something like that for a colleague. I don't think Roy had heard that old saying, or at least it didn't mean anything to him. I tried to decline, but he would have none of it. This was the way it was, and there was no further discussion.

Roy, of course, was right. There did come a time in those weeks when I needed to use his clinic. A small dog with a ruptured bladder after being hit by a car required abdominal surgery. Most people can relate to cooking in someone else's kitchen where you don't know where anything is at. You ought to try doing surgery in someone else's surgery suite sometime. But I got through it, and I was forever in Roy's debt in my view of the world.

After they got home Sandy and I took Roy and Jenny to dinner at the Hereford Steer in Albany. In those years, the Hereford Steer was about as upscale as one could get in Albany. It was small payment for their generosity and allowed us to build on a new friendship. Sandy and Jenny got along well. Roy was much more of a talker than I, and dinner was just beginning when the storytelling started. I had not been in the profession nearly as long as Roy, but I was in a busy dairy practice in Enumclaw, so I had my share of stories also. People often complain about how veterinarians can talk shop and tell stories over dinner, but for us, it is just the way it is. Veterinary medicine in the 1970s was a lifestyle as much as it was a career. Solo practice was the norm. That meant many long hours of work in professional isolation with few specialty people to send severe cases. If it was going to get done, it would be done by my hands. Family plans were often dashed due to the last-minute phone call, and the phone often started the day as early as 3:00 a.m.

Roy's voice was loud in normal conversation, and after a couple of drinks, I would guess it probably got deafening. With dinner over, we continued the storytelling and relaxed over a little Kahlua on the rocks. The evening wore on. We told stories of complicated deliveries, gaping wounds, abdominal surgeries, maggots, and pus.

It was in the middle of one of Roy's stories when I looked around and realized that we were alone in the middle of the large restaurant. The other folks and their tables had been moved as far away from us as possible. Some of the people were trying to ignore our discussion, and some were watching with horrified expressions.

It had been a great evening in our view. New friends and a colleague who I knew I could always depend on. My only concern was how was I going to be able to repay this man. The waitress, on the other hand, was very prompt when I raised a finger for the check. ~

Ageless Ida and Kitty

Ida was sitting beside her daughter, waiting patiently, with Kitty nestled in her lap. Ida was my oldest client, a tiny, frail old lady with snow-white hair. She lived by herself, but her daughter, Lila, was close at hand. Lila was no spring chicken herself.

Ida drove until a couple of years ago. She had expressed her disappointment to me when they took away her driver's license. She was fiercely independent, and she hated to have to impose herself on her daughter.

Kitty was an old tabby cat with a white blaze and a white chest. The record did not have a birth date for Kitty. That meant the girls probably disagreed with Ida's guess. Maybe I should resolve that issue today.

Ida slapped at her daughter when Lila tried to help her stand up with Kitty. She also refused the helping hand offered by the girl showing her to the exam room. She ambled toward the exam room with measured steps and cradled Kitty in her arms.

"Kitty has not been feeling well for several days," Ida said as she carefully positioned her on the exam table. "I had to crawl under my bed to get her this morning."

I had to take a moment to process that statement. I am not sure I could crawl under a bed to retrieve a cat, and I am a young man. Imagining this frail little lady crawling under her bed was difficult to conjure up in my mind.

"Ida, you shouldn't be doing that at your age," I said. "You should get one of your grandsons to help."

"They're always busy, and Lila is in worse shape than I am," Ida said. "Besides, if you quit doing things for yourself, pretty soon, they stick you in one of those prisons that they call all sorts of fancy names today."

"That's pretty good advice," I said. "Let's look and see if I can find out what's wrong with Kitty."

"Kitty is very old, she is twenty-six years old now," Ida said.

"That's pretty old for a cat. Are you sure of the date?" I asked.

"David, I got her as a kitten for my seventieth birthday," Ida said.

"I should know her age. I named her Kitty because cats never pay attention to a name but always come when you call kitty."

"I had no idea she was that old," I said. "I don't think I've seen another cat near that age. I did have a client who moved here from California with a seventeen-year-old cat. That cat aged two years every three months, according to the owner. It was twenty-five when he died a year later."

"I have a picture of Kitty and myself at my birthday party," Ida said. "That was the last birthday party I allowed Lila to give for me. They are sort of silly for old folks. They just use them as an excuse to take their picture with you. Just because you might not be around next year."

Kitty was lying on the exam table, unmoving through all this discussion. I petted her head and then ran my hand down the length of her body. There was a bump when I crossed her abdomen. I felt closer. It was a tumor, the size of an orange.

I looked at Ida, and she had a tear on her cheek.

"I felt it last week," she said. "I prayed it would go away, but that didn't help."

"Sometimes, we can remove these with surgery," I said. "That might be difficult at Kitty's age."

"No, I told her I wouldn't let you do any of that to her," Ida said, tears streaming down her cheeks now. "I don't know what I am going to do without her, Doctor. She's all I have to talk with now, all my friends are long gone."

Ida was purposely avoiding the discussion of euthanasia. I knew it had to be discussed, but I wanted her to bring it up. Maybe that wasn't going to happen.

"You should get a new cat," I said. "We could find you a kitten." "That wouldn't be fair to the kitten, David," Ida said. "I am not going to be around forever, you know."

"You could have your granddaughter help pick her out," I said. "She could know that it would be her responsibility when the time came."

"That might be a thought," Ida said. "But what are we going to do with Kitty? I don't want her to suffer."

"Is she eating at all?" I asked.

"She has been under my bed for three days," Ida said. "That's why I had to crawl under there to get her."

"I think she's waiting to die," I said. "Maybe it is time we talk about making that an easy process for her."

"Yes, I think that's what I thought when I called Lila this morning," Ida said. "Then I can take her home and bury her beside her favorite place in the back yard."

"You should get one of your grandsons to help you with that chore," I said.

"The ground is still soft, David," Ida said. "I'm not helpless. That's something I would like to do privately."

"It will only take a moment for me to put her to sleep," I said. "You can wait out front if you like, and we can bring her out in a small box."

"I think she will like to be looking into my eyes when she goes, I will wait right here," Ida said. "And I will take her home wrapped in her blanket. She would like it that way."

And that is precisely how it was done. Ida carefully wrapped Kitty in her blanket and wiped a tear from her eye before gathering her into her arms.

"Thank you, David," Ida said. "I will think about that kitten."

I watched as Lila helped her mother out the door, Ida slapping at her as she tried to hold Kitty.

That was the last time I saw Ida. Her obituary was in the paper a few months later. ~

Gus and the Manure Piles

Manure piles were—and still are to some extent—standard fare on Oregon farms. They were located around the barn somewhere, were built in many shapes and sizes, and served multiple uses. Smaller places had a simple pile outside a doorway where the barn was cleaned. Larger farms had more elaborate piles. In my experience their edges were the easiest place to collect a can of worms for a day's fishing. They also were used to dispose of small animals that were casualties during the year on the farm. They were the ultimate compost piles.

Gus was a typical barn cat, well past middle age when I first met him when I came to Sweet Home in 1976. Gus was lucky to have been neutered early in his life, but still had his share of scraps defending his turf. He was nothing special, gray tabby in color and not large, maybe eight pounds. He lived with his extended family on a small acreage on a hill outside of Sweet

35

Home. Grandma and Grandpa lived on the "farm." It was not much of a farm but enough for a few cows and sheep and a small barn. The son and his family lived about a quarter mile up the road on a neighboring tax lot. When Gus came to the clinic he came with Carol, the daughter-in-law.

Over the first few years of practice in Sweet Home, Gus was approaching his golden years. In those times I didn't see neutered male cats over fifteen years of age. This was before the advent of the feline leukemia vaccine, and diets did not address urinary tract and heart issues. For barn cats to reach that age was truly exceptional. One cold winter morning Grandpa hurried into his pickup truck in the carport on the side of the barn. It was cold and he was anxious to get the truck started. "Thump, thump" came from under the hood. Gus had sought the warmest spot he knew of to sleep the night before. The warm engine block was one of his favorites. Usually he was able to scramble out before the engine started, but this morning it didn't work.

Grandpa knew what the noise meant. He had seen more than one cat caught in a fan belt on cold mornings. He was disappointed when he found Gus, he had been such a good cat. Gus was a mess, broken leg with bone poking out, left eye hanging out of the socket, several large lacerations and bleeding from his mouth. In Grandpa's mind there was only one thing to do. Picking up a hammer, he made a quick whack to the back of Gus' head. Disposal was easy. Gus' final resting place was the manure pile on the other side of the barn.

In most cases that would be the end of the story, but remember, cats have nine lives and Gus had already used several of his just surviving to this advanced age. Now he would need to cash in all the others.

Carol had noticed that Gus had not been to his dish on the back porch for several days. She mentioned his unusual absence to Grandpa. Grandpa was quiet, knowing Carol would have rushed Gus to clinic and spent a lot of money on an old cat.

The next morning, she heard a noise on the porch. She opened the door and was aghast at the scene. There was Gus. Covered with manure, left eye hanging out, broken and torn. How had he managed to make it to the door? How had he known which door was the one to provide him help? She carefully boxed Gus and headed for the clinic. Grandpa was outside as she drove by so she stopped to show him what she had found. Grandpa had no choice but to confess. He said that the vet could do a better job than him, assuming that Gus would be put to sleep. In those years, in Sweet Home, if a cat couldn't be fixed for a hundred dollars it probably was not going to be fixed. Gus would surely be well over that figure. Carol laid Gus on the exam table and related the story. She wanted to know her options. Gus looked hopeless to me. Gus was a pitiful sight as he lay on the table, looking cautiously at me out of his one good eye.

What are your options, Gus? I thought to myself as I pondered the situation.

My initial thought that Grandpa had Gus' best interest at heart; he just didn't do the job very well. I'm not sure that was what his owner wanted to hear.

"We have a lot problems here" I started. "Contaminated compound fracture of the tibia, fracture of mandible, an eye that needs to be removed, broken teeth and multiple lacerations that are very contaminated. The first question we need to discuss is, do we want to put him through all this over the next few weeks?" Carol was quick to respond, "We are not going to put him to sleep, not until we don't have any other option. I don't care what it costs. If we have to, Grandpa can log a few trees. That's the least he can do after what he did to this cat."

I knew Grandpa. He would log his trees for his family or for the grandkids. I wasn't so sure about a cat.

Now we were on to option number two. Referral was out of the question. There were no specialty clinics around at that period of time. If Gus was going to survive it was going to be by my hands only.

We have several things to do, first we need to sedate him and get him cleaned up, get him on some fluids and antibiotics.

The wounds are too contaminated to close. If we clean them up and remove the grossly contaminated tissues, they'll heal if he lives long enough.

I can probably wire the jaw and remove the broken teeth. The eye is toast and has to go.

"The fractured tibia is too contaminated to fix, the ends of the bones are likely dead. The leg has to go."

Carol finally spoke, "I want to save the leg!" "Can't be done." I responded.

Again Carol spoke, "I want to save the leg, we can try!" "Okay, we can try, but if it happens it will be a miracle. And the leg will be short. We'll try. He'll have to stay a few days. I don't know what this will cost."

Carol left, convinced that Gus was going be back to his old self in a few days. Might take a little longer than that, I thought. We sedated him with a dose of ketamine and got him under the spray nozzle in the tub. After cleaning the manure and dirt, it looked like things were almost doable. We got him dried off and an IV started. Antibiotics on board and warmed up a little, he was ready for the first of several procedures.

Putting Gus on some gas anesthesia, we started cleaning wounds and shaving hair from the wounds. We removed contaminated tissues and packed with Furacin Ointment (the best topical antibiotic ointment I had at the time).

I worked on the tibia next. The ends of the bone were dry and brown with debris stuffed into the ends. I cleaned the wound as best I could but calculated that I would have to remove bone from both exposed fragments. I couldn't make myself think this was going to be anything but a waste of time. We packed the wound with antibiotic ointment and would do the repair tomorrow.

The left eye was hanging out of the socket and did not require much to remove. I placed a single suture around the optic stalk and removed the eye. I could deal with closing the socket later.

The mouth was clean compared to the rest of the cat. Gus was missing both upper canine teeth and one lower canine tooth. His jaw was fractured on the left side and separated at the symphysis (the mid point at the front of jaw were the mandible bones join in a non-movable joint).

The symphysis was repaired by passing a twenty-gauge wire around the mandibles just behind the lower canine teeth, exiting on the ventral midline where I twisted the ends to tighten the ligature. I cut the ends short and buried with a single suture. The fracture of the mandible was stabilized by wiring around two teeth on each side of the fracture. Probably will need to do more but later. The next morning Gus was looking pretty good and actually was ready to get out of here and back to his barn. We gave him a few laps of gruel and continued the fluids. We were going to tackle the leg later today. I still felt this was a waste of time.

* * *

With Gus under anesthesia, I went to work on the exposed bone. To my surprise, I did not have to trim too much bone before I came to bleeding bone. The marrow cavity appeared pretty clean with the superficial debris removed. I repaired the fracture with a threaded intramedullary pin I inserted at the knee and threaded down the marrow cavity to the fracture site. Placed the ends of the exposed bone into normal position and seated the pin into the distal fragment. This was the common repair at that time. We will have problems due to the contamination at the fracture site. I cleaned up the wound as best we could and closed this wound.

Gus was ready to go home for a few days before we started the next round of repair and treatment.

Both Carol and Gus were happy to see each other. Gus was actually stepping on the fractured leg. Cats always make surgeons look like they know what they are doing.

Over the next few weeks, Gus became a regular visitor to the surgery room. We would clean his open wounds, which were granulating well. We closed his eye socket and placed an additional wire in his jaw to improve the repair. On each visit I was more and more cautious on how the leg was healing. The soft tissues were looking well, but I was still skeptical about the bone. Carol was in great spirits, and I think that Grandpa was getting to come out of the doghouse once in awhile.

Finally, push came to shove. It was time to x-ray the leg to see how the repair is going. Gus is still quite a sight. One eye and one lower canine tooth protruding out on the outside of his upper lip.

Larges patches with no hair, but the wounds are mostly healed. Probably as good as they would have healed had they been sutured. He would purr and he was bearing weight on the fractured leg.

The x-rays were better than I expected. There was some healing but not what was needed. We would have to try something different.

So at six weeks from the time of injury I removed the IM pin. There was a pretty good fibrous union of the fracture, but no bony union. The next try was an external fixation device, four small pins driven into the bone, two above and two below the fracture site and bolted to an external pin to fix the bones in position. A tall order for a cow doctor but I got it done.

Another four weeks and we were done. The leg was healed, Gus was happy, Carol was happy. I don't know about Grandpa. The total dollars are lost to a clouded memory. Anyway, it was never about the money.

The last time I saw Gus was almost a year later. Into his golden year now, and with none of nine lives to spare, he was truly an old cat. He was in for routine stuff, an abscess on the side of face—left side, he probably didn't see the punch coming —and tapeworms. Still defending his turf and still able to catch a mouse or two. I always wondered about his final resting place. Was it the manure pile, again? ~

Charlie and Betty Land, Breeding Mares

I pulled the fingers off a plastic OB sleeve and pulled it on my left arm. After the fingerless sleeve was in place, I pulled on a latex exam glove. Then I pulled on a second OB sleeve, also with the fingers removed. This would allow excellent protection from the 'elements' and still allow for excellent sensitivity at my fingertips. I applied a good squeeze of KY to my hand and arm. I struggled to maintain a safe position behind this large quarter horse mare. She moved from side to side as I eased my gloved hand into her rectum. Standing at her right hip, I hold her tail with my right hand and lean hard on my elbow firmly planted on her rump.

It was apparent who had the most muscle as we danced from side to side in the stall.

How many times have you bred this mare?" I asked Charlie as I advanced my arm into her rear end.

"This is the third visit for her this year. I had problems with her last year and didn't get her pregnant. The owner really wants to get her in foal with Carbine," Charlie answered.

Charlie had related the problem when he stopped by our house on Ames Creek yesterday. I was out front with the kids, picking some corn in the garden, when Charlie pulled into the driveway in his old blue Chevy pickup. He was on his way home from work when he saw us out front.

"Hi, I'm Charlie Land, I have a little horse ranch up the creek. I just wanted to introduce myself and ask if you had time to look at a mare for me this weekend," Charlie said as he walked across the lawn with his hand outstretched.

"Dave Larsen," I replied as we shook hands. "We're going to be home on Saturday. I could run up and look at her in the morning. Not terribly early, I'm not much of a morning person and like to sleep in when I get a chance."

"This is a mare that I have been trying to get pregnant for a couple of years," Charlie explained. "I lease this big quarter horse stud, Carbine. He's a pretty valuable horse and has a great record on the quarter horse track. I generally have mares lined up all spring. This mare didn't get pregnant last year, and I only get paid for a pregnant mare."

***

My hand reached the brim of the pelvis, and I swept from side to side to find the uterus. I carefully ran my hand along the length of the uterus, starting at the tip of the right horn and continuing to the tip of the left horn.

"Not pregnant, and the uterus feels pretty normal," I said, almost to myself as I reached the left ovary. "Normal left ovary," I said, returning to the right ovary, "The right ovary is normal, and a large follicle is present, this mare should be in heat very soon," I said as I pulled my arm out and peeled the OB sleeve and gloves off. I breathed a sigh of relief as I pushed myself away from the mare. I was always told the only way to be safe around a horse was to be in the right place at the right time. To be in the right place at the right time, you have to be in the right place all the time. Doing a rectal exam on a poorly restrained horse was one of the most dangerous positions to be in, both for the horse and for the examiner. It is easy to receive a kick, and ruptured colons are also possible for the mare.

"If she doesn't get pregnant with this breeding, she goes home," Charlie said. "What do you think we can do to get her pregnant?" "Well, Charlie, I will be honest with you. I'm much more of a cow doctor than I am a horse doctor," I said as I pondered the problem in my mind. "The horse guys like to culture a mare and treat any infection according to the culture results. That procedure takes almost a week to complete if we start today. She's going to be in heat in the next day or two."

"This heat is her last chance this year," Charlie said. "She goes home after her next cycle."

"In the cow, I do a post-breeding infusion," I explained. "The day after breeding, I infuse the uterus with an antibiotic that is easily absorbed by the uterine lining. This clears any infection in the lining of the uterus and gets it ready for the fertilized egg, which reaches the uterus usually three days following breeding. My guess is if you call a horse vet, he'll shudder at that strategy. I don't know why, it might be a money issue. Their procedure runs up quite an expense. Might just be that they listen to the experts more. In the cow, we're working a herd, not an individual."

"You make sense to me," Charlie answered. "I'll breed her when she cycles and give you a call. Or just stop by your house. I thought, how lucky can a guy get when you came to town, then I thought I had died and went to heaven when you moved in down the road."

"Whatever works, you're more than welcome to stop by the house anytime. We haven't been in town too long, people are just now learning I'm around, so I am not too busy just now," I said. "The clinic won't be completed until this fall."

***

Charlie pulled into the driveway on his way home from work on Tuesday. I recognized the old blue Chevy pickup and stepped out of the garage, where I had been putting things away. "I bred that mare last night after work," Charlie said as I walked up the driveway toward his pickup. "I was hoping you could come up this evening."

"It'll take me a couple of minutes to get things ready," I replied. "If you get home and get her in a small stall, I should be there by then." It didn't take long. I just needed to make sure everything was in the truck. I ran through a checklist in my mind as I looked through the back of the vet box. Plenty of water, a vial of IV ampicillin, infusion pipettes, tail wrap, OB sleeves, bucket, boots, coveralls, Betadine scrub and solution, and plenty of lube. I ran into the house and told Sandy that I would back before dinner. Charlie's place was only a couple of miles up the creek.

Charlie was waiting in the stall with the mare haltered when I stepped through the open barn doors.

"Push her over against the wall on her left side," I instructed.

I wrapped her tail and did a preliminary scrub of the rectum and vulva with Betadine surgical scrub. After mixing the three-gram vial of ampicillin, I did another scrub of her rear end and then flooded the area with Betadine solution. I drew up the ampicillin in a 60-cc syringe and stuck it in the chest pocket of my coveralls. I held the infusion pipette in my teeth as I pulled on an OB sleeve and applied ample KY.

Again, standing at her right hip, I eased my left hand into her vagina. She tensed a little but tolerated the intervention far better than the rectal exam the other day. I moved more behind her now, took the pipette in my right hand, and directed the tip into the palm of my left hand. I advanced my left hand and arm into the vagina until I encountered the cervix. Holding the pipette steady, I attached the syringe to the pipette with my right hand. With my index finger in the cervical orifice, I advanced the pipette into and through the cervix. Then I slowly infused the ampicillin solution into the uterus.

That accomplished, I withdrew my arm and pipette, moving out from directly behind her as I did this maneuver. I rinsed her off thoroughly and removed the tail wrap.

"That's all there is to it," I said to Charlie. "Now we wait to see what the next couple of months give us. Since there's no rush to make a pregnancy diagnosis, I would wait at least sixty days before checking her. Obviously, if she continues to cycle, she's probably not pregnant."

"I doubt if the owner will be able to wait that long before a check for pregnancy. But that is his problem, she's going home this week. I'll let you know when I get the news either way," Charlie said.

"Everybody's in a hurry for an answer, but if it doesn't make any plans change, time will give you the same answer as an early pregnancy exam," I said as I loaded things into the back of my truck. "I'll be as anxious as everybody to hear the news, you let me know either way."

It was just short of fifty days later, and Charlie's pickup skidded to a stop in our driveway. Charlie jumped out and ran to the door, getting there before I could navigate the way across through the toys scattered around the living room.

"Good news," Charlie said as soon as I opened the door. "You are my hero now, that mare is pregnant, and the owner is happy as can be. I think I like the way you treat cows."

Charlie pulled a wad of bills out of his front pocket and peeled two bills off the roll. He reached out his hand with two hundred-dollar bills. "This is for your good work," he said.

"No, Charlie, I'm no damn lawyer, I charge for what I do, I don't take from your profits resulting from my efforts," I said. "You just call me next time, that's rewarding enough."

"Call you next time!" Charlie said, "I'm thinking that next year we should be infusing every mare. You'll make me a lot of money if we can speed up the process and get more mares serviced and pregnant."

"That might be overdoing it a little, but we can work out the details next spring," I said.

As time went by, my relationship with Charlie grew with every mare we treated. This was a simplified procedure but worked well. Mares were seldom bred more than one time, and the pregnancy rate was very high. Charlie remained a happy and loyal client. ~

Fetotomy on Whiskey Butte

J ack had called first thing in the morning. He had a wild little heifer with a calf half hanging out of her. His directions sent me over the top of Whiskey Butte into some country I had not been through before. By the time I made the turn to his place, I was close to Cascadia. It would have been quicker to have come up the river on the highway.

Jack was talking from the moment I stepped out of the truck. He wanted me to know he could take care of this if he wasn't so damn old. He also wanted me to know that he didn't think much of that last vet he had out here from Albany.

"That guy was afraid of cows," Jack said. "He didn't even look at her, just handed me a little medicine and told me to give her a shot. Charged me forty dollars for nothing. Why, I would shoot her before I called that guy again."

We stood at the edge of the corral, and I flinched as the heifer charged the fence. Jack was watching me with a wary eye. It didn't look like we were going to get much accomplished standing here watching her. I started over the fence with my lariat in hand. Jack stood by, watching with a sly smile on his face.

Jack was a big man, standing well over six feet and weighing close to three hundred pounds. His large belly would shake when he laughed. He had a large pointed nose and thinning grey hair topped his weathered face.

"I have a squeeze chute, but it's at the corral in the lower meadow," Jack said, in a voice that matched his size.

I swatted the heifer on the nose with the lariat as she charged the fence as I was climbing down. That changed her attitude enough to allow me to get on the ground and throw a quick loop over her head. I took a wrap around the nearest post and slid out to the end of the rope. I snubbed her close to the post. Jack was watching open-mouthed as I reached through the fence for the second rope. I put the second rope on the heifer with a loop across her nose to fashion a halter. She was already choking herself on the rope around her neck. I tied her with the second rope giving her ample slack as she needed to lie down. Then I released the tension on the first rope.

With her safely tied, I jumped back across the fence for my equipment.

"My God, where did you learn to handle cows like that, Doc?" Jack gasped as I hauled my OB bag and bucket over the fence.

"It just comes from growing up around them," I said. "I get surprised by one every once in a while, but most of the time, I know what they're going to do before they do it."

This heifer had a dead calf hanging halfway out of her. She was actually in pretty good shape, considering this calf had been hip locked for most of the morning.

"What are you going to do, just yard it the rest of the way out?" Jack asked as I started cleaning up the heifer. "I used to just hook on to 'em with a tractor and pull 'em out," Jack continued. "If that's the only thing you can do, I know some of 'em never get up again." "No, Jack. This calf is long since dead, there's no sense making it any harder on her than necessary. We're going to do this the easy way," I explained.

Jack was quiet, thoughtful, rubbing his chin as he pondered what I was up to.

"So what are you figuring to do, Doc?" Jack finally asked as I begin assembling the Fetatome.

"This rig here that looks like a little trombone is a Fetatome. I'm going to use it to cut this dead calf into several pieces so we can get it out of there without damage to the heifer," I explain.

Jack is quiet, but quite watchful now. I thread a length of OB wire through the tubes of the Fetatome, leaving a large loop hanging from the front end of it. I worked the loop over the head and feet of the dead calf and worked it down to the mid-abdomen.

I ran the Fetatome along the side of the calf to the leading edge of the hip bones. Then I hooked the T handle on the side of the instrument to the chains on the front feet. This would hold the end of the Fetatome in position as I made the right angle cut through the calf's body.

Jack's son, Gene, arrived just in time to lend a hand with the sawing. "This will work a lot better if you can give me a hand with the saw as I hold the Fetatome in position," I say to Gene as I encourage him to climb into the corral.

After getting everything in position, I clamped the handles on the OB wire and instructed Gene on how to saw with long, slow but strong strokes.

Holding the end of the Fetatome against the calf's hip to stabilize it, Gene started sawing with the OB wire. The heifer has been pretty still through all of this, concentrating on pulling against the rope tying her to the fence. The OB wire made a rapid cut through the calf, and the front part of the body fell out of the heifer in short order. Gene was not prepared for that event and dropped the handles as he moved to the far corner of the corral.

"Don't take off on me now," I kid Gene. "The real mess is still to come. We still have to get the hips out," I explain.

"I'm O.K," Gene replies.

Jack snickered, enjoying the whole scene.

"I'm still not sure how you're going to get the butt out," Jack says. "Well, I'm going to split the thing in two, Jack, and it will slide right out," I explain as I tie the OB wire to a long OB chain. I had the chain in a bunch in my left hand, and I reached in passing my hand over the rump of the calf. My arm is into the heifer to my armpit. I dropped the chain over the back of the calf, reached along the belly between the hind legs, fishing for the chain. Finally, my fingers found it. I retrieve it, pulling it out between the calf's legs. I pull the chain out with trailing OB wire around the rear end of the calf. I quickly threaded the Fetatome and positioned the front end of it against the severed end of the calf's backbone. "O.K. Gene, here we go again!" I say.

Gene begins sawing as I hold the Fetatome. This is a difficult cut, cutting through a lot more bone. But the bone is soft, and after a brief rest by Gene, the OB wire slid through the last of the fetal pelvis. I removed the Fetatome, reached in with my left hand, and pulled out one leg and half of the pelvis. When I pulled out the second half, the fetal membranes followed with a gush.

"I'll be damned," Jack said, shaking his head. "I been around cows my whole life, I've heard about this kind of stuff, but I never seen it before." I cleaned up the heifer and placed five grams of tetracycline powder into her uterus. Then I gave her a dose of extended-release sulfa boluses. I knew that when we turned her loose, it would be \some time before she let anybody on this ranch catch her.

"She should be fine," I told Jack as I turned her loose. "You might want to send her down the road, Jack. She won't provide you any production for another year."

"Aw, she's a big heifer, she'll be fine next year," Jack said.

From that day on, Jack would always tell everyone within earshot about my ability to handle cows and how I cut that dead calf out of that heifer, not hurting her a bit in the process. He always spoke in a loud voice and seemed unaware of who might hear him. He proved to be one of my best advertisers, often calling to me in his loud distinctive voice across crowded restaurants or meeting halls. It never failed; right after the greeting, he would start explaining to anybody close to him.

"Best damn vet I ever did see. I tell you what, you should see him handle a cow. I had the wildest cow ever trying to have a calf, and he just crawled down into that corral and roped and tied her just like that," he would say, snapping his fingers. And in a voice about as loud as the greeting. ~

Block and Tackle C-Section

Another 3:00 a.m. emergency, I thought to myself as I started loading things up for my trip to the barn. Glenn Hill was not a regular client but often helped out down the road at Ayer's place. This large old barn told a familiar story of bygone days, once a thriving little family dairy farm. Now the kids are grown, Glenn old enough to just being able to manage a few cows and the market for milk from small dairies has long since dried up.

I shook off the chill of the early morning air, hopeful it would be a little warmer in the barn. Glenn was waiting with the large barn door pushed open slightly.

"Morning, Doc," he said with a smile, "Sorry to call you so early, but she's been at it for several hours with no progress."

I could see the heifer tied to a center post. A large Simmental heifer with a single foot visible at her vulva. The foot was huge, this was not going to be a simple morning.

I approached the heifer cautiously and scratched her forehead. I should have known, she was like a pet, probably the only replacement heifer Glenn had and a far cry from a wild range heifer. I adjusted the halter to make sure it would not choke her if she went down during the exam and then moved to her rear end. The second hoof was just inside the vulva, the soles of the hooves were up. These were hind feet and they were very large, nearly filling the entire birth canal.

I tied a length of twine on the switch of the tail and secured the other end in a loop around her neck. This held the tail out of the way. Then I scrubbed the vulva with warm water and Betadine surgical scrub. After pulling on a plastic OB sleeve I carefully inserted my hand and arm into the vulva to explore the situation. There was just enough room for my arm and the two legs of the calf. I could reach the cervix and palpate the calf's hocks. This was a massive calf. I strained to reach past the hocks to the rump of the calf. No vulva, this was a bull calf. I inserted a finger into the rectum. There was a strong tightening, he was alive.

"Glenn, this calf must weigh a hundred and fifty pounds. His two legs and my arm fill the entire birth canal," I explained. "The only way he's coming out of her is if we do a C-Section. He's in posterior presentation and alive, but I don't know if you and I can lift him out of her."

I thought about the situation. Glenn was a small man but I knew he was no weakling. I have had difficulty in the past bringing the uterus up to a flank incision when the calf was in a posterior presentation. It would be best to use a ventral midline incision. Laying the heifer down would be no problem, but then lifting this calf out of her was going to be tough.

"Glenn, do you have a block and tackle?" I asked.

"Sure, Doc, what do you want to do with it?

I pointed to a spot in the rafters that could hold the block. "Let's hang it there, I'll lay this heifer down and roll her onto her back. Maybe we could block her in place with a couple of hay bales."

Glenn hung the block and tackle while I got things together for a C-Section. It looked like it could lift a thousand pounds. These things always took me a couple of hours, probably no chance of getting back to bed before office hours.

We moved the heifer over to where I wanted to throw her, tied her to a post and placed a flying W on her. This is a standard rope throw that I often used. I put the rope over her neck in the middle of the rope, tied a loose knot that fit between her front legs. Then I threw each end over her back so they crossed in the middle of her back. After that I put the ends between her hind legs, exiting on each side of her udder. I grabbed these ends, pulled hard and leaned to the right at the same time. The heifer made a hard flop onto her left side. Glenn looked at me and smiled. By his reaction, I am certain he had never seen that before. I rolled her up on her back, and tied each hind leg to the rope so when she strained or kicked against the rope it would put more pressure on flying W and increase the restraint. Then we placed a bale of hay against each shoulder to maintain her on her back.

This done, I stood up and stretched a little. "I hope you can get me an extension cord?" I asked.

Glenn had one hanging on the wall near the door and he had it plugged in and stretched out in no time. I plugged in my clippers and clipped the ventral abdomen from the umbilicus to the udder and to both sides. I scrubbed it with Betadine and wiped the incision area clean. I used 2% Lidocaine for local anesthesia, about 90 cc and left 30 cc in the syringe in case I needed more.

I did a second prep of the area and wiped it with alcohol, then sprayed it with Betadine solution. I laid out my surgical pack on a hay bale and opened four packs of #2 Dexon suture material and a scalpel blade. Then I put on a pair of surgical gloves and dropped to my knees beside the heifer. I made an incision through the skin on the midline, about twelve inches long, extended this though the subcutaneous tissues and exposed the linea alba (white line in Latin, that fibrous band on the abdominal midline). There I made a small incision and inserted a thumb forceps to protect the abdominal tissues from the blade. I opened the linea the full length of the incision.

I pulled the omentum forward and there was the uterus filling the abdomen. With one hand I tried to externalize the uterus, but I could hardly move the head. I found a foot and moved it to the incision. I incised the uterus using the space between the toes as a guide to the incision. With this foot exposed through that small incision, I attached a nylon OB strap to it and hooked the loop of the strap to the hook on the tackle block.

"Take up some slack and put just a little tension on this foot," I instructed Glenn.

I enlarged the incision just a little to allow me to reach in and find the other foot. I pulled it out and attached it to the other end of the OB strap. "A little more tension," I said.

As the legs extended through the uterine incision, I enlarged it toward the head of the calf. Now, with most of weight on the block and tackle, I could lift the head of the calf up to the incision. I worked the head through the incision, looked at Glenn and said, "Pull."

The calf glided out through the incision with ease. I guided the hind feet out and away from the cow and Glenn lowered it to the floor. Indeed, this was the largest calf I had delivered, every bit of a hundred and fifty pounds.

The calf snorted, and shook his head. Glenn was all smiles. I took a towel and wiped the mucus from the calf's nose and mouth and rubbed his chest a little. "He'll be up before his mama," I said. I changed gloves and started back to work on the cow. I removed some of the membranes through the incision but most were left to pass vaginally. I dumped a package of five grams of Tetracycline powder into the uterus. I closed the uterus incision with #2 Dexon in a continuous Utrecht closure. I returned the uterus to the abdomen and covered it with omentum. Then I started on the closure of the linea alba. I closed it with an interrupted sliding mattress using doubled #2 Dexon sutures. Then the free edge was closed with a simple continuous suture using #2 Dexon.

With this done I relaxed a little. If I dropped dead now, the rest of the incision would probably heal on its own. About this time, the heifer strained against the rope. The right foot came most free and she kicked hard. The hoof caught me on the left side of my jaw and felt like a very solid punch. It was hard enough to set me back on my butt. I shook my head and realized that I was okay, got back to my knees, and retied the foot with an extra wrap or two. I changed gloves and completed the closure. I used a simple continuous in subcutaneous tissues and a standard mattress on the skin, all with #2 Dexon: I didn't want to have to crawl under this heifer to take out any sutures. I sprayed the incision with Furacin spray and the whole area with fly spray. Done at last, I thought, as I stood up, pulling my gloves off.

Glenn had the calf on his feet already. I took a bottle of Betadine and filled his umbilical cord, saturating the surrounding area.

Then I gave him a two-hundred-pound dose of MuSe, a vitamin E-selenium supplement. This calf looked a month old already.

We untied the ropes and moved the hay bales. The heifer rolled to her side and onto her sternum in one motion. When Glenn pushed the calf toward her, she jumped to her feet and took control of the calf. I gathered up my stuff and got everything back in the truck. We untied her tail and removed the halter.

"I'll leave her here for now," Glenn said.

"Yes, I would keep her close for a few days, just to make sure everything is okay," I said. "Call if you have any concerns, but I would expect things to be fine. She should pass the rest of her membranes tomorrow or maybe the next day."

I got back in the truck and rubbed my jaw a little. Opened my mouth wide, everything was okay. My guess is that the foot had been slowed down by the rope, otherwise it would have been worse. As I headed back toward town, the sky was starting to show some light in the east. I would get home in time for a shower and breakfast before I was due at the office. No rest for the wicked.

Sort of reminded me of my Army days. ~

My First Ellwood

T he pup tried to lift his head as he laid on the exam table, but he just didn't have the strength to accomplish the feat. He let it settle back to the towel on the stainless steel tabletop, resigned to his fate, whatever that may be.

"I don't know anything about him, Doc," Paul said. "I was working on the house I'm building in Liberty, he walked out of the brush and collapsed at my feet. I guessed that meant it was up to me to try and save him. I am just happy that you can look at him on a Sunday afternoon."

Cachexia was one of those words I was forced to learn in vet school. Dr. Kainer, the freshman nemesis, seldom remarked about the words he heaped upon us. Still, he had indicated that we would rarely need to use cachexia in our records. But if anything described the condition of this pup, it was cachexia. He was literally skin and bones, and completely out of strength. Most likely he has been looking for a place to die, or maybe hoping for a miracle.

"Just off the cuff, my guess is his chances are slim to none," I said. "We will spend a little money to figure out what's wrong with him unless we get lucky. And then treatment is going to be more expense."

"I have an extra hundred dollars in my pocket today, Doc," Paul said. "If that will buy him a new start, that would be great. If not, at least we tried."

This was something I learned early when I came to Sweet Home in the middle 1970s. If you could save a pet for a hundred dollars, they would do it. If it was going to be much over that, there would be careful consideration of the options.

I opened the pup's mouth, it was almost dry, the saliva was white and mucus-like—extreme dehydration. His tonsils stood out like bright red grapes hanging in the back of his throat.

As I ran my hands over his body, I could feel every bone. He was like a skeleton covered with skin. He weighed twelve pounds, and as a young shepherd cross pup, he should be over forty pounds. Every lymph node was enlarged, noticeable enough that I didn't have to palpate them. His abdomen was empty but gurgled with my palpation. The mercury in the rectal thermometer was just a little over ninety-five, quite low for July afternoon. A drop of liquid stool hung on the thermometer when it was removed from his rectum. I carefully transferred that drop to a microscope slide. "I'll take a second to look at this under the microscope," I said to Paul. "If you would, make sure he doesn't jump off the table." "Surely you jest," Paul said.

I mixed the small sample with a couple drops of flotation solution and put a coverslip on the slide. Under the microscope, a diagnosis was confirmed with just one glance. Nanophyetus salmincola eggs covered the field. This pup had salmon poisoning.

"Paul, this pup has a very advanced case of salmon poisoning," I said. "Actually, I have never seen a case this advanced. Most dogs are dead before they get this bad. I don't know if we can help him, my guess is we will be throwing your money down the drain."

"I said a short time ago, I have a hundred dollars to put into him," Paul said. "You haven't had to do any fancy blood testing to find out his problem, let's put the rest of it into some medication and see how he does."

"Okay, we can wing it from here," I said. "Ideally, we should check to see how his liver and kidney function is doing, but I'll put him on an IV, run some fluids, and give him a couple of miracle drugs. We will see what morning brings."

Working on this unnamed pup by myself was no problem. He did not move a muscle, not even a flinch when I inserted a catheter in his vein. I started a bottle of fluids at a slow drip. Then I gave a dose of oxytetracycline as a slow IV injection.

I drew on the experience of a couple of the men whose shoulders I stood upon. Doctor Annes at Colorado State always said that no patient should die without the benefits of steroids. And Doctor Haug from Myrtle Point always treated his salmon poisoning patients with oxytetracycline and an equal volume of dexamethasone. I usually gave a small dose of dexamethasone on the initial treatment for salmon poisoning. Still, looking at this guy, he could probably benefit from Doctor Haug's larger dose. I gave the larger dose of dexamethasone as a slow IV injection.

Scratching his head, I wished him luck and turned to fill out the records. "Name of Pet" jumped out at me from the top of the paper.

"So, guy, what are we going to call you?" I asked the pup. He sort of raised one eyelid, the first real response I had seen from him. I pondered the name.

"I think you might make a pretty good Ellwood, at least for the next few hours," I said. "But, I am telling you, Ellwood, you had better get well quick. The ticket is for a short ride. I'll be back and check on you after dinner."

Anyone who has been around salmon poisoning knows that the odor of the diarrhea is most offensive. I have had clients tell of waking at three in the morning after their dog has had an explosive event in the hallway. Everyone in the house wakes up with a headache from the odor. The same thing can happen in the veterinary clinic, especially in a patient who is so dehydrated that their diarrhea has stopped. When they get some fluids, an explosive event often follows.

After dinner, I was a little apprehensive about opening the clinic door. I hoped I would not be greeted with a clinic filled with a salmon poisoning dog's pungent odor. No odor, that was good. Now all I needed was for Ellwood to still be alive.

Much to my surprise, Ellwood was up, resting on his sternum with his head up and watching for me as I came through the kennel room door. He was a completely different pup.

"Well, I'll be, Ellwood, you might just live after all," I said as I looked him over. "You're so thin, I wonder if you would eat a bite." Because salmon poisoning dogs lose their appetite early in the course of the disease, many will not eat for several days after treatment is started. And there is often some residual vomiting if food is given too soon. But I opened a can of mild intestinal diet food and placed a spoonful between Ellwood's paws. It disappeared so fast that I almost questioned myself whether I really put it there.

"Wow, one more spoonful tonight, then we will give you more in the morning if this stays down," I said. I thought I saw a slight wag of the end of Ellwood's tail as I placed the second spoonful between his paws. Again it was gone in an instant.

In the morning, the bottle of fluids was empty, and Ellwood was standing up, wagging his tail. I could almost say he was bright and alert.

"You are a sight, Ellwood," I said. "How can you stand with those muscles of yours?"

I placed several spoonfuls of the canned food in a small bowl. Ellwood wolfed it down and wagged his tail. I put a small pan of water in the kennel, Ellwood lapped it up in short order.

"I think you're well, Ellwood," I said. "Never in my wildest dreams would I expect it today, especially on your budget."

When Paul arrived at the clinic later in the morning, I think he was worried if he was going to have to dispose of the body or if we would do that for him. He was pleasantly surprised to see Ellwood up and wagging his tail.

"I think he had survived the disease," I said. "He just needed some fluid replacement and drugs. I think you have a new pup."

"I didn't expect him to be alive. I was thinking I was going to have to dig a hole for him," Paul said. "Do you think he's going to be okay?"

"I'm not sure my opinion means much concerning Ellwood," I said. "I didn't expect him to live through the afternoon yesterday." "Where did you find his name?" Paul asked. "I looked for a tag, and I couldn't find one."

"That's just a name that I thought would fit him," I said. "He is sort of a fighter, a little like an Ellwood I know."

We fixed Paul up with Ellwood's special diet, medication, and instructions for the next week. Paul stood at the counter with Ellwood on a leash, while I finished calculating the bill.

Paul noticed my diploma on the wall behind the counter. My full name was clearly spelled out on the diploma. Paul smiled, and held his hand out to shake.

"Good job, thanks, Ellwood." ~

Gus and Blackie

We watched as Blackie hurried across Main Street, coming our way, almost in the crosswalk and with no regard for the traffic light, his long leash trailing behind him. Blackie was a dachshund cross, mostly black in color, and the structure of a dachshund.

Blackie was always in the lead and always seemed to know where he was going. And not too far behind came Gus with his narrow-brimmed hat, cocked to the side of his head and sporting a grouse feather stuck in its band.

Gus was much slower afoot than Blackie and walked with a broom, a little bent over, favoring his lower back. He always gave the appearance of someone who just got out of bed and dressed quickly, never getting everything on just right. His shirt was half tucked in and his greying hair was sticking out from under his hat in all directions.

Blackie was at the clinic door now, patiently waiting for Gus to arrive, the leash strung out on the sidewalk behind him. This leash was Gus' way of complying with the city's leash law. Gus was schizophrenic. Medication kept him functional in the community, but if he is off medication, he has problems and he is well known to the police.

Ruth opened the door for Blackie and waited a couple of minutes for Gus.

"What are you two up to today?" she asked.

"Blackie thinks he needs to see the Doc," Gus replied, leaning on his elbows on the counter to catch his breath.

"Come on, Blackie," Ruth says, as she gathers up his leash. "Let's go get your file."

Gus always played the role of being a little dense or slow, but in reality was he was as sharp as a tack. If you wanted to know what was going on in town, all you had to do was ask Gus. He knew everything about everyone and every business. He just had difficulty articulating the facts in a manner that anyone could understand. Blackie was due for his annual exam and vaccinations and a heartworm test, and we would have mailed Gus a card tomorrow.

That is how well he kept track of things.

Blackie was an excellent patient on the exam table as long as you talked with him and took things slow. If you tried to zip through the exam and stick him with a needle without adequate conversation, he would get a little snappy.

"Gus, I see that Blackie is doing well," I said.

"He does okay, you send the bill, Cindy over at the DQ has a problem," Gus stammers.

I have found that Gus will carry on two or three conversations at the same time, giving snippets of each sentence stitched together in a manner that is almost incomprehensible if you don't listen very carefully.

"John takes care of it, I think her boyfriend left," Gus continues. "I will get your sidewalk, maybe she is pregnant."

Gus kept track of all the drama in town. I never knew how he came up with his information. I think maybe people didn't pay attention to him, thinking he was never listening.

"I ran a guy off last night, John says Blackie owes some money," Gus continued.

"Blackie's bill is fine," I said. "You don't worry about Blackie.

We will take care of him."

"They didn't like me in that jet," Gus said. "That guy next door doesn't like me. In Korea, they were mad. I only moved it a little."

Gus must have been in the Air Force, he often spoke of being in a fighter jet and taxiing it a small distance. I would guess that probably ended his military career. And there were several folks in town he had altercations with in the past. Those seemed to stick in his mind and come out once in a while.

He was not allowed in any of the bars in town because if he drank, especially if he forgot his medication, he would become violent and unmanageable. It was not unusual for Gus to require a few weeks in the state hospital in Salem to get straightened out. John, Gus's attorney, related one trip he made, taking Gus to the state hospital. He said that Gus babbled all the way to Salem and then was real quiet when they were waiting to see the doctor. A new, young doctor was interviewing Gus that day and Gus was as normal as John had ever seen him. Just when the doctor was getting ready to send Gus back home, Gus snapped back into his incomprehensible babble. John said the doctor's eyes just popped. But for all his problems, Gus did pretty well. His family had provided him a small house and Gus worked every day, sweeping and cleaning up small areas. He had funds that John managed for him. They were probably disability insurance, and maybe some state funds from time to time. I took care of Blackie, the A&W fed him lunch and dinner at times—although he usually had to eat outside. Some of the women in town would clean his house on occasion.

If everyone on public assistance did a fraction of the work that Gus did, communities would be far better off. And that segment of the population would be looked upon with better favor. ~

Pat's Menagerie

The mouth was wide open, and saliva dripped from the gleaming white teeth. The snarl could have come from a timber wolf. As I reached around to his rear end, the mouth snapped viciously at my arm. My arm would have been chewed to pieces if Joleen hadn't had a death grip around Paco's neck.

Once Joleen was able to get that grip on Paco, we were committed to complete the procedure. There would be no fooling him a second time.

Paco, one of our most unmanageable patients, was in for a much needed and overdue neuter. His black color made his white teeth more obvious and ominous. Soaking wet, this Chihuahua weighed maybe four pounds. Joleen, who is no small girl, needed most of her strength to direct Paco's slashing teeth away from my hands.

I applied a rubber band tourniquet to his forearm as Joleen continue to struggle, directing his bites away from me. I slipped a small needle into his cephalic vein, and the effects of a low dose of Pentothal was rapid. Joleen turned Paco to his side and relaxed her grip. I could feel myself relax as we inserted the endotracheal tube and moved Paco toward the surgery room.

With Paco clipped and prepped for surgery, I placed sterile towels around the surgery site and covered those with a sterile drape. I pushed one testicle forward out of the scrotum. Then because we didn't want Paco returning to remove sutures, I made a short midline incision over the testicle. I squeezed the testicle out of this small incision. The second testicle was externalized similarly. I generally open the tunic covering the testicles and ligate the vessels separately. With a small dog, like Paco, I placed a couple hemostats on the cord and ligated the cord without opening the tunic. Now, with Paco's jewels on the tray, I could rest assured that there were going to be no little Pacos running around to eat my fingers.

I closed the skin incision with a single mattress suture placed under the skin. With this method I would avoid seeing Paco a second time for suture removal.

Pat was happy to be able to pick up her Paco that evening. Paco was wagging his tail rapidly and when Pat opened the cage door, he jumped on her shoulder. It was hard to believe this was the same dog we had on the exam table that morning.

As I watched Pat and Paco walk out the door, I couldn't help but remember one of my calls to Pat's farm on the top of Scott Mountain Road.

It was a warm afternoon in August when Pat had called about her old horse, Dan.

"Doctor, I am hoping you can get a look at Dan today," Pat said into the phone. "He hasn't been his self for some time now, but today he's out in the pasture just wandering in circles. I'm worried sick that there's something terribly wrong with him."

"Pat, I can get up there in the early afternoon. That will give me time to get any lab samples ready for the courier this evening." Pat was waiting for me in the front yard. I could see her wringing her hands and wiping a tear from her cheek.

"I am so glad you could come this afternoon," Pat said. "Your old horse is not doing well?" I asked.

"Yes, it's Dan," Pat said. "He is old, but there's something terribly wrong with him. Look at him." Pat pointed to Dan, who was slowly walking in a wide circle in the middle of the pasture.

"Let's go get a look at him," I suggested.

We walked around the small shingled farmhouse to the gate into the pasture. As we walked out to Dan, I scanned the small farm. Pat had several horses, a small flock of about forty sheep, a couple of pigs in a pen by the old barn, with ducks and chickens scattered everywhere. The pasture was dotted with tansy ragwort. Tansy is a poisonous weed that seemed to be everywhere in the 1970s. It is bitter tasting, and most grazing animals would not touch it. However, for some reason, an occasional horse would develop a liking for it and seek it out. It was toxic to the liver, and the toxicity was cumulative. A nibble here or there, over time, became a lethal dose.

When we got to Dan, Pat stepped in front of him. He stood there, pressing his head into her chest and grinding his teeth. As I worked through an exam, Dan did not move. His mucus membranes and the whites of his eyes were noticeably yellow. To me, the diagnosis was tansy toxicity and Pat was going to need some time to come to grips with the finality of that diagnosis. I drew some blood to send to the lab.

"Pat, Dan is probably in liver failure," I said. "You can see how yellow his membranes are by looking at the whites of his eyes." I lifted Dan's head to a level that Pat could see his eyes a little better.

"What does that mean for him?" Pat asked.

"It is seldom good," I said. "I'll send in this blood and they can tell us how advanced things are. This is likely tansy poisoning. If that's the case, Dan is going to die."

"I was so afraid of that. I knew he was very sick. When will you hear on the blood results?"

"I will hear in the morning," I said. "Is he suffering?" Pat asked.

"If this is tansy, there's nothing we can do for him," I said. "It would be best to consider putting him to sleep. I'll give him a couple of injections to make him more comfortable for tonight." I had no hope of helping Dan with any injection. I could just remember a couple of mentors admonishing me to always give an injection, even if it is sterile water. That way, if the patient dies, at least you tried in the eyes of the client. And then, if there is a miracle recovery, you get all the credit. And in school, they always said no patient should die without the benefit of a steroid. "I'll give you a call as soon as I get the results," I told Pat as I was leaving.

There were no miracles. Dan's days were numbered. The blood test showed he had advanced liver failure. I took a deep breath and called Pat.

"Thank you for the call and for your efforts," Pat said. "I need to spend some time with the old boy. We've been through a lot together over the years. I'll call when I'm ready."

"That's fine. I know it's never easy," I said. "But if you wait too long, Dan is going to go down and have an awful death struggle."

It was a few days later when Pat called. I again made the trip to the top of Scott Mountain and quietly put Dan to sleep while Pat waited in the house.

It would be another dozen years before the imported Cinnabar moth would give western Oregon some relief from the losses associated with tansy ragwort.

***

As I sat down to fill out Paco's surgery record, I scanned through the old records. Dan's file was still there. Pat had sent me a poem after that event. I looked for it, but it apparently did not survive the years. Probably not clinical enough, I guess. ~

Two Down at Once

The appointment said 1:30. I looked at my pocket watch. It said 1:30. I stood in the driveway, wondering what to do now. At least I wasn't far from the clinic.

Finally, Paul came out of the house and down the walkway to my truck.

"Sorry for the hold-up," he said as he extended his hand. "Sue was supposed to be here by now. It's her horse, but I guess I can give you a hand, up until there's blood. I don't do blood."

Paul is a big guy, well over six feet tall and well-muscled. He stands and watches as I get my things together. Horse castrations were basic surgery, but I wouldn't say I liked the procedure. I guess that's why I am not a horse vet. A lot of guys did the procedure with the horse standing, but with most owners lacking adequate facilities, I was reluctant to do standing castrations. That, and the fact that I watched a classmate lacerate his arm with a scalpel doing a standing castration in school. I've always found that a good dose of Pentothal works wonders. It laid them down comfortably, and recovery was fast enough and smooth for the most part.

"Where is the horse?" I ask.

"He's out in the pasture. Sue thought that would be the best place to do this," Paul said. "He's not a problem to handle. Sue said, you were going to sedate him."

"Yes, I give an anesthetic, lay them on the ground to do the surgery. They recover without much of a problem."

"Are you going to be okay if I leave after you get him on the ground?" Paul asked.

"Yes, I'll be fine. I tie a leg up, and the surgery is relatively rapid." "I would do more, but blood is just one of those things I can't handle," Paul said with some anxiety in his voice.

"Well, there's not much with this, and once we get him on the ground, you can just walk away," I said.

I handed Paul a few things to carry, and stood, waiting for him to lead the way to the pasture. I was hoping that he was correct about the horse being no problem to catch. Often the owner has that story, and when the vet arrives, the head goes up, and there is no catching him.

There was no problem today. I picked a nice level spot in the pasture and put my things down. Paul brought Pepper over with a lead on his halter, and we were set to go.

Pepper was a gray roan, a nice-looking young horse, probably less than two years old. That probably led to his name.

I soothed Pepper a little. I had drawn up three grams of Pentothal into a 60-cc syringe. I stood at Pepper's left shoulder, and Paul was standing at my shoulder, holding the lead. The horse was as calm as one could expect. I held off the jugular vein with my left hand, palpated it with the back of my right hand, and then slipped the needle into the vein. I glanced at Paul, and he was doing fine. I drew back on the syringe to ensure I was in the vein. A small bellow of blood came into the syringe. It looked like an upside down reddish mushroom. With everything in place, I started the injection. Then I glanced back a Paul.

There he was, flat out on the ground behind me. That small bellow of blood in the syringe was all it took. He was out like a light. At least he had some soft ground to land on. My problem now was I had started the injection and couldn't stop midstream. I gathered the lead rope in my left hand and delivered a full two grams into the vein.

I was able to guide Pepper's fall back and to his right side so he would end up well away from Paul. Then, with Pepper on the ground, I slowly gave the other gram of Pentothal to get him well under anesthesia.

With Pepper under control, I went over to check Paul. He was starting to come around when I got down beside him. I helped him sit up, and then after a moment, I helped him onto his feet.

"I'm sorry, Doc," Paul said. "It doesn't take much blood to do me in, I guess. Are you going to be alright here? I think I'm going back to the house."

With Paul under control and gone, I put a sideline on Pepper and took a wrap on his left fetlock. Then I pulled that foot forward and up, securing it out of the way. Then I prepped the scrotum with Betadine Scrub and sprayed it with Betadine.

Everything was set for surgery now. I incised the scrotum over each testicle, extending the incision into the testicle, so the tunic was also incised. Then, hooking my finger in the pocket formed by the everted tunics, I pulled both testicles, and their tunics, out of the scrotum. This freed all the tunic attachments.

Then I clamped an Oschner forceps across the cord and removed the testicle and tunic with the emasculator. I held a firm grip on the emasculator for a moment to ensure a good tissue crush. I sprayed the cord with an antibiotic and released the forceps. This allowed the cord to retract into the scrotum. The next testicle was removed the same manner. Then with scissors, I removed the bottom of the scrotum between the two incisions. I stretched the opening to ensure adequate drainage and sprayed the area with an antibiotic spray. I sprayed a large area with fly spray, including the tail. With everything done, I picked up everything and moved out of the way. I removed the sideline and grabbed the lead rope. While I was waiting for Pepper to recover, I gave him a booster to his tetanus vaccination. And since Sue was usually at work during office hours, I gave him a good dose of Dual Pen. I didn't use antibiotics following surgery if there were no problems, I just thought this might save me a return trip.

It was not long, and Pepper opened his eyes, then with one motion, he righted himself to rest on his sternum. Then he stood up, I needed to steady him a bit, but he was good to go in no time at all. I removed the lead rope and gathered my stuff, putting almost everything into the now-empty bucket.

After getting everything put away in the truck, I glanced out to the pasture. Pepper was grazing, almost as if nothing happened. I went to the front door and knocked. Paul was a little slow to open the door but looked okay when he did.

"I was just checking to make sure you were okay," I said.

"I'm okay, Doc," Paul said. "I'll have Sue stop by your office to pay the bill and get any instructions."

"Good enough, you take care of yourself," I said. "Pepper is up and eating. You don't need to worry about him, Sue will check him when she gets home."

I could never understand why it works the way it does. A great big man and a few drops of blood, and bam! He hits the ground like ton of bricks. It always seems to fit the old saying, "the bigger they are the harder they fall." ~

A Little Bit of Magic
Helps Sometimes

How long has she been down, Dick?" I asked, standing over a young heifer that had just delivered a calf.

"When I got back this afternoon, she had this calf hanging halfway out of her," Dick said. "The calf was dead, I hooked onto it with the tractor and drug her and the calf around the pasture. On the second time around, we hit a bump, and the calf popped out. When she wasn't up when I got home after the football game this evening, I figured I had better give you a call."

"I think you would have been better off if you had called me before hooking up the tractor," I said. "When I have a calf in a hip lock, and the calf is dead, I cut the calf into a few pieces to get it out without doing any more damage to the heifer. But that's water under the bridge now. Let me check her over, and we can talk about what needs to be done at this point in time."

"What do you do if the calf is alive?" Dick asked.

"That's my worst nightmare," I said. "We have a few options today, but it's a nightmare. Decisions are often made based on economics. How much is the calf worth versus how much is the heifer worth."

"This calf was half Simmental," Dick said. "They say she would be worth twelve hundred dollars. That's a lot more than the four hundred dollars this heifer is worth. Or should I say, was worth." "Sometimes, we can manipulate the calf in the birth canal," I said. "If we can turn the calf ninety degrees so the hips are up and down in the birth canal instead of across the canal, we can sometimes pop the calf through. If the hips are only slightly too wide, pushing them higher in the birth canal will do the trick. The heifer's pelvis is wider at the top. Then there is a high-risk procedure for the heifer. If the heifer is young enough, we can split the pelvis bottom and get the calf out."

"That doesn't sound like fun," Dick said.

"That's what I was saying," I said. "It's my worst nightmare. Luckily, we've solved the problem somewhat by measuring the pelvis on the heifers before breeding. That, and people are learning that these big Simmentals don't make the commercial producer any more money than the standard breeds."

We were in a small pasture on the top of Marks Ridge, overlooking the entire town of Sweet Home. It was quite a view at ten o'clock in the evening, with all the lights shining brightly.

"You have quite a view up here," I remarked.

"Yes, I really enjoy it," Dick said. "But it's one hell of a drive to town in the wintertime. The wife worries herself sick about one of the kids killing themselves going down the road in the snow."

"I guess there are pluses and minuses to any location," I said.

I cleaned up the heifer and did a vaginal exam. Somewhat to my surprise, there were no vaginal injuries. Her hind legs had very restricted function, however.

"Dick, this heifer has obturator paralysis," I said. "When that calf was stuck at his hips in the birth canal, and then you pulled her out in the manner you did, the obturator nerves were damaged. Those are the main nerves going to the inside muscles of the hind legs." "I suppose I have nobody to blame except myself," Dick said. "Is she going to be alright?"

"Time will tell," I said. "Some of these cases never get up again. Some get up in the first few days of injury, and some get up after a week or two of working with them. Some veterinarians hoist these cows up with a medieval contraption that clamps on the hips bones. It takes some pressure off the muscles when a cow is down for an extended period. I've never liked those. After a few days, you end up with damage up here on the hip bones. If these cows are going to walk again, they'll do it in a few days. Beyond that time, the odds are not good."

"What do we do with her tonight?" Dick asked.

"I am going to give her a big dose of magic," I said. "That sounds like witchcraft," Dick said.

"The good thing is we are not long after her injury," I said. "My magic is in a dose of dexamethasone. This is a potent steroid, a big anti-inflammatory medication. With a little luck, we can reduce the inflammation around those injured nerves. If we get really lucky, she might be on her feet in the morning."

"That would be good," Dick said. "If not, I would guess I should be moving her to get her undercover."

"Yes, but we have to do that carefully," I said. "Many of these heifers that would get up end up being injured because they're moved around or picked up with all sorts of jury-rigged contraptions. Many times, those injuries end up being fatal. For tonight, we'll just leave her here. You give me a call first thing in the morning, and I'll run up here and help you move her if she's not up."

"Will do," Dick said. "And you need to take it slow going down that hill tonight. There will be some frost on a couple of those corners this time of the year."

***

Dick called first thing in the morning. He was in a jovial mood. "Your magic seems to have done the trick," Dick said. "That heifer was up waiting at the feed rack when I went out this morning. Thanks for your good work and quick response last night." "We got a little lucky," I said. "What I want you to do now is go out and tape my phone number on the steering wheel of that tractor. Just so you remember to call me before you try to pull out another calf with that thing." ~

73

Harry's Place

"Hi Doc, I'm glad you could come this morning," Harry said as he stepped out of the mobile home into the morning mist. "I have a couple of new calves with diarrhea. They're still up and around, but I don't want to take a chance on losing them." A couple of young girls, about and five and seven, followed Harry out of the house as he motioned me toward a small shed down the trail. The morning mist was getting heavier, almost alight rain, and there was still some fog that hung over the river.

Harry was an older man than I. Tall with thick dark hair that had just a touch of gray, probably in his fifties. His features were rugged, telling of hard work in his life. His voice was different for Western Oregon, a strong Southern drawl was my first impression, but that didn't really fit. Maybe from the Appalachian regions, I was guessing now.

"Did you get these calves from the sale?" I asked.

"No, I know a guy who got them from a dairy, out in the valley," Harry said. "I know better than to buy those poor baby calves at the sale barn. They get exposed to every bug in the county. Some of them don't last a week."

I started looking the calves over. They were bouncing around and sucking on my pants leg or anything else they could get their mouth around. Their temperatures were normal, and their navels were okay and looked like they had been treated with iodine. The shed was not much, but it was watertight and windproof.

The girls were joined by a boy now, maybe six years old. They were hanging on the fence rails of the calf pen as I was trying to crawl back out. I don't think Harry had stopped talking the whole time I was looking at the calves. I admit that I am not always a good listener when I am working, but he was talking about raising calves in North Carolina, Tennessee, or someplace back there. "Harry, I think these calves are going to be fine with a little medication," I said. "They're probably just a little upset with the move and the change from milk to milk replacer. I'm going to give them a dose of BoSe, which is a selenium and vitamin E supplement that calves need here, some antibiotic tablets, and a couple of doses of oral fluids to use this evening and in the morning instead of their milk replacer. That will give their gut a chance to rest a bit." After treating the calves and giving Harry the additional medication, we started walking back to the truck. Harry proved to be much more of a talker than I was.

When we got to the truck, and I put things away, got out of my boots and coveralls, Harry was still standing there in the rain with no hat, talking away.

"We come here to take care of these kids," Harry says. "Their father died last year, and then their mother, our daughter, was killed in a car accident this summer."

I didn't know what to say. I wished then that I had been listening to him a little better when he was talking earlier. What kind of a man, a couple, does it take to pull up roots to take care of their grandkids? And what an undertaking, to raise young kids at his age.

Harry didn't let my lack of response slow him much. He continued to talk. The rain was dripping off his eyebrows and his nose. He didn't notice. We stood there in the rain and my schedule faded into the background as Harry talked and I listened. My respect for the man grew by the minute, which probably came close to an hour.

Harry had a lot of knowledge of livestock, but it was from a background that was not familiar to me. Most of his understanding seemed close to correct, but just seemed based on a different set of standards than what I was used to, sort of like something you would read in the Foxfire series of books.

The kids would come and go, mostly because they tired of standing in the rain. Harry would put a hand on their head or shoulders as they stood close, but it did not slow his conversation. We were both soaked when I finally got back into the truck.

***

I would see Harry from time to time, for little things mostly, but it was a couple of years before he called for some cow work. He had moved to a small farm on Hamilton Creek at the time. He had a heifer that needed to be dehorned.

Harry and his crew of two of his kids were racing to the barn as I came to the end of the long driveway. The kids were older now, and they were actually helping instead of just being in the way. I know how that made them feel because I was always at the barn from the time I was three. I always felt almost grown-up when I could actually do something helpful.

"I got this heifer for an excellent price," Harry said. "She is pretty handy with those horns, though. I don't know why people don't get them off when they're babies. It is so much easier at that age." "This won't be a problem for her," I said. "We're early enough that flies won't be a problem and late enough to be done with most of the rain."

"The kids are worried that it is going to be painful," Harry said. "I'll show them how I give an injection of Lidocaine," I said.

"We'll numb these horns up, and she won't feel a thing."

Deshawnda and Nathan had the heifer in her stanchion and a rope halter on the heifer already. I think they didn't want me to use my nose tongs. I pulled the head to the right and tied the lead rope to hold it there.

I drew up ten ccs of Lidocaine in a syringe and pointed to the four points I was going to inject to completely deaden the horn.

Actually, when I did a group of heifers, I would only block the main nerve at the base of the horn at the six o'clock position. The injections were completed effortlessly with the head well secured. "This is going to smell a little bit, sort of like burnt bone," I said as I place an OB wire saw around the base of the horn.

I leaned back, putting a lot of my weight on the wire. I wanted to go quickly, but also I wanted the wire to get hot enough that there would be little or no blood.

With a number of long strokes of the wire saw, the horn popped off. It was a clean-cut, and the vessels were sealed from the heat of the wire, and not a drop of blood for the audience. The frontal sinus was open, leaving a gaping hole, which was typical for this age of heifer.

Harry picked up the horn from the ground and glanced at it.

His face fell as he dropped the horn back to the ground.

"Oh no," Harry said as he turned and stepped into the barn.

I repeated the process on the other horn and pulled all the vessels so there would be no bleeding. I covered the openings to the frontal sinus with a patch of filter paper. It would only last a couple of days and probably served no real purpose, but I thought it might make Harry feel better.

I was just finishing up when Harry came back from the barn. "How bad is it, Doc?" Harry asked. "She's such a nice heifer, it makes me sick."

"How bad is what, Harry?" I asked.

"Hollow Horn," Harry said. "I saw the horn, how bad do you think it's going to be for her?"

"Harry, in a heifer of this age, a hollow horn is normal anatomy," I said. "The frontal sinus extends out into the horn. The old disease called Hollow Horn was one way of explaining what was wrong with a cow when they couldn't know what was really wrong. Those names and disease explanations were used before we knew much about parasites, viruses, and bacterial diseases."

"You think she's going to be okay?" Harry asked.

"She's going to be fine," I said. "This dehorning is not going to slow her down one bit. Those holes into her frontal sinus will heal with no problem."

"Okay, Doc, I trust you," Harry said. "I've heard of Hollow Horn my entire life, but I'd never seen it before."

We turned the heifer out into the field, and she joined the others and started grazing as if nothing had ever happened. ~

A Few Precious Hours

I launched the drift boat at the Rock Creek Campground boat ramp after parking the pickup and trailer. The kids decided that they needed to run back to the camp for one last item. "Okay," I said, "I'll pull the boat down by the camp and wait for you there."

With that, I got in the boat and rowed down the bank, so it was close to our campsite. Now I just waited for the kids to show up. Time away from the practice was precious to me. It was rare that everything lined up in a manner that would allow us a weekend away. Crane Prairie Reservoir, on Century Drive south of Bend, was one of my favorite places to fish. It held large rainbows and was big enough that you could avoid the crowds. It was also far enough away from Sweet Home that it would be rare for me to be recognized.

When I was away from town, I always avoided any mention of being a veterinarian. Any mention of my profession, even to complete strangers, would prompt a long story of their dog or cat and their trips to the vet clinic. Being an introvert at heart, I hated such conversations, especially from strangers.

I pretty much only fly fished. There were times when we would fish with bait with the kids, when we could harvest the catch. But we had learned that the fish out of Crane Prairie tasted like mud this time of the year. You almost couldn't use enough tartar sauce to make them palatable.

When we were loaded up, I rowed out to Osprey Point and dropped an anchor from each end of the boat. This would keep it from swaying in the wind. I had made fly poles for the kids. I used inexpensive fiberglass rods, seven and a half feet in length, and rated for line weight of four. Since kids cannot cast too far, and the most expensive part of a fly setup is the line, I took double taper floating lines and cut them in two. This gave each rod a thirty-three-foot tapered fly line. This was almost perfect for young kids.

At Osprey Point, there was a deep hole just off the point and large fish for the taking. It was also an area were the kids could fish with their floating fly lines. By using a nymph, about six feet under a strike indicator used as a bobber, they could hook their share of fish. This allowed me to fish the deep hole with a sinking line. I would drag an olive Wooly Worm across the bottom of the hole. This made for wild action most of the time.

I always believed that when you were fishing with kids, the action was urgent. The quickest way to sour a kid on fishing was to make them sit in a boat or on a bank for hours with nothing happening. We would hook fish in the first fifteen minutes or a half an hour at most, or we would go do something else. When a kid asks when do they know they have a bite, you have waited too long before going to do something else.

We managed to get everyone hooked up with a fish in a short time, but that was enough for most of them. We headed back to camp to drop off the kids. Derek was the only one who wanted to fish more but we needed a lunch break anyway.

When I was ready to go back out in the afternoon, Derek was dragging around a little.

"I will wait for you at the boat," I said as I headed down to the shoreline.

I was standing there leaning against the side of the boat when I noticed the group of boys. There were four boys, walking along the shoreline, coming from the direction of the boat ramp. They looked like they were somewhere around ten years old and were checking out everything that looked movable as they came along the bank. One of the boys was carrying something.

When they reached me, they stopped, and the one boy handed me a bird he had been carrying. It was a starling with a blowgun dart that had pierced through its back just in front of the wings. The wound was days old, maybe a full week. There was extensive tissue necrosis around the dart that extended across its back. Its wings were not functional so even with comprehensive medical treatment at this point, this bird would never fly again. My impression was this bird would not survive, even with medical treatment.

The larger question was how had this group of young boys found the only veterinarian standing on the banks of Crane Prairie today. Even when I thought I had made a clean escape from town, even when I was as anonymous as it was possible to be, they still found me.

I knelt down to talk to the boys at their level.. This was no rag-tag group. These boys were well dressed for a fishing lake shoreline. I would guess they were all from well-to-do families and were probably reasonably well educated, if that can be said for a group of ten-year-old boys when they were grouped with their peers.

I point out the extent of the wounds caused by this dart.

"I hope the guy who shot this dart is proud of his skill," I said, hoping to instill some pity for the bird and to just maybe educate the boys on the ethics of killing an animal. "This bird has been suffering for several days, maybe a full week. You can tell by looking at the rotten flesh around the dart."

They carefully examined the wound, probably for the first time. I wiggle the dart a bit, to illustrate that the tissue infection has allowed the dart to loosen in the tissue.

"Hunting, and fishing, is something that we do as a people," I said. "Some people would say this bird should not have been shot, but this bird is one of the birds that people are allowed to shoot. But to shoot the bird and not finish the kill is cruel to the bird."

The boys have some chatter over those statements. Each one of them repeats their interpretation of what I have just told them in some fashion.

"I don't think this bird is going to survive," I said. "For us to finish the kill would probably be the best thing we could do today. This bird has suffered enough, and we should bring that suffering to an end."

So now I was in a corner. With four boys watching, how was I going to euthanize this bird?

One of the boys who was wearing a cub scout shirt I had just noticed, took the lead.

"Set him on the ground, and I'll get a rock," the young scout said. "I can crush him with a rock."

"That might work," I said. "But you might miss, that wouldn't be very fair to the poor bird."

"How should we do it?" the young scout asked.

"I'll take care of him," I said, hoping the boys would continue their exploration of the shoreline.

No such luck, they all stood there, looking at me for the answer. I gripped the bird in my right hand and held it so the body would not respond. Then I took a firm grip on the head with my left hand. With a quick jerk, I pulled the head off the bird. The body quivered in my right hand for a few seconds.

"Oh! He pulled the head off!" the young scout said.

"That was the quickest way to do it here," I said. "Now he's not suffering anymore. You guys remember, if you shoot something, you make sure it's dead."

Then it is over, the boys continue along the shoreline, I toss the decapitated bird into the grass. Derek comes down from the camp about then, realizing he had missed something, but not knowing what to ask.

We loaded up and went out to fish for a few precious hours.

Surely, they won't find me out on the lake. ~

Blackjack and Newt

J oleen, are you still feeding that feral tomcat out the back
door?" I asked.

"I don't think he's really feral. I'm going to catch him one of
these days."

"Catch him. If you get hold of him, it will be a question
mark as to who has caught who," I said.

Our original clinic on Nandina Street had a large patch of
berry vines across the alley from the clinic. That patch of briers
was home to a sizable population of feral cats and Joleen had
taken a liking to this young black tomcat. She was convinced
she could catch him and tame him down.

A couple of weeks later, Joleen came out of the back and
washed her hands at the front sink.

"I got him," she said as if it was no big deal. "I threw him
into the isolation ward. It wasn't so hard. I didn't even get
scratched."

"What are you going to do with him?" I asked.

"I figure if we neuter, vaccinate and deworm him, then leave
him in a kennel for a time, he should tame down just fine. Then
I'll either take him home—or we could make a clinic cat out of
him."

"I'm not sure about a clinic cat," I said.

And so began Blackjack's sojourn in the clinic.

Our first adventure was transferring him from the isolation room, a small bare room at the time, into a cage in the kennel room. He was not going to be fooled by Joleen's gentle nature again. It took a capture pole and a lot of clawing and biting at the end of the rod to accomplish the transfer.

Finally secured in a kennel, we made plans to secure his future. "We're not going to have a tomcat in here for long," I said. "There is nothing that will stink up a vet clinic worse than tomcat pee." "We have time; you can neuter him this afternoon," Joleen said.

One more wrestling match, and I had an injection of ketamine into Blackjack. Joleen took the opportunity to comb him out. He was a short-haired cat, black as could be, but he had been living in the briers for some time now and needed to be spruced up a bit.

Then we neutered, vaccinated, and dewormed him.

"He'll be a new man in the morning after his brain surgery," I said.

Blackjack tamed down in a surprisingly short time. In a couple of weeks, he was given a limited run of the clinic. It was not long before we recognized that he enjoyed people and the cats that were with them. Coming off the street, he was very dog-wise and could greet a few of the dogs that came through the door, but most of them he avoided with the skills learned only by a feral lifestyle.

He was controlled by the smell of the canned food. Joleen would pop the seal on a can of cat food, and Blackjack would come running from anywhere.

Then came a day when Blackjack wanted out the door.

"Do we dare let him out?" Joleen asked, more to herself than to me. "I think he knows where his home is by now. My guess is he'll be back before closing time."

That was the case. About four, Joleen heard him meowing at the back door. He came in for his can of cat food and then headed to his kennel for the night.

It was not long before he would come and go by the front door. He learned to scurry through the door as a client would enter or leave, jumping up on the counter and almost scaring some woman who had not noticed him following her through the door.

Most clients loved Blackjack, and he loved to sit on the front counter and accept any pats handed out by clients. Unfortunately, not all clients felt that way. One of our 'Cat Ladies' thought we provided Blackjack a terrible existence.

"It is not right for him to be cooped up in here all the time," she would say. "He should be in a home, where he is loved."

"Mary, he has the run of this place," I said. "He can come and go as he pleases, and his life here is far better than his old life."

"Well, that may be, but I think he deserves a real home," Mary said.

It was some months after that conversation that Blackjack left by the front door of the clinic one afternoon and never returned. We looked on the neighborhood streets and through the feral cat colony. There was never a trace of him.

"I bet she took him," Joleen said. "Poor Blackjack, his life here was far better than she will ever provide."

"There is no way we'll ever know. There are a hundred ways that a cat can meet his fate in this world. We gave him the best we could while he was in our care. I doubt she would have been capable of catching him out on the street."

We were still grieving a bit over Blackjack's loss when Kathy burst through the front door with a limp kitten in her hands.

"The highway crew found this guy in the ditch by our house," Kathy said. "It looks like he has taken a big whack on the head, but he's alive. If you guys can do something for him, that's fine," Kathy said. "I can't afford to do anything for him."

"We'll look him over and see if he is savable," Joleen said. "If he recovers, we can maybe find him a home."

This kitten was about six weeks old and had a patch of hair gone on the top of his head. Still unconscious, he must have been hit by a car. When I started handling the kitten, he began to stir a little. Other than the patch of missing hair on his head, he looked fine. I gave him a dose of dexamethasone, and Joleen went back to settle him in a kennel. Or so I thought. She carried him around in a towel for the rest of the morning. By noon, the little tabby kitten was back to normal function.

We offered him some canned food, and he acted like he hadn't eaten in a week.

"It looks to me like you have your next clinic cat," Joleen said.

After devouring his lunch, he was screaming for more. And I did say screaming.

"He sounds like he would make a good Speaker of the House.

Maybe we should name him Newt," I said.

Newt grew up in the clinic, spending most of his first year in the clinic. This was his domain where he had free run of the place during the day, and we would put him in a large kennel overnight.

His voice was the first thing heard when we came through the door in the morning. He knew he got his breakfast and that the kennel door would be left open.

Newt enjoyed people, and they loved him. He would often perch on the front counter, acting as a greeter. He seemed to have no interest in going through the front door.

He was close to a year old when Bill and Opal were in with Mucho for a check-up. When they completed their visit, they purchased a twenty-five-pound bag of C/D cat food. We were a little surprised when Opal came back into the clinic with the bag of food.

"This bag has a hole in the corner," Opal said.

Sure enough, there was a small hole in the bag and evidence of scratch and bite marks.

"That looks like Newt has been helping himself to some free meals," I said. "We'll refund that money. Do you want to keep this bag, at no cost, or do you want another one?"

"Oh," Opal said. "We can keep this one if you can tape it up. We really don't want our money back."

I grabbed some packing tape and closed the hole. "You really don't have any choice, Opal," I said. "Sandy has already reversed the charge. If I take it back, we will just throw it away. So you may as well get the use of it."

When Opal left, I went back and inspected our inventory. Newt made good choices. The bland diet foods for liver or kidney failure were not touched. But every bag of C/D had a small hole in the corner.

"Newt, I think you just got canned," I said. Newt looked at me in a very aloof manner. "I think you earned a trip to the house. I can't afford to lose hundreds of dollars in inventory to a cat that doesn't produce any income for the clinic."

That night Newt went home with us. This transition to our house went off without a hitch. He was quick to stake out his corner on the foot of our bed as he settled into a long life in the Larsen household. ~

The Wicked Witch of the West

S andy went with me on this late afternoon call to Lacomb.

With the kids visiting our parents, we had planned to stop for dinner on the way home.

I leaned against the rail of the log corral. On the far side of the corral stood this evening's patient, a Scottish Highlander cow, with a long set of horns. She was eyeing me as carefully as I was her.

Then she charged, and she covered the ground across the corral with surprising speed. I stepped back from the rail just before she struck the fence and swept her horns through the slats, side to side. "I told you she was mean," Jean said. "We are hoping that dehorn-

ing her will help to calm her down."

"I see what you mean," I said. "Dehorning her will remove those weapons, but she might still be dangerous to have around. Sometimes you're better off to send these cows down the road."

"She gives us a nice calf every year," Jean said. "These cows are small and really are not profitable beef animals. They're mostly just pets."

"If you keep a cow with this kind of behavior, five years from now, you're going to have four of them to deal with," I said. "Behavior is pretty heritable, like mother, like daughter."

"Well, to start with, let's get those horns off," Jean said. "Is that something you can do?"

"It would be a lot easier, and cheaper, if you had a squeeze chute," I said. "But I can probably get it done. I'll have to get a couple of ropes on her and cross tie her to get close enough to restrain her head. If I can do that, the rest is easy."

The cow stayed against the far fence in the corral now. I walked around to her side of the corral. I jumped as she again butted the rails and slashed at me with her horns. When she backed up a couple of steps, I dropped a lariat loop over her head and took a quick dally on the nearest post. Her first reaction was to run. I held tight when she hit the end of the rope. Then she gave me enough slack so I could get the dally tied on the post. I moved around the corner and tried to get her to come up to the fence. No way. She stood at the end of the rope, as distant from me as she could get. I moved back to my original position with Jean and Sandy. The cow moved back to her place near the post where the rope was tied. "I guess if I'm going to get another rope on her, I'm going to
have to crawl over the fence," I said.

"You be careful," Sandy said. "I don't like the way she's acting." "Yes, I wouldn't trust her at all," Jean said.

I crawled up to the top of the fence, hoping to entice her to move closer to me. I threw a loop at her from this position, but it fell short. After recoiling my lariat, I crawled down into the corral.

She watched me closely as if measuring me up or measuring how much rope she had to play with. I took a couple of steps toward her. She bellowed and charged.

The charge took me by surprise. I thought I knew cows pretty well, and I was expecting her to move away once I was on the ground in the corral, but here she came, at full speed.

I knew I didn't have time to turn and run, so I backed up quickly. My back hit the fence. Both Sandy and Jean were too frightened to scream. She was almost on me, but then she hit the end of her rope. She slashed her horns back and forth, the tips coming only inches from my chest. I waited for a second to allow my breathing to quiet, then I dropped the loop over her head.

With both ropes her now, I could cross tie her in the far corner of the corral. Once I had her cross-tied, I grabbed her with my nose tongs and tied her short.

The dehorning was almost a pleasure at this point. I gave some thought to doing it without anesthesia, but that would be taking advantage of my position to get back at her. I clipped the hair away from the base of her horns and scrubbed the area with Betadine. Then I did nerve blocks on each horn.

After removing both horns with a wire saw, she looked almost like a nice cow. I sprayed the wounds well with antibiotic spray and fly spray even though we were probably too early for flies. Now all I had to do was to turn her loose.

I had quick-release hondas on both lariats, so they were quickly removed. Now she was only secured by the nose tongs, and she was pulling against them.

Standing on the fence's bottom rail, I made a quick, coordinated motion to untie the nose tongs and shake them loose from her nose. She took a step back and then charged the fence, knocking me to the ground when she struck the rails, swinging her head, not yet aware that her wicked horns were gone.

Both Sandy and Jean rushed over to help me to my feet. "Are you okay?" Jean asked. "I told you she was a mean one."

"I'm fine," I said. "She's not mean, she's a wicked Scottish witch, that is what she is. At least, pretty soon she'll learn that her horns are gone. Most of her herd mates have probably been hoping for this day."

My nerves were almost back to normal as they seated us by a window in the restaurant at Pineway Golf Course.

"I think I deserve a beer before dinner tonight," I said. ~

Egor

E gor was a large mix breed dog. He was large enough that he could have had some Saint Bernard in that mix. His massive head sat on a body with a broad flat back that reminded one of an aircraft carrier's flight deck. He weighed over one hundred and ten pounds and was generally treated on the floor for apparent reasons. Joe first called for me to see Egor in September of 1976. I was doing house calls then because the clinic was still several months from completion. Egor was nine years old at that time, and he was beginning to show his age.

"Good morning, this is Joe, I was hoping you could look at my dog, Egor. He has a torn toenail."

Joe and Kathryn lived in a small house. The living room was cluttered with knickknacks, mostly old clocks, and antiques. Then, when you put a couch and two chairs in the small room, there was little room to work on a large dog. We moved to the front yard. "This toenail is broken back into the quick," I explained. "This is going to be painful for a couple of days, even after I clip it. We are going to have to do a nerve block on this toe, and that might be painful also. Hopefully, Egor is going to let me do this."

"Egor is a tough dog," Joe said, breathing hard from the short walk to the front yard. "You can do anything to him, and he won't move."

I had Egor sit and picked up his paw. When I inserted the needle in each side of his toe and injected a good dose of Lidocaine for a nerve block, he did not even flinch. We waited a few minutes to make sure the nail was numb. Joe's breathing was improved with the short rest, but you could still hear every breath as he struggled to exhale.

I wiggled the broken portion of the toenail, watching Egor closely. If he felt anything, he was not showing it. I took my nail scissors and snipped off the broken portion of the nail. The blood flow was enough that I was glad we were outside. I held a cotton gauze on the bleeding nail for a moment and then put a silver nitrate stick on the point of bleeding. It took a couple of minutes, but finally, the bleeding stopped.

"What if that starts to bleed after you're gone?" Joe asked.

"All bleeding stops, eventually, one way or the other," I replied. Joe did not understand the comment, or he didn't think it answered his question.

"If it starts bleeding, you give me a call, and I'll come back. I'm not too busy yet, and I live just a little way up Ames Creek," I replied.

That was the first of many visits with Joe and Egor. It was always a sight to see Egor coming to the clinic door with Joe hanging onto the leash, struggling to keep up. They would come through the door, and Joe would grab a chair, entirely out of breath. Egor would be wagging his tail as he went into the exam room. Joe always waited in the chair.

In April of 1978, Egor developed acute kidney failure. His prognosis was poor.

"He means the world to me, Doc," Joe said. "I can't give up on him. If you can do whatever is possible to save him, I'll find a way to pay you."

"He's a huge dog, Joe," I said. "There's less than a fifty percent chance he can survive, and treatment is going to be expensive."

"My wife has all sorts of antique clocks," Joe said. "You can have your pick of the collection."

"Okay, Joe, we'll do as much as we can. But you must know, there are no promises. Sometimes, all the money in the world cannot buy a cure."

"I understand that, Doc," Joe said. "But without Egor, I won't last a week."

"We'll keep him at least three days, probably more likely a week," I said. "I'll keep you posted on Egor's progress."

"I can't take him home at night?" Joe asked.

"I'm going to be running IV fluids around the clock," I said. "He is going to need to stay if we are going to have any chance of saving him."

Egor was a great patient. He was very ill, had IV tubes hanging everywhere, and we were coming at him with needles for a blood draw or an injection multiple times a day. His tail always wagged. He hated the bland food he was allowed, but he would lick your hand when the bowl was put in the kennel.

After three days, he greeted me with a bark and a bounce when I came into the kennel room. He was feeling better. His kidney numbers edged back toward normal. When I called Joe, I tried to instill only cautious optimism.

"Good morning, Joe," I said into the phone when he answered, only allowing a single ring. "Egor is improved this morning. His kidney numbers are close to normal this morning, and his urine has some concentration to it. He's not well, but much to my surprise, he's improved."

"Does that mean I can take him home?" Joe asked. "I have been worried to death that he's going to die down there, Doc. I know we all have to go sometime. I would just like to be with him when it's his time."

"I'd like to keep him one more night," I said. "I'll take him off the IVs, and we will see if his kidneys can maintain him on just water." Egor bounced out of the clinic the next day. He almost knocked Joe over, he was so happy to see him. Joe had no understanding about how incredibly lucky we were to be seeing Egor go home. We loaded him down with a case of kidney diet food and oral antibiotics. I was not confident that Joe would have the strength to keep Egor on the special diet for an extended time, but for today, everybody was happy.

"You and your wife come by the house this evening and pick out a clock," Joe said as he and Egor went out the door.

"Do you think they have a clock that is worth enough to cover this bill?" Judy asked.

"I guess the value of an antique is based on perceived worth," I said. "Seeing those two go out the door together is a pretty precious event in itself."

Sandy and I dropped by Joe's house that evening. Egor greeted us at the door as if he hadn't seen us in weeks. Sandy and Kathryn looked over the clocks as I sat and talked with Joe and Egor.

Sandy selected a modest mantle clock. Kathryn had some large clocks that she felt had a higher value and tried to get Sandy to make a better selection. We had discussed our needs before we stopped, and we needed a clock that we could display, not one that took up a lot of space.

Egor did well over the next months. Not perfect, but pretty well. The bland, low protein, diet required in Egor's long term management did not appeal to either Joe or Egor. My guess was that Joe tried but likely cheated some.

Egor was losing a lot of protein in his urine and losing weight. His kidney numbers continued to hover close to normal, and he maintained his high spirits. But when he would drag Joe into the clinic, it was evident that neither one of them were their old selves. Joe died in October of 1979. The family decided that Egor was too ill, and too lonely without Joe, to go on. They brought Egor to the clinic for the last time, a couple of days following Joe's death. We were busy that day, and Egor was left in a kennel for a short time before I could find a few minutes for him. This should have been nothing for Egor. He had been in this very kennel for days at a time in the past.

Egor sat in the kennel and howled a loud, mournful howl, as I have never heard a dog howl before or since.

If ever a dog knew his fate, it was Egor! ~

Charlie and Betty at the Track

I have a hot tip on a horse running in the third race at the State Fair Friday night," Charlie said into the phone. "I'd like to take you and Sandy up there with Betty and me if you can get free. This is a solid tip. We can make some money. Sort of like insider trading."

"I think we can get a babysitter and would be happy to go with you. Thanks for the invite," I replied.

Charlie and Betty were right on time to pick us up Friday night. Charlie seemed excited to be on the way to the horse races, almost jovial.

"This is a solid tip I have on this horse," he said as we sped through Sweet Home. "You probably knew that betting the horses is filled with pitfalls. You have to have good information from the trainers to make any money at it. Occasionally, a race comes along where the trainers stick a horse in the race to get track experience. Rarely do one of these races end up with one good horse, and all the others are just there for the experience. But this race is a sure bet. I hope you brought enough money to make a good bet."

"I brought some money," I said, "but I probably have a different experience at the track than you have, Charlie. My experience has been based on luck, and I've suffered from overconfidence at times." "I'm telling you, and you can take this to the bank. This is not overconfidence, this is the closest thing to a sure thing at the track you will ever see," Charlie said in a stern voice, seeming to be irritated that I might question this tip.

Friday night and the state fairgrounds were packed. We did find a parking spot. Charlie walked at a fast pace. I think he was excited. I could keep up with him, but Sandy and Betty lagged far behind. They did not catch up with us until we were standing in line to buy admission tickets to the races.

"This is a good thing," Charlie said. "A large crowd means a bigger payout."

We picked up hot dogs and a beer at the concession stands and found our way to a set of seats about a third of the way up the grandstands. The good thing was that it was close to the betting windows. After downing the hot dogs, Sandy and I set about picking a horse for the first race.

"I'm telling you, Doc, don't waste your money on two-dollar bets. You need to take all your money and put it on the number six horse in the third race," Charlie said in a hushed voice, not wanting to give away any information to somebody who might overhear the conversation.

"I'm pretty conservative at betting, I try to pick the best horse and bet him to show," I explained.

"You won't win enough to pay for the gas getting here," Charlie snorted.

Sandy and I went along with Charlie and watched the first two races. As the third race was announced, Charlie sprang to his feet. "Give me your money and I'll buy the tickets. I don't want any mistakes on this one," Charlie said with his hand outstretched.

I handed him a ten-dollar bill and shuddered a little, remembering the horse race in Boston where I was overconfident and lost ten dollars on a horse that I bet to win.

Charlie must have been first in line because it was not long, and he was back. He handed me our ticket, and we stood to watch the race, not really looking at the ticket. Charlie was all smiles and a little agitated. I was guessing that he was starting to question his tip. Horse races don't take long to run. They spend a lot of time getting the horses out on the track and parade up and back to allow adequate time for the betting to take place. Once in the starting gate, they are off in short order. The number six horse had a good start and was in the lead by a full length at the first corner. There was never any question after that point, and he won with a solid lead. Charlie almost threw Betty in the air. We were happy also. This horse had pretty favorable odds, something like six to one. Charlie and I headed to pay windows. I started to get in line for the ten-dollar window, and Charlie grabbed my arm and pulled me over to the high stakes window. Now I looked at my ticket, it was a ticket for number six to win in the third race, but it was a hundred-dollar ticket.

"You must have got your tickets mixed up," I said to Charlie. "No, that's your ticket. I assumed the risk. You can pay me back out of the winnings," he said, handing me my ten-dollar bill back. I collected the six hundred dollars and handed Charlie his hundred. I am not sure how much Charlie had bet on the race, but he had a lot of money in his hands.

"Now we have enough money to bet a few quinellas or trifectas. I'll teach you how to win a little money at the track. But remember, you have to have an in with the trainers, and you have to trust their tips. If you don't know Randy, I'll introduce you one of these days." Sandy and Betty were awaiting our return. Sandy was feeling pretty frisky thinking we had won fifty or sixty dollars, so she was a little surprised when I handed her a couple hundred dollar bills. "Charlie insured our bet at a little higher value than my ten," I told her.

Charlie and I won a little more money as Charlie tried to teach me everything he knew about betting the horses. But with every bet he placed, he always came back to the original statement. "You have to have inside information to really win at the track. Always remember that when you're betting." ~

Don't Give That Injection

I looked at the clock, five-thirty in the morning. I had no idea how long the phone had been ringing. I rolled over and stretched to lift the receiver. "Good morning," I say.

I can hear an elderly woman on the line and she sounds frantic. It took me a couple of minutes to collect my thoughts and I finally sat on the edge of the bed.

"I'm sorry, it's early, and I didn't catch much of what you said," I said.

"This is Opal," the woman said. "I live in Albany and go to a veterinary clinic here. Julie works at this clinic, but she takes her animals to you. Mucho has diabetes, and the doctor here has been having trouble getting him stabilized on a dose of insulin. Julie told me yesterday that this doctor didn't know what he was doing and that I needed to get Mucho in to see you."

"I know Julie," I said. "I'm a little surprised that she would suggest that to you."

"She said that Mucho will die if I don't get him in to see you right away," Opal said. "He has been having little seizures all night long. And I am supposed to give him another injection at six thirty." "I could probably see Mucho if you have him at the clinic at eight this morning," I said. "But if you're going to bring him to see me, you don't give that injection this morning."

"But those are the instructions that I have from my doctor here," Opal said.

"This is what I am telling you, Opal, if you give that injection, I will not see Mucho," I said. "If you give that injection, you go to see your doctor this morning. And if Mucho has been having seizures all night, you probably better call him before you give that injection."

"Okay, I will not give the injection, and we will be at your clinic at eight," Opal said.

"Do you know where we're located?" I asked. "Yes, Julie gave me directions," Opal said.

"Okay, I am going to try to get an hour of sleep. I will see you and Mucho at eight."

Julie was a good client, and we had talked about her situation several times. She knew that she could get her veterinary services at much-reduced fees at the clinic in Albany, but just preferred coming to me. I am sure that she would lose her job if her clinic knew she was actively sending clients to my clinic.

Opal and her husband, Bill, were waiting in front of the clinic when I arrived at seven forty-five. They were an older couple in their mid-seventies, both short and slightly built. Some would call them trim. Bill's hair was thin on top and gray in color, and he had a well-trimmed mustache. Opal's hair was white. Opal was the commander of the group. Bill followed and carried things.

Mucho was a white poodle, immaculately groomed without a hair out of place. He looked older and somewhat heavier than he should be, but I would stop short of calling him obese.

"Good morning, Doctor," Opal said as I unlocked the door.

I held the door open as Opal and Mucho entered. Bill took hold of the door and motioned me to go ahead of him.

99

"It's going to take a few minutes for everyone to get here and set up to see you," I said. "You can make yourself comfortable, and we'll get you looked at as soon as possible. Do you have any records?"

I knew that was a mistake as soon as I said it. Opal pulled out a folder that was an inch thick.

"These are my records," Opal said. "I didn't want to ask our doctor for records because I didn't know if Julie would get in trouble or not."

I took the folder from Opal. "I'll glance through these while we're waiting for the rest of the staff to arrive."

At about the same time, Ruth came through the door, and Mucho stiffened in Opal's arms, pulled back his head back, and started twitching.

"On second thought, maybe we should take Mucho and get a look at him immediately," I said.

"He has been doing this for most of the night," Opal said.

We got Mucho into an exam room and collected a blood sample for a blood glucose level. The test would take a little time. While we were waiting for the test result, we got an IV catheter in place and started a slow drip of D5W. I was sure that his glucose level was going to be quite low.

Just how low was the question; his blood glucose was 42. Had Opal given the prescribed dose of insulin at 6:30, Mucho would have never made it to Sweet Home.

Talk about an instant cure, with a small bolus of fifty percent glucose, Mucho was up and wagging is tail.

"That is amazing, Doctor," Opal said. "What did you give him?" "I just gave him a little glucose," I replied. "You see, the insulin dose you've been giving has been too large. It just keeps making his blood glucose a little lower each day, then finally, it's too low. So we have to do a couple of things. Number one, we need to get him through today. And then, number two, we need to start him back on a low dose of insulin and adjust it slowly every couple of days until we get him where we want his blood level."

"How will we keep this from happening again?" Opal asked. "I'll do things a little different than your doctor in Albany," I said. "I'll go slowly, making sure his diet is the same every day, and adjust his insulin dose, so his symptoms are relieved. That means we will adjust his glucose to a level that you and Mucho can live with, not what some book says it should be."

"That sounds a little complicated," Opal said. "I want you to know that I won't leave Mucho here. We will have to do this at home." "Except for today, that should be no problem," I said. "It might mean that you will need to travel back a forth every couple of days, but we can do most of this as an outpatient."

"You said, except for today," Opal said.

"We need to keep Mucho for a couple of hours anyway," I said. "Just to make sure he's not going to have a seizure on your way home. We need to know that he's out from under the insulin dose from last night. You guys could probably go eat breakfast. If you eat slowly and talk to each other a little, that would probably be long enough."

And so it began. Opal and Mucho were nearly constant clients for a time. That first day went well, and we let Mucho go home without any insulin for a couple of days so we could get a fresh start on stabilizing his dose.

Mucho did prove to be quite a challenge, however. We ended up having to use a split dose of regular insulin and NPH insulin. He did very well for many years. Getting his insulin every twelve hours and eliminating all the little goodies from his diet pretty much did the trick.

This entire time, I worried about Julie's job status. If Opal's previous veterinarian knew she had sent Opal over here, he would not be happy. The problem was solved in a couple of months when Julie informed me that they had purchased a small farm in upstate New York and would be moving shortly. Things worked out just fine. ~

Bill and Mary Jane

I turned off of McDowell Creek road into the barnyard. I could see only a few cows in the holding pen and a couple of guys heading up the hill to the upper pasture. I looked at the clock to make sure I wasn't early for the appointment to do the fall pregnancy exams on the herd.

Bill came out of the barn to greet me.

"I'm sorry, Doc," Bill said. "The boys are having a heck of a time getting the cows down. They smell a rat, I guess."

"We could reschedule for another day," I said. "I figured this will take the better part of the morning, and I have some afternoon work to do."

"I think they'll get the rest of them on this trip up the hill," Bill said. "Maybe we could take you over to look through one of the chicken houses, if that would interest you."

"I have a lunch planned for everyone when the work is done," Mary Jane said. "That should get you back to the office on schedule." "Okay, you twisted my arm just hard enough," I said. "And yes,

I would love to look through one of your chicken houses."

"We don't allow many people into these houses," Bill explained. "It's upsetting to the birds when a stranger shows up. We try to have the same worker handle each house. That way, there's no upheaval. We'll be okay today if we just step through the door and stand and look."

We stepped inside. This was a sizable open chicken house, constructed of steel, and it reminded me of the Quonset huts on the Army bases in Korea. These were about thirty feet wide and over one hundred feet long. It was all open area on the inside except for a small room for feed and supply storage. The chickens ran free. And there must have been a thousand birds in this house. "The company owns the birds," Bill said. "They supply everything, the feed and the medical care. We just supply the house and labor. We get paid when they go to the market. It's to our benefit to have rapid growth and good survival. But if these birds grow too fast, they have heart problems. Their hearts sort of explode, sort of a heart attack, I guess."

"Chicken medicine is a real specialty in veterinary medicine," I said. "You just about have to go to vet school in Georgia to get any real education in chicken medicine. Just like swine medicine, you have to go to Missouri or Kansas to get much in the way of swine medicine."

"If we have any losses, the veterinarian comes by and autopsies a few birds and gives us the answer and directions on what to do," Bill says.

"Yes, chicken medicine is population medicine," I said. "I had a virology professor who went to vet school in Georgia. He told a story of his diagnostic lab rotation during his senior year. A group of four students would spend a couple of weeks running the diagnostic lab. People would bring in several birds and they would have to fill out a questionnaire. Then the students would euthanize the birds and do a necropsy, the veterinary term for autopsy. That way they could come up with a flock diagnosis. His group came up with a plan to finish the work faster so they could have time for a morning cup of coffee. One guy would check in the birds, pass them to the back, and then fill out the paperwork. So by the time the paperwork was done, the birds were euthanized, and the necropsies were complete. This one day a lady brings in a big rooster. The guy up front passes the rooster to the back and the group started the process back there. The guy up front starts going through the paperwork. 'What signs of disease do you see in your birds?' he asks. 'He has diarrhea,' the lady replies. Noticing this comment, he asks, 'How many birds are in your flock?' "One,' replies the lady."

"Oops," Bill said.

"Let's go see if they are ready to get to work on the cows," Mary Jane says.

With the cows lined up in the crowding ally and a crew of several young guys pushing the cows, the pregnancy exams go pretty fast. The pregnancies are spread out more than I liked. They ran from forty days to five or six months of pregnancy.

The good thing was that almost all the cows were pregnant. They had only one open cow. The spread was something I would need to talk with Bill about. He was going to be delivering calves for over four months instead of the month and a half that I preferred.

But getting there was a multi-year project that required increasing your replacement heifer numbers and doing some selective culling. That discussion would need a couple of sit-down sessions.

The best part of the day was lunch. When the herd was done, we all went to the house. I spent the most time at the sink and was able to get myself mostly clean. Only a small manure stain on my shirt at the left shoulder remained. Had I known lunch was on schedule, I would have brought an extra shirt to wear for the occasion. Mary Jane set a table that reminded me of the lunches during silo filling when I was young. They resembled Thanksgiving dinner more than lunch. We had roast beef, potatoes and gravy, veggies, and a salad. And then to top it off, apple pie with a scoop of ice cream.

We had plenty of time to talk following lunch. I told a bit about my early days of growing up in Coos County, and how many farms were located in the little valleys.

"When I was a kid here, the school bus was always full," Bill said. "There were family farms on the road all the way to town. Those are all gone today."

"It's interesting, I've been transcribing the journals of my great-grandfather and my great-uncle," I said. "My a Chichutalks about selling a bull for eleven cents a pound in 1890. And my great-uncle sold a bunch of steers for fifty-four cents a pound in 1952. It just seems like those were pretty good prices for those days. Today, a young person cannot buy a ranch and make a go of it."

"I think it is pretty sad," Bill said. "The loss of the family farm has been a major change in society today."

When the talk was over, I gathered my things, thanked Mary Jane for the super lunch, and headed back to the office to finish my day.

**

I noticed Bill standing at the front counter. He looked a little agitated as he was waiting for his turn to talk with Sandy. I went out and shook his hand.

"Doc, I've got to show you this," Bill said. "I've been up most of the night after we discussed your great-uncle's journals."

We moved into an exam room, and Bill laid out a crumpled piece of paper that he had been using for a scratchpad.

"If your great-grandfather sold a bull for eleven cents a pound in 1890," Bill started, his hand shaking as he pointed to the paper, "the closest figure I could find was a Model T in 1908 that cost eight hundred and fifty dollars. Figuring eleven hundred pounds for a bull approaching two years of age, he would have needed seven of those bulls to buy that car."

"That's interesting," I said.

"Oh, there's more here," Bill continued. "In 1952, my father went down here to Lebanon and bought the best, top of the line, Buick that they had on the lot. He paid thirty-two hundred dollars for that car. If your great-uncle was selling steers for fifty-four cents a pound in 1952, figuring those steers were five hundred pounds, he would have had to have twelve of those steers to buy that car." "I am betting that you are trying to say things have changed a little," I said.

105

"Changed a whole lot, I would say," Bill said. "I could sell every darn animal I have out there, and I wouldn't come close to being able to buy a decent car."

"Those are interesting figures, they show the status of the farmer in the country today," I said. "When I was in dairy practice in Enumclaw, I was told that the guy who delivered milk to the store got more out of that gallon of milk than the dairy farmer."

"It is no wonder that a guy can't make a living ranching today," Bill said.

Bill had hit the nail on the head. When I was a boy, a family could purchase a farm and it would pay for itself with some hard work. When I was out of high school, it couldn't happen without one or both of the couple working at an outside job and running the farm also. Today, even that is difficult or impossible. For a large part, farming has become land speculation. ~

A Kitten's Tale

I noticed her sitting in the far corner of the reception area, patiently waiting for the crowd to clear. She was an older woman with white hair, short and petite, well dressed for Sweet Home.

She was tanned to a rough brown, and her face and hands showed the wrinkles that came from years of outside work.

My curiosity was getting to me. I stayed up front to see what she was going to want.

"Ma'am, is there something that I can help you with?" I asked. She approached the counter with slow, measured steps.

"Are you Dr. Larsen?" she asked. "I have heard a lot about you from my friends. I am June. I have a small place up on Forty-third. My husband has been gone for several years now. It is just my cats and me now."

"Yes, I'm Dr. Larsen," I said. "I hope that your friends said good things about me."

"Oh yes, Doctor, you are well thought of by most people in town," she said.

"So, what is it that brings you to see us today?" I asked.

"If I had a kitten that needed its tail removed, is that something you could do?" she asked.

"Yes, we do just about anything here," I said. "What happened to the kitten's tail?"

Ignoring my last question, she continued. "And how much would such a procedure cost?"

"That depends on how large the kitten is and if the tail problem needs any additional treatment," I said. "If it's infected, there might be charges to take care of that infection. That's something I could give you a close estimate for when I look at the tail."

"I mean, if there is nothing wrong with the tail, how much would it cost for a three-day-old kitten?" she asked.

"You're asking about docking a kitten's tail?" I asked. "That's not something that is done in most cases."

"You dock puppies' tails," she said in a matter of fact voice. "There can't be much difference, most of those pups have no real reason to have their tails docked."

"You make a good point," I said. "Some breeds need their tails docked, others it's purely cosmetic, or for some breed standard. If you've ever lived with a cocker spaniel in a western Oregon winter, you would understand why we dock some tails."

"I don't see a difference," June said. "I have a litter of kittens, six of them that I would like to have their tails docked."

"I'd have to think about that one," I said. "You're asking me to stretch my ethics a little."

"Now listen, young man," June said in a stern voice. I wondered if she had been a school teacher in her day. "There are not many options for these kittens. Placing kittens in homes is difficult these days. All my cats are fixed, but this little mamma cat shows up and has this litter of kittens in my woodshed. I can leave them there and let them grow up wild. They will probably die from distemper next year that way. Or I can find them homes. If a kitten doesn't have a tail, it is easy to find them a home. I never call them Manx, I just say they don't have tails. My husband used to cut off the tails with his pocket knife. Now I need you to help these poor little kittens find homes."

"What do you tell folks when they try to breed these kittens, expecting to get kittens without tails?" I ask.

"That only happened once," June said. "Most people have them fixed like I recommend. That one time, I just said, what do you think I am, some sort of a geneticist? That word shuts up most folks around these parts."

"You win the argument about the ethics of tail docking," I said. "I'm not comfortable with you deceiving people about what kind of cat they are getting."

"So you would rather I got the neighbor boy to put them in a gunny sack and drop them in the river?" June said.

"Okay, I'll dock the tails for you if you get it scheduled before they're five days old," I said. "But, if any of these kittens end up here for their shots or to be fixed, I won't be a part of your deception. If asked, I'll tell the truth."

"I see, you would rather have them search for a real Manx kitten," June said. "Half of which will have bowel and rectal problems for their entire life. Many of those will not reach adulthood. My kittens save a lot of little girls a lot of heartaches."

"Your husband must not have won many arguments," I said.

June had the kittens in the next morning. The procedure was brief, I prepped the tail, snipped the tails with scissors and closed the wound with a drop of Nexiban surgical adhesive. The kittens were asleep before they left the office.

I didn't charge June. I felt her intentions were sincere. In those years, I donated a lot of services to the humane society. June was serving in the same capacity. I only hoped that the humane society didn't get wind of her philosophies. ~

Saved by Daisy

I just don't know what's wrong with her, David," Violet said. "She won't jump up on the bed, and she cries if I try to pick her up."

Violet was one of my older clients. She was a tiny woman in her nineties with snow-white hair, and still very spry. She still lived by herself, her sole companion was a Shih Tzu with a dirty white coat. Daisy was at the center of Violet's activities.

I had noticed that Daisy was walking very carefully this morning. She was usually bouncing around when Violet came into the clinic. Today she tensed when I reached down to pick her up and whimpered as I placed her on the exam table.

"She is really sore, Violet," I said. "How long has this been going on?" "I noticed her moving slowly yesterday, and then she wouldn't jump up on the bed last night," Violet said. "She didn't say anything when I put her on the bed last night, but this morning she cried when I lifted her down."

Daisy tensed under my slightest touch. I ran my hands over her body, looking for a sore spot. I started with some gentle palpation of her abdomen first, then down her spinal column. She cried out as I came to the middle of her spinal column. I repeated the procedure, and she cried out again.

"Violet, she has hurt her back," I said. "Most likely she has a herniated disk, right in the middle of her back. That's a common location for a middle-aged Shih Tzu"

"Is she going to be alright?" Violet asked. "I just don't know what I will do if I lose her."

"Usually, there's little or no progression of signs as long as we get some anti-inflammatory medication on board," I explained. "But I should get a set of pictures just to make sure there isn't anything else." "David, I just can't afford to spend a lot of money today," Violet said. "You know, Social Security just doesn't pay an old lady much

these days. And I have just about outlived my savings account." "I'll get a set of x-rays," I said. "And I will worry about how to pay for them. We keep a little slush fund for just such an occasion. But you have to understand, x-rays often don't show a lot on a case like this where there is no nerve dysfunction."

"Then why do you want to take them?" Violet asked.

"I just want you to know what we can expect tomorrow and next month," I said. "It really doesn't matter what the x-rays show us. Daisy is not a candidate for surgery, and she will have to have some lifestyle changes."

"Lifestyle changes!" Violet says. "Now really, David, she lives with this old lady, we don't have much of a lifestyle."

"Little changes," I said with a chuckle. "Things like no jumping and no stairs, keeping four feet on the ground. Making her a bed on the floor and maybe losing a little weight."

"We don't have any stairs. Keeping four feet on the ground might be a challenge as Daisy likes to stand up for treats," Violet said. "Making her a bed on the floor will be difficult for both of us." "The bed on the floor might be the most important," I said. "We'll see what her back looks like on x-rays, but just one jump off the bed, and she could end up paralyzed."

The x-rays didn't show much. That is often the case with middle-aged Shih Tzus. There was just some narrowing of one intervertebral disk space in the middle of her back.

"This is just what I expected," I said as I reviewed the x-rays with Violet. "Daisy is going to do well. We'll put her on some anti-inflammatory medication for a few days and provide her with some cage rest while on medication. We can keep her here for the cage rest if you would like."

"I most certainly would not like, David!" Violet said with a stern voice. "I could not live without her for those three days. My daughter has a kennel, and if she doesn't, I'm sure my neighbor does."

So Daisy went home with Violet. I would have felt better if she had some help at home, as we loaned her a kennel for the trip to her house.

"You need to call your neighbor and have her help you get Daisy into the house," I said.

"Yes, David, I will give her a call as soon as I get home," Violet said. "I will have a lot to talk to her about, with all of Daisy's problems."

Violet's neighbor was most helpful, indeed. She got Daisy into the house for Violet and loaned her a large kennel. Then she brought the small kennel we had loaned Violet back to the clinic. We made sure that she knew everything that was to be done over the next few days.

We expected things to be uneventful for Violet as Daisy mended her back. Nothing could be further from the truth.

The following morning Violet made an early morning call to her neighbor. Violet complained that she could not sleep with Daisy now sleeping on the floor, and Daisy whined all night because she was not on the bed with Violet.

Then the unexpected happened. Violet passed out in the middle of the conversation, her neighbor heard her hit the floor, and she hung up and dialed 911. Then she rushed over to Violet's house to find Violet completely unresponsive on the kitchen floor.

The EMTs were there within minutes. Violet was in cardiac arrest. A couple shocks with the paddles, and she was revived. The neighbor took Daisy to her house, and Violet spent several days in the hospital. But she did return home and lived in an assisted facility several more years.

Numerous studies show pet ownership is a big plus for older people. People with pets tend to have fewer medical problems themselves and, in general, live longer than their non-pet owning peers.

In Violet's case, it was undeniable that Daisy was instrumental in her living longer. Had Violet not been on the telephone to her neighbor that morning, they would have found her dead on the kitchen floor. ~

Charlie and Betty and Foster

Charlie's horses were pretty well managed, and after the breeding season, there was not a lot to do around the farm.

Betty managed to keep their account pretty active.

"What brings you in today?" I asked Betty when she eased through the front door. Betty was a slightly built woman with black, shoulder-length hair. She seemed a little shy most of the time when Charlie was around, but I suspect that she could hold her own in most situations.

"This darn cat of mine is peeing everywhere," she said with some concern in her voice.

This darn cat was named Foster; he was an old guy. He was approaching the golden year for male cats in the 1970s. I seldom saw a male cat over fifteen years, and if I remembered correctly, Foster was going to be fifteen this summer. Betty had found him as a kitten under the dumpster at Glen's Market in Foster. He pretty much had the run of the place now.

"Peeing all over the place, small puddles or large puddles?" I asked. "Oh, they are large puddles when they're on the floor. He peed on the bed this morning. That's why I'm here, it woke up Charlie,
and he was none too happy," Betty explained.

"Well, let's get him in an exam room and look at him and see if I can get some urine out of him."

Pulling him out of the carrier, I noticed that he was much thinner than he was in the past. There was urine in the kennel. "Oh my," Betty exclaimed, "how could there be so much urine already?" "We'll get a quick look at this urine first, then I'll do an exam,"
I said as I drew up some urine from the kennel.

This urine would do fine for a dipstick but we would need a better collection if we were going to have to do additional testing. I handed the syringe to Dixie and returned my attention to Foster. He was quite thin, ribs showing through his hair coat. His eyes had early cataracts, sometimes these old guys just have trouble finding their way to the litter box. He was dehydrated also. My guess was either advanced kidney failure, the most common cause of death in an old cat, or possibly diabetes. I seldom saw diabetes in the cat, but it was definitely on the list.

Dixie popped into the exam room and laid the results of the dipstick on the counter. A four-plus urine glucose and normal specific gravity just about confirmed a diabetes diagnosis.

"Betty, Foster probably has diabetes. We need to do some blood tests to make sure and to check his liver and kidney function. Then we need to give him some fluids and get him on a stable insulin dose. He's probably going to have to stay with us a day or two."

"Doc, I can leave him for the day, but I don't want to leave him overnight. If he's going to die, I want him to die at home," Betty said in a stern voice. I had not heard that voice from her before.

"We can probably work with that, but I'll need to see him every morning for a week or so. We'll start off with a pretty low dose of insulin and work it up slowly," I explained.

"The other thing we need to discuss is what we can expect with his treatment. He's almost fifteen, and I don't see very many male cats older than fifteen. Diabetes is a difficult disease to live with for people. For people to manage the disease in pets is even more difficult. Top that off and cats are also difficult to treat when they have diabetes. A high percentage of pets with diabetes are euthanized within six months of diagnosis, just because of the difficulty of living with the disease."

"We'll do whatever we need to do to keep Foster alive," Betty said. "I know he's old, and I know he won't last forever, but we won't be the ones to give up on him."

With that, we kept Foster for the day. His blood glucose was well over four hundred, and other blood tests were normal. We gave him 300 ml of Ringers Lactate by subcutaneous injection and started him on a low dose of insulin.

Betty was waiting at the door every morning with Foster. My guess was the barn chores would wait until his treatment was done. Testing at the time was cumbersome. The first few days, we did both a blood test and urine glucose. Foster was obviously feeling much better, looking brighter, and Betty reported him to be much more active and peeing less. My goal was to get his glucose to somewhere around two hundred, just to a level he could live with and not have much in the way of a hypoglycemia risk.

By the third day, we were there. "I think this is the dose we use for a couple of weeks," I explained to Betty. We had been showing her how to do the injections all week. "I still want to see him for a couple of days, just to check his urine glucose and give the dose in the morning, Then we'll turn you loose at home."

Thursday morning, expecting a quick check, Foster's urine showed no glucose. Great, so much for a simple case. We drew a little blood. Blood glucose was fifty, pretty low.

"No insulin for Foster today," I explained to Betty. "Sometimes, in the cat, we'll see a remission or sometimes a fluctuation in insulin requirement. So no insulin today, and we will check him in the morning."

Friday morning, and there was still no glucose in his urine. We decided to go the weekend without insulin and recheck on Monday. This might prove to be a complicated case to manage.

On Monday, Foster's urine showed a 4+ glucose, and his blood glucose was over three hundred. So we started over where we left off. "That would be great if you could check his urine every morning, but I'm not sure that you could get urine out him," I said. "We'll have you check his glucose every morning, give insulin if it's positive, That's not perfect, but we'll l see how that works.

You just call in the mornings and let Dixie know how things are going so she can keep his record up to date."

So that was the program, Betty was happy, Foster was delighted, I was hopeful that we would not have a wreck. I could not believe that Betty could get urine every day.

Two weeks later, when Betty was in for a recheck, I noticed that the daily record was complete. There was a two-day stretch where she did not give insulin. Foster had gained almost two pounds and starting to look like his old self.

"Things look like they're going well," I said. "But it looks like you're going have to check his urine every day, his insulin demands are just going to fluctuate enough that we have to have a daily check. My concern is, how are you going to get urine out of him every day?"

"That's no problem, I just have him pee in a coffee cup," Betty said with no expression, just like that was something everybody would do.

Betty was able to manage Foster for another three years with this simple program of monitoring. Consistently during those years, Foster would have several days each month where he would have no need for insulin. We could have managed him closer and done away with those days, but I am not sure that his quality of life and the quality of life for Charlie and Betty would have been improved. ~

The Wolf Hybrid

Sandy and I had a dinner meeting with the local group of veterinarians in Albany. It was always a hassle to go out. First, we had to get out of the clinic on time, and then the babysitter had to show up on time.

When Sandy and I were finally dressed and in the car, we glanced at each other and stifled a laugh. We were escaping for a few hours by ourselves.

Pulling out of the driveway, we headed toward Albany. We were almost to Bauman mill, halfway to Lebanon, when the red light came on, and the car was overheating. We pulled off the road, and I looked under the hood. Unlike many of my high school friends, I was never a car guy. In this case, even I could see the remains of a fan belt.

I looked around and saw a house a couple hundred yards down the road. I told Sandy to sit tight and headed down the road to the house.

Knocking on the door, an older lady, probably in her fifties, answered the door.

"It looks like I lost a fan belt, and I was wondering if I could use your phone to call a tow truck?" I said.

"Where are you at?" she asked.

"We are at the pullout, a couple hundred yards back up the road."

"My husband has a shop at a service station in town," the lady said. "We are just finishing dinner. He and my son will come tow you to town in a few minutes."

"That is far more than I would expect," I said.

"It's no problem," she said. "They will be happy to help."

I walked back to the car. Sandy was glad to see me.

"I hate sitting alone in a car beside the road," Sandy said. "I am scared that some idiot will come and run off with me."

"Well, we are in luck," I said. "The guy at that house has an auto shop in Lebanon, and he and his son will be here shortly and tow us to the shop. Hopefully, they can put on a new belt."

It wasn't long before Adam and his son Dan pulled up with a pickup. Adam checked under the hood at confirmed it was a fan belt.

"These Chevys are notorious for losing this belt," Adam said. "We will tow you to town, and I will get a new belt on that in a jiffy."

"That would be great," I said, not wanting to ask how much this would cost. Whatever it costs would be fine.

They hooked a tow line to the car, and Adam reviewed the procedure with Dan.

"Dan will drive your car," Adam said. "We have done this before, and it is better that way."

We loaded up, and Adam pulled out onto the highway. It wasn't long, and we pulled into the service station where they had their shop. Dan unhooked the car while Adam grabbed a fan belt. Five minutes later, we were ready to go.

"How much do I owe you?" I asked.

"We are fine, you were in need, and we were glad to help you out," Adam said. "You don't owe us anything."

"You can't make a living giving everything away," I said.

"No, I'm serious. You don't owe us a thing," Adam repeated.

"I should at least pay for the fan belt," I said.

"When you need some work done, just remember where we are located," Adam said.

I reached for my wallet and pulled out a business card.

"Listen, I have started a new veterinary clinic in Sweet Home," I said. "If you need any services, just give me a call, and I will return the favor."

"Fair enough," Adam said, handing my card to Dan. "We have a few critters. We might be able to take you up on that if you remember who we are."

"I have a good memory," I said. "If you have any needs, just call and ask for me."

We pulled out onto the highway and probably drove too fast, trying to make it to our dinner meeting before we were left out.

We had a reserved room upstairs at The Hereford Steer. We were the last to arrive but made it in time for dinner. This was a small, almost informal group of local veterinarians. I would guess that we fell under the auspices of the Oregon Veterinary Medical Association, but there was no formal organization to this group.

The Reid brothers, Bob and Dick had organized this meeting. We had a medical doctor give a program on his trip to Nepal to climb a mountain. I forget the mountain, but I think it was K-2.

Other veterinarians in the group included Roy Craig, Don Myrtue, and Fritz Kaiser. The wives were all in attendance, but most of their names were lost to my memory.

Other local veterinarians who occasionally attended meetings were Phil Brittain and Ben Bratt. They were not in attendance this evening.

After dinner, we had the program. The mountain climbing was interesting, but we would never be doing that any time soon.

The doctor ran into some interesting ethical issues on the trip. Their group traveled through the back country of Nepal. Most of the villages were very poor and had virtually no access to medical care. When the word got out that a member of their group was a medical doctor, there were always people waiting to see him in every village.

He had brought a small inventory of medical supplies and antibiotics, in case the climbing party ran into a medical problem. It was soon apparent that the villagers' needs were going to deplete those supplies. Should he treat the lady with a life-threatening infection with antibiotics that could be needed by the climbing group? Of course, he gave the antibiotics to the lady, thus saving her life via a chance meeting for an exam.

***

Weeks, then months, flew by and the events of that evening faded into my memory when there was a phone call from Dan.

"This is Dan," Dan said. "Do you remember when we towed you to our shop in Lebanon?"

"Yes, I remember," I said. "What do you have going on, Dan?"

"Well, we have this wolf hybrid and also a little chihuahua. She is in heat, and he is going crazy because they just don't match up, size-wise."

Great, I thought. Wolf hybrids were illegal in the county then, and I had refused to treat several of them. Now I was stuck. I couldn't refuse Dan.

"I was wondering if you could spay her while she is in heat?" Dan asked.

"It's not the best practice, but I have done that before," I said. "People think that solves the problem instantly, and that doesn't happen. It takes several days for the odors and swelling to go away. But several days are better than a couple of weeks."

"That would be great," Dan said. "When can we get it done?"

"It just happens that we have some time in the morning," I said. "Can you bring her in about eight? Make sure she doesn't have anything to eat or drink at night or in the morning."

"Thanks," Dan said. "I will have her there in the morning."

I hung up the phone with a sour look on my face.

"That look tells me you didn't like that call," Dixie said.

"A few months ago, we lost a fan belt in the car," I said. "Dan and his father towed us to Lebanon and replaced the belt at their auto shop. They wouldn't take any money for it, so I told them when they had a dog problem to bring it to me, and I would take care of it."

"That sounds like a good way to get even," Dixie said. "So, what is the problem?"

"The problem is they have a wolf hybrid in heat, and they want her spayed," I said.

"Oh, no," Dixie said. "Do they know they are not supposed to have one of those in this county?"

"I didn't get into that," I said. "I couldn't renege on my offer. They really got us out of a pinch that night. They saved our night out. I am really in their debt, so I need to do this for them. I just hope we can handle the dog."

"I hear some of those hybrids are really hard to handle," Dixie said.

"If she is a problem, I guess we could get a dose of Rompun into her before Dan leaves," I said.

"Now, you are going to have trouble getting to sleep tonight," Dixie said.

***

Dixie had been right on the problem of getting to sleep. I lay awake half the night, worrying about all the issues we would face in the morning.

The legal issue was not a big concern. There was little enforcement of such ordinances. As long as nobody got bit, it would not be a problem. The problem would be if the people with other hybrids learned that I would work on them, they would flood the clinic.

Not only that, but it was spaying a large dog in heat. There were more possibilities of complications that would require a recheck. By the time I got to the clinic, I was sick with worry.

I busied myself setting up the surgery room. I was glad that we had a slow morning. I could bring the dog right into surgery without putting her in a kennel that we might have trouble getting her out of. I was running everything over in my mind. I was sure there would be a problem somewhere.

Dixie interrupted my struggles.

"Dan is here with our spay," Dixie said with a smile.

I dropped what I was doing and walked to the reception area to greet Dan. There he was with his Chihuahua sitting on his lap

I laughed at myself out loud.

"What's the matter?" asked Dan, somewhat confused by my laugh.

"I was planning to spay a wolf hybrid," I said. "I guess I got the sexes mixed up when you told me your problem."

"Oh, I am sorry about that," Dan said. "I guess it would have been the same problem the other way around."

"Who do we have here?" I asked.

"This is Roxy," Dan said. "She is pretty hungry. She was upset that her dish was empty this morning."

"The day is set up so we can go right into surgery with her this morning," I said. "She should be ready to go home any time this afternoon."

"Good, I have some stuff to do this evening, so I will be here right after lunch," Dan said. "How much am I going to owe for this?"

"You're going to owe just what I had to pay for that fan belt," I said.

Dan smiled, "That's good, thanks a lot."

Dan left and Dixie and I took Roxy into an exam room to get started on the day.

"I was never so relieved to see a Chihuahua in my life," I said.

There's Gold in Them Hills

It was a little after eleven in the morning, and Bob should be coming through the door any minute. He was sort of the highlight of our morning in the office. Bob had been our postman ever since the office opened. He was older, probably getting close to retirement, but he was a joy to talk with.

I think he must have scheduled us for his break on his route because he always seemed to have several minutes to talk. Bob was a Sweet Home native or as close as one could be to a native. He knew everyone in town so if we wanted to know about someone, Bob could give a pretty good synopsis.

Bob could talk gold. He knew where to look in every stream, and he shared that information only to a trusted few. I liked to think I was one of those entrusted few. The reality of the thing was he knew I was too busy to chase any of his stories.

Bob had lost a son who was my age, a lieutenant in the Army. In those years of the Vietnam War, Bob was probably preparing himself for his son serving in the war. Instead, he was driving home from the East Coast, and died in an auto accident.

We bumped into Bob one afternoon when he was panning gold with a friend. Bob took the time to give the kids and me a lesson on how to work the pan. We came up with a lot of black sand but no color. Bob truly enjoyed teaching his hobby to the kids, including myself, although "hobby" wasn't entirely accurate. I think gold was Bob's true vocation. His postal job and any other work in his life only allowed him to pursue his real life's work.

Bob told me a story one day about one of his trips to the California goldfields. He and a group of friends would make an annual trip to the areas out of Sacramento, California to pan for gold. This was a working trip for this group of guys. They would rework some of the same streams that were the site of the 1849 gold rush.

Bob said that on one of these trips, they had a new guy along. He was always underfoot and trying to learn every little thing he could from these old guys. Bob finally tired of putting up with the newcomer. Bob pointed to a distant sandbar up the creek.

"Why don't you go up there and work that sandbar," Bob said. The guy took his shovel and pan and headed up to the sandbar, leaving Bob and the rest of the crew to continue to work with the dredge where they had been all morning.

"That was the biggest damn mistake that I ever made," Bob said to me. "Just before quitting time that afternoon, this guy comes down the creek with a gold nugget the size of the end of your finger. I was so mad at myself after that, I almost couldn't eat dinner." One August afternoon, a new client, Rob, came in with his dog, Yoda, a pit bull cross. Yoda had a pretty severe laceration on the large pad of his right front foot. Yoda had been camping with his owner way up the Calapooia River at the mouth of State Creek. "Yoda spends most of the day in the river with me," Rob said. "If he is not in the river, he's chasing a squirrel somewhere up the creek. I don't know when this happened, I noticed him licking his foot last night, and then this morning he was limping on that foot quite a bit."

Yoda was an excellent dog, and he didn't flinch while I examined his foot. This was a deep laceration that extended halfway across the carpal pad, front to back. This was going to be challenging to get healed, especially in a dog who was used to spending a lot of the day in the river.

"Pad lacerations are difficult to manage in the best of circumstances," I said to Rob. "In a dog who's spending a lot of his time in the river, it might be impossible."

"I can keep him out of the water for a couple of weeks," Rob said. "I am not on any schedule. I'm just spending the summer up there panning for gold."

"I suture most of these," I said. "By suturing them and keeping them wrapped for a couple of weeks, most of them will heal. If we can't keep a dry wrap on the foot, there is little chance that the sutures will hold."

"When can you do this?" Rob asked. "Keep in mind, I'm a long way from camp."

"I can probably do it shortly," I said. "But it's going to take a little time for Yoda to wake up."

"This dog is the toughest dog I have ever owned," Rob said. "You could probably sew this up without giving him anything. Is there any chance you could do it with local anesthesia?"

"We can try," I said. "Yoda will let us know if that is an option or not."

We moved Yoda into the surgery room and laid him down on his side. He did not react as we started scrubbing the wound. Rob stood on the opposite side of the table from me and scratched Yoda's ears.

I drew up a syringe of Lidocaine and looked at Rob.

"We're going to find out right now. This stuff stings a little, I hate it myself," I said.

Avoiding the laceration, I slid the needle through the skin at the front edge of the pad, injecting a little at a time as I advanced the needle under the pad. I injected half the syringe here and then repeated the process from the back edge of the pad.

After a few minutes, I parted the edges of the laceration. There was no response from Yoda. Spreading the wound wide, I scraped the deep crevice of the wound. I applied some Neosporin into the crevice and wiped it out with a sterile sponge. Then I draped the wound.

Taking a deep breath, I stabbed the pad with a suture needle. There was no response from Yoda. I glanced at Rob and smiled as I continued to close the wound. In this type of deep pad lacerations, I would use a deep vertical mattress suture using stints on each side to spread the tension across the wound edges so the stitches would not tear the tissues.

Closure took only a few minutes. And then I applied a wrap that extended halfway up the leg.

"The key to healing this wound is the wrap," I said. "If it gets wet, it needs to be changed. Otherwise, we'll change it every third day. Is that a schedule that will work for you?"

"I can work with that schedule," Rob said as he let Yoda stand up on the table.

"I'll put him on some antibiotics just to make sure we keep the infection down as much as possible," I said.

With that, Rob and Yoda headed back to camp. We started on their schedule of regular visits. Rob did a great job of keeping the wrap dry, and the wound looked better with each wrap change. After two weeks, we had a decision to make.

"We could go without the wrap starting now," I said. "This wound looks good, but I really would like to go one more week."

"The squirrels are going to love you, Doc," Rob said.

The following week we removed the wrap and the sutures. This wound healed as well as any pad laceration that I had managed. I patted Yoda on the head when I set him down on the floor.

"It's been fun working with Yoda," I said as I shook hands with Rob. "It's been good working for you, too. How long are you going to be around these parts?"

"I'll probably break camp in a couple of weeks," Rob said. "You never know about a guy like me, I might back next year, or I might be in Colorado."

As the days passed, Rob and Yoda sort of slipped to the back of my mind. I was a little surprised when Rob was in the reception room one afternoon. He motioned to me, indicating he had something to show me. I invited him back into the exam area, and he looked at an empty exam room and stepped into it.

"I have to show this, Doc," Rob said. "I saw this under a large boulder, and it took me three days to get to it."

Rob had something wrapped in a square of rawhide in his left hand. He held his hand out as he peeled back the folds of rawhide.

There, in the palm of his left hand, was the largest gold nugget that I had ever seen. I didn't have words.

"Wow!" I said.

"This is what keeps us guys with gold fever going," Rob said.

It was a few days later when I had time to meet Bob when he came through the door with the mail.

"Bob, I have a story to tell you," I said.

"Well now, that is a switch," Bob said, "you telling a story."

"Bob, I just spent a few weeks working on a dog for a guy who was camped up the Calapooia River at the mouth of State Creek," I started.

"I know the area," Bob said.

"He came into the clinic the other day with a nugget wrapped in a piece of rawhide," I said. "This nugget covered the palm of his hand and was over an inch thick."

I motioned on my hand the size of the nugget. Bob grabbed my forearm, his eyes wide open, and his pupils expanded as wide as possible.

"No!" Bob said, "I have been all over that river and that area. There is gold there, quite a bit of the stuff. But it is all small, tiny stuff really. I have never seen a nugget come out of the Calapooia." "Well, I don't know," I said. "That was the biggest nugget I've ever seen."

"That's a twenty-thousand-dollar nugget, maybe thirty thousand dollars," Bob said. "But I can't believe it came out of the Calapooia." "I guess, when I think about it, he never specifically said it came out of the Calapooia, I just assumed it," I said. "He has been camped up there most of the summer."

"Now you've done it," Bob said. "I'm not going to be able to sleep until I can get up there and start looking through the place myself."

Had Bob lived a couple of generations earlier, I am sure he would have been one of those guys with a crooked hat and burro, chasing gold stories up and down the streams around here. ~

The Birds and the Bees
and Basset Puppies

We had just finished dinner and were supervising the girls as they cleaned up the dinner table when the telephone rang. "Good evening, Doc," Sandi said into the phone. "I hope you've finished dinner. Betty has been pushing for about three hours. She has broken some water, but there is no evidence of a pup."

I cared for quite a few basset hounds for a group of women who showed these dogs. They were relatively valuable dogs, and the women wanted meticulous veterinary care. Betty, a champion basset, had been in labor for nearly three hours.

Her owner, Sandi, had been through this on multiple deliveries. Three hours of contractions without a pup was cause for intervention, and with each passing minute, the puppies were more at risk.

"It sounds like we should get a look at her," I said. "I can be at the clinic in twenty minutes."

Of our four kids, Amy, our second grader, took the most interest in the goings-on at the clinic. She liked the people and the animals and showed compassion for both. She was ready to go to the clinic with me in an instant.

Sandi came through the door with a very pregnant Betty and two women friends, recruited to help.

We carefully lifted Betty onto the exam table.

"Judging from the size of this stomach, this is going to be a large litter," I said.

"She had ten puppies in her first litter," Sandi said. "I'm guessing there is more this time."

I cleaned Betty up. She did have some greenish fluid dripping from her vulva. This was an indication that her water had broken some hours ago. A quick vaginal exam failed to reveal any pup in the birth canal.

"You know the story," I said to Sandi. "Betty has been in labor for several hours, and there is no pup in the birth canal. The longer this goes on, the more the puppies are at risk. Our options are to try some oxytocin or to go right to a C-section."

The oxytocin injections could work magic, but it could also mean a long night. When bassets have large litters, you can end up with a C-section for the last pup or two because the uterus runs out of strength for continued contractions. With the extended time of labor, those remaining puppies are often lost.

I enjoyed working with Sandi on these deliveries because she would always be quick to elect a C-section. I agreed with her in most of the cases. It made for a shorter night for me and usually a more successful delivery.

"Let's not spend all night here. Let's just go to a C-section, and everyone will be better for it," she said.

I called Dixie, my right hand at the clinic, to come help. Sandi had a couple of friends in tow. That would mean we had four gals to tend to the puppies, plus Amy. Sounds okay, but my guess was over ten pups, maybe twelve or thirteen. We are going to be very busy for a few minutes when I start handing out puppies.

While waiting for Dixie, I got the surgery room set up, giving Amy several chores to help. She conducted herself like an old pro. "Amy, you need to bring a stack of towels and put them on that little table in the corner," I said. "When we do this surgery, the puppies are surrounded by a lot of fluid, and it generally spills off the table onto the floor. We will need towels down to mop up that fluid."

I had Amy help hold Betty after I rolled her onto her back. It probably wasn't necessary to keep her on her back. Betty was sort of like a turtle on her back. Her belly spread out enough that she couldn't right herself if she tried. I clipped her belly, and we placed an IV catheter and got some fluids going.

As soon as Dixie arrived, we moved Betty into the surgery room and gave her a dose of IV Innovar, the morphine combination drug. This provided strong sedation, and we secured her to the surgery table and did a surgical prep on the abdomen. Then we used Lidocaine for local anesthesia at the incision line. This would allow us to deliver the pups with the least depression from anesthesia.

"Now we start the surgery," I said more like an announcement but specifically to Amy.

The surgery went well, and I had the abdomen open in short order. I started pulling the uterus out of the abdomen, one pup at a time. I laid it out across the drape on moistened towels. One puppy, then the next, and it kept coming. Finally, I had it all out, twelve pups, six in each uterine horn. This uterus, a pencil's size in its non-pregnant state, laid out on the drape and towels. It was too large to stay up on the abdomen. Several puppy segments hung over the abdomen on each side, reaching the surgery table's surface: quite a remarkable organ, the uterus.

I made an incision on one side of the uterus and quickly started extracting puppies. I handed this first pup to Dixie, and she gathered it up and headed back to the heated box and the reversal syringes. Now pups came in rapid succession. I would squeeze a puppy through the incision, clamp the umbilical, sever the cord, and hand the puppy to the next pair of hands.

"They look like they are doing well," Sandi said as she took the next pup and headed back to Dixie.

This continued. Finally, Amy's was the only set of hands available. She caught the pup in a towel and followed the girls to the puppy basket as if it was nothing out of the ordinary.

Everybody was back for their next pup, and Amy assumed her place in the line. Finally, the last puppy, number twelve, was delivered. I double-check the birth canal just to make sure there is not a pup hiding there.

Amy was back to watch the finish. "Now, I just have to remove all the placentas and make sure there's nothing left in the uterus," I explained. "Then, I just close the incisions, and we're done."

With the uterus closed, I return it to the abdomen and closed the abdominal incision.

"Nothing left except to wake up Mom and introduce her to her new family," I explain to Amy.

Once everything was closed up, I gave Betty a reversal drug, and she recovered rapidly. We returned her to the kennel, and she was awake before we knew it. She was an experienced mother, and she took the pups as soon as we showed them to her.

There was fluid covering the table, and the floor was soaked. My tennis shoes will be retired to the work shoe shelf. The towels that Amy laid on the floor have soaked up most of the fluid. Now there was a little time to relax. Twelve live pups, Sandi and her friends were pleased.

We sent Sandi, Betty, and pups home as soon as Betty could stand. She and her puppies will do better at home under Sandi's watchful eyes. I relaxed a little and looked at Amy. She has done well this evening.

"What do you think about all of this commotion tonight," I asked.

She just shrugged, didn't say a word, displaying a nonchalance that she probably got from me.

The C-section became a forgotten evening until we went to a parent-teacher conference some weeks later.

Mrs. Rose, Amy's second-grade teacher, was a little gray-haired woman who was very prim and proper. Adored by her students and their parents alike, she was an old-time teacher, very much into the three Rs. She kept a tight rein on her classroom, ruling it with a tender heart.

Mrs. Rose went over Amy's progress, which was exceptional, and then looked at us with a wry smile.

"A few weeks ago, the whole class had quite a learning experience about where puppies come from and how they get here. Amy was very excited about her experience and very descriptive of the surgery she helped you do. I don't generally worry about discussing the birds and the bees in my classes. Your daughter sort of changed all of that," she said. ~

The Salamander's Tale

J ake lifted his young son out of the pickup and handed him off to Sue as he opened the tailgate and let Bruiser jump out of the pickup bed.

They could already feel the cooling breeze coming from the river and providing some welcome relief from the mid-Willamette Valley's August heat.

Bruiser was excited, he had been here before, and he strained against Jake's hold on his collar while Jake struggled to attach a leash. Sue was double-checking everything in her bag. She didn't want to make a trip up the bank to the pickup for some forgotten item. Finally, she was ready.

"Okay, let's get to the water," Sue said as she jostled Benny on her hip.

Bruiser strained at the end of the leash, trying to reach the trail leading down to the river. Jake had to lean back against the pull to keep from being pulled off his feet.

"Why don't you just let him go?" Sue asked.

"We don't know who's down there. I don't want to end the day with a dog fight."

They threaded their way down the trail to the river from the highway. The far shoreline was filled with people, kids, and dogs. This side was a little more challenging to get up and down from the road, but it was much less crowded for that very reason.

"I wish that the Cascadia State Park side wasn't so crowded," Sue said. "It's so much easier to get down to the river."

"We'll enjoy the day so much more on this side," Jake said. "Bruiser can run off-leash, and we won't have to worry about all the dogs on the far bank."

There was a small beach with soft, warm sand on this side of the river. Everywhere else was just smooth bedrock that the river flowed over. Several large holes of deepwater offered prime swimming areas. They were connected with short rapids as the water cascaded over the shale.

The breeze coming up the river was most refreshing, and Sue spread the large beach towel out on the soft sand and sat down with Benny. The little beach was shaded by the large maple trees that lined the river, so she didn't have to worry about smearing sunblock on Benny.

"This feels so nice here. I wished we lived closer, so it wasn't such a chore to get here," Sue said.

"It would be nice," Jake said as he released Bruiser from the leash and started to wade into the water. "When I was young, and we lived Sweet Home, it was an easy trip. But from Albany, it just seems like it takes forever."

Jake dove into the deep pool. He popped up and looked back at Sue and Benny on the little beach. The cold water was a refreshing contrast to the valley heat.

Sue tried to get Benny to look at his father, and Bruiser was standing in the river with the water touching his chest. Being a pit bull, he was not a good swimmer and did not like the deep water.

Jake thought he would do a deep dive and then take Bruiser up to the shallow water beyond the rapids above this hole. Jake dove to the bottom of the hole.

This was a hole carved into the smooth bedrock of the river. The hole's bottom was littered with large river gravel—rocks worn smooth from being tumbled down the river during the rainy season. As Jake turned to head for the surface, he noticed several trout feeding in the area where the water spilled into the rapids' deep hole. They seemed oblivious to his presence.

Jake returned to the beach and grabbed Benny from his toys on the beach towel. He tossed him a few inches in the air. Jake would have thrown him high, but Sue would not allow that. Then he took Benny to the water's edge, put his feet in the water, and splashed some water on his bare belly.

"Would you play with Benny in the water while I take Bruiser up to the shallow water?" Jake asked Sue.

Sue set her book down and jumped up to take Benny. Jake motioned to Bruiser and headed up the stream toward the shallow water.

Bruiser plowed into the shallow water above the rapids. He splashed and ran, piling up a wake in front of his broad chest. Jake watched him and smiled. He liked this place so much as it reminded him of his days as a child. Few people knew of the little sandy beach. It was always like their little private spot.

Jake stood and surveyed the scene in front of him. The cool breeze coming up the river was in his face. Sue and Benny were playing in the water at the beach and the mass of people frolicking on the rocks at the deep holes down the river by the park. It was just about a perfect day, an ideal place.

Jake turned around and looked at Bruiser. Bruiser was standing in a shallow pool and had a yellow-bellied newt hanging from his mouth by its tail.

"Put that thing down!" Jake yelled at Bruiser.

Bruiser looked at him, then slurped the salamander into his mouth, chomped a time or two, and swallowed it.

"I hope that tasted good, you dumb dog," Jake said. "Come on, let's go back to the beach."

Jake turned and started back down the stream to where Sue had just started drying Benny off with a large beach towel.

He looked to make sure Bruiser was following. Bruiser was foaming at the mouth a little and shaking his head, scattering foam into the water on both sides of him.

"I told you to put that thing down, now look at you. Come on, let's go get you cleaned up."

Bruiser started to follow Jake down the stream, staggering a bit as he ran across the rocks.

"What in the world happened to Bruiser?" Sue asked as they approached the beach.

"He ate one of those salamanders that are all over here this time of the year. I think they call them newts."

"I seem to think that they might be poisonous. Just look at Bruiser now. He can hardly walk."

Jake turned to look at Bruiser. He was stumbling and staggering to keep up with him. His chest was covered with the thick white foam that he continued to shake out of his mouth.

"I'll wash out his mouth. That should make it a little better."

"I don't think so. I think this is serious," Sue said. "I think we should take him to the vet. There is probably one in Sweet Home." "Maybe you're right. Let's load up and run down there and have him checked."

Sue hastily packed her things into her bag and grabbed Benny, and started up the trail. Jake put the leash on Bruiser and gave it a tug. Bruiser did not respond.

Jake looked closely at Bruiser. Bruiser's eyes seemed unfocused. Jake pulled on the leash again. Bruiser tried to take a step but fell face-first into the sand. Jake was anxious now.

He gathered Bruiser up in his arms and clambered up the trail to the pickup.

"He's getting worse by the minute," Jake said to Sue as he lowered the tailgate and slid Bruiser into the bed of the pickup. Bruiser looked up but did not try to stand. The pupils of his eyes were widely dilated, and he seemed to look without focus.

"Let's hurry. We can stop at the store and get directions and have them call for us," Sue said.

They loaded everything into the cab and sped off down the road to the store.

Sue ran into the little store. Joyce was behind the counter. "Our dog swallowed a salamander, and he was foaming at the mouth and staggering by the time he got out of the water. I don't think he can stand now. Can you call the vet for us in Sweet Home and let them know that we are on our way?"

Joyce gave Sue directions to the clinic and said she would call.

"You guys drive safe going down that road out there. The traffic is pretty heavy today."

Sue looked at Bruiser as she walked around the pickup to get in on the passenger side.

"He looks worse by the minute," Sue said. "She is going to call, so they'll be waiting for us."

Jake pulled out onto the highway and turned on his emergency flashers. Then he pushed the gas pedal to the floor. It was going to be a challenging thirteen miles.

Sandy took the call from Joyce.

"It must be bad," Joyce said. "She was really frantic. They should be there shortly if they don't crash on the way."

Sandy relayed the information to Terri and me. "What do you for that?" Terri asked.

"Those newts are highly toxic. This is probably going to be a dead dog. There's nothing to be done. A young guy in Coos County swallowed one on a dare when they were partying on the river bank a few years ago. He died."

"So, these folks are going expect us to do something."

"Let's set up the endoscope. Maybe we can retrieve the thing from his stomach and reduce the dose. It will look like we are trying, but it's going to end with a dead dog."

When I was in school at Oregon State studying under Dr. Storm in the Zoology Department, he talked about one of his graduate students' studies on these newts in Western Oregon. They are called the Rough-Skinned Newt and are very toxic around here, less so in some areas. I didn't know at the time, but the student was from Myrtle Point. Older than me by a few years, but he was in high school with my brother. We called him Butch. He is pretty much the expert on the newt."

We were all set up for Jake and Sue's arrival with Bruiser. They came through the door in a rush. Bruiser was limp in Jake's arms, Sue was carrying Benny on her hip. We guided them to the treatment table, where Jake laid him out on the table.

"I think he's dead," Jake said. I checked. He was dead.

"We should have been faster," Jake said.

"I'm sorry, Jake. This is a hard way to lose a friend, but being faster would have made no difference. Bruiser signed his death certificate when he ate the salamander. There is nothing to be done to treat this toxicity."

"Do we owe you anything?" Sue asked.

"No, not at this point. Do you want us to take care of him for you?" I asked.

Jake gathered Bruiser up in his arms, "No, we will take him home. We have a place to bury him."

With that, they were gone, almost as fast as they came. "That was sad," Terri said.

So many people have no idea those little things are so deadly. As a kid, we played with them all the time. I never heard of a problem with them until I was in school at Oregon State. ~

The Painful Quill

D oc, my old Tank dog just came home tonight with a few porcupine quills in his mouth," Ed said into the phone.

I wonder why they either call at dinner time or three in the morning, I thought to myself as I listened to Ed, hoping I could get back to the table before everyone was done eating.

"I hear that I should be able to pull them out myself," Ed continues, "What do you think of that idea?"

"Some guys do it," I said. "I don't know how they get it done. Most of the time the dog is going to get real tired of the process pretty quick. I just put them under an anesthetic before I start. It's a lot easier that way, and you don't end up with a lot of broken and buried quills."

"He's not too bad," Ed said, "I might try to pull a few tonight and see how he does. If I have any problems, I'll just bring him into the office in the morning."

"That will be okay," I said. "Try to get Tank there early, right at eight, and I'll have some time to take care of him. I have a farm call scheduled for ten, and it's going to take me a few hours."

"If I'm coming, I'll be waiting for you at eight," Ed said as he hung up the phone.

Ed was waiting at the door with Tank when I pulled up to the clinic. I could see from the truck Ed's assessment of quill numbers was a bit off. He said a few quills, but old Tank's mouth and face was a mass of quills, probably two hundred. You could never trust a client to evaluate the number and severity of porcupine quills.

"I would say that Tank has a few more quills than a few," I said to Ed as I was unlocking the front door to the clinic. "I'm going to have to get started on him right away, or I'll be behind schedule all day."

"I pulled a couple of quills out last night, and Tank said that was enough, in no uncertain terms," Ed said as Dixie took Tank and headed for the treatment table.

"We'll get him taken care of right away," I said. "It will take him some time to wake up, and I'll want to check him when I get back from the farm call. We'll have him ready to go home anytime after three."

With that, we had Tank on the table, and I gave him a dose of IV Pentothal. Placing an endotracheal tube in a dog with a mouth full of quills can be a painful experience. My usual procedure was to hold the mouth open with a mouth gag, pull the tongue forward with my left hand and hold the epiglottis down with my index finger of the left hand. I could then guide the tube in place, with the whole procedure taking only a few seconds. With a mouth full of quills, there was no way I could stick a hand in that mouth. I would have to use a laryngoscope, it would work okay, just a little more cumbersome.

Tank was under anesthesia, and we started pulling quills. The porcupine quill is barbed. Under the microscope, the tip of the quill looks like a shingled roof. When they are pulled, it takes slow, steady pressure or you will break the tip off. I always hear from clients that it is easier if you cut the back end of the quill off, allowing the air inside the quill to escape, and pulling them is easier. I have never found that to make any noticeable difference.

I pulled the quills with a forceps, holding the skin in place with a finger so as not to bury any small quills in the area. Pull a quill, place it in a pan of water to facilitate getting it off the forceps and easier cleanup. With this many quills, the whole process takes an hour. I have to hurry to keep on schedule.

I would see most porcupine quills in the fall. I think this was because the porcupines are forced to come down out of the trees for water at the end of summer's dry period.

Most of the time, one episode was enough to teach the dog that he didn't want to mess with the critters. One time in Enumclaw, I saw the same three dogs, daily for three days. Each day one of the dogs would have the majority of the quills, and the other two would only have a couple of quills. On the third day, the owner confessed that he was going to have to go porcupine hunting.

Another dog, Jack, was the one exception to the rule. Jack was a cocker spaniel. Like all cockers, his activity level often exceeded his judgment. I pulled porcupine quills out of Jack at least five maybe six times.

I have seen a couple of cows with quills in their nose. I have never seen a horse with quills. One cat came in with quills completely through his front legs. It looked like he must have jumped on the porcupine.

***

"Hello, this is Cathy. The pups have been gone since dinner time, and they just came home," she says. "Kirk has porcupine quills. Could you take care of him tonight? I would hate for him to have to suffer until morning."

"I could probably meet you at the clinic," I said. "Did you check Spock? Many times if one has a lot of quills, the other one will at least have a few."

"Sam checked them both over pretty well," Cathy said. "Kirk is the only one with quills. It will take us half an hour to get to the clinic."

"I'll meet you there," I said.

Looking at Sandy, I said, "I hope this isn't an all-night affair. People are just not able to make a good judgment call evaluating porcupine quills."

Both Sam and Cathy were waiting when I pulled up the front of the clinic. They came up behind me when I started to unlock the front door. Kirk was standing with his head sticking between them. He looked at me with his mouth open, tongue hanging out, and panting. Kirk was probably still excited about the hunt and the ride to town. He had two quills stuck in the end of his nose.

I hooked a finger behind his canine tooth and raised his nose so I could get a good look to make sure there weren't any quills in his mouth.

"Is that all he has?" I asked Sam. "That is all I could find," Sam said.

I put my door key in my pocket and, with one quick motion, grabbed both quills and plucked them out of Kirk's nose. I brushed the blood droplets that sprang from the holes with the heel of my hand. Kirk stood there with his tail wagging.

"Let's go home. Do you want these?" I said, holding the two quills out to Sam. "They are sort of interesting if you can get them under a microscope."

Sam took the quills, looking a little confused at how fast the problem was handled.

"Do we owe you anything?" Cathy asked.

"I didn't have to open the door, I think we're square," I said.

~

Rosie

Rosie was a quiet Lab who lived with her family up the river from Cascadia. Their driveway was nearly a mile long and joined the highway just below Mountain House. Tall Douglas fir trees lined the road in this area and the river ran along the south side of the highway. The timber provided shade from the summer sun and the bubbling river provided additional cooling of the area. Even on the hottest day of summer, the upper reaches of the Santiam River provided a gentle breeze and mild temperatures.

Mountain House was the last semblance of civilization for the next fifty miles. Just past it the road started a steep climb to the Santiam Pass in the Cascade Mountains. The history of Mountain House goes back to the early years of Linn County. It was a hotel to begin with, serving clients who visited the soda springs in the area. Now it was a backcountry inn and general store. With no phone lines in this last vestige of civilization, you were isolated.

The road had its share of curves, so any travelers were moving slowly. People who took this route over the mountain were not in a hurry. They would turn off their air conditioning and open the windows so they could enjoy the fresh mountain air, hear the rushing water of the river, and hope to see some deer, elk, or any of the numerous birds in the area. Maybe even be lucky enough to glimpse a Big Foot. This area was as wild as any area in the state. Rosie's family was small. Her owners were an older couple who had lived in their little house on the banks of Soda Fork for many years. George and Alice Dunn relished the quiet and isolation. They seldom came to town, preferring to get what supplies they needed from the Mountain House. If they needed something special, they would order it, and the Mountain House would pick it up for them when they went to town for supplies.

Rosie shared this family with an old dog, Nick, an old black Lab, very arthritic, who didn't often get off the porch. He provided Rosie company, and while she licked his ears, she could share her adventures of the last squirrel hunt or the fishing trip in the deep holes of Soda Fork Canyon. Then they would curl up and sleep on the porch, Rosie keeping one eye open for the raccoons who would come by in the night. She hated those raccoons.

Life on the banks of Soda Fork was not without its challenges. A garden near the house was impossible because of the shade from the timber. They would grow their vegetables on some of the clearcuts located along road higher up the creek. They had learned to carry water to these gardens from the marijuana growers in the Cascadia area. They used an old waterbed mattress in the back of their pickup truck, would attach a hose to the outlet of the waterbed, and water the garden as needed.

Their meat supply came from the game harvested from the area. They took only the meat they needed, and they used every part of the animals collected. Whether a deer, an elk, or a couple of squirrels, they only took what they needed, and they gave thanks every time. The short canyon up Soda Fork provided some excellent fishing, especially in the spring and early summer. The access to the canyon was too difficult for the fishermen from town, so hunting and fishing seasons had little meaning for them, as they did not hunt or fish for sport but for subsistence. Game wardens only ventured into this area during hunting season when there were enough other people to make it safe for them to be off the main road.

We did not see the Dunns often. They would bring the dogs in for their rabies vaccination every three years. They felt they were isolated enough that they did not have to worry about the other vaccines.

"Your isolation might make those other vaccinations more important," I explained on one of their visits. "Dogs in town get a vaccination as a puppy, and then they see many other dogs in their lifetime. They are likely exposed naturally to most of the important viruses. Their immunity is likely to last for several years. We recommend boosters just to be sure because a disease like canine distemper is often fatal, and parvovirus can be extremely expensive to treat. Your dogs seldom see another dog, their immunity probably weakens much sooner than the town dogs who are likely to come into contact with those viruses naturally. Something to think about when considering their vaccinations."

During these routine visits, Rosie enjoyed the clinic and the treat jar. Nick, on the other hand, hated the trip to town and shook the entire time in the clinic. He would take a treat, only to drop it on the floor for Rosie. He would not be bought.

Nick continued to age and his arthritis became so severe that he could hardly get around. There was not much that we had to offer, medication wise, at that time. That last visit came when Nick could no longer get off the porch to do his business.

"Doc, we feel terrible about this, we wanted to wake up some morning and find that he had passed away in his sleep," George said. "Are we doing the right thing? We don't want to do this if you think we should wait."

"It's always a hard decision, but once you make it, you don't want to put yourselves and Nick through the struggle again. He isn't going to get any better, and life is going to be miserable for him from here on out. It's better to make this decision one day too soon than a day too late."

Alice signed the release. "I'm going to wait outside, George. You stay with him. I wish we had brought Rosie," Alice said as she slipped out the door, wiping tears from her eyes.

"What happens now, Doc?" George asked.

"I'm a farm boy, George. Life comes, and life goes. I believe that when the decision is made, and we're all on board, we get it done. No ceremony, get it done, and then we all can get on with grieving."

"Okay, Doc, I'm ready."

I dropped to my knees. Nick was lying on the floor. He hated the exam table. I lifted his head by his chin. His eyes were half-closed, cloudy mucus filled the corners of his eye. There was no longer any black in his muzzle, and gray hair streaked the rest of his coat. I stroked his head and allowed him to lower it back to his paws. I placed a rubber band tourniquet above his elbow and felt to make sure he had a favorable vein. This needed to be a quick procedure. Nick hated this place, and I didn't want to put him through any more than necessary.

I took his left paw in my left hand and slipped the needle into his vein in one movement. I drew back on the syringe just a little, making sure I was in the vessel, released the tourniquet, and started the injection of a massive dose of pentobarbital. Nick was gone before the dose was fully delivered. I checked his heart and pulse, nothing there. No reflex in his eyes.

I stood and looked at George. "That all?" he asked.

"That's all, he's gone. Do you want me to take care of him?"

"Oh no, we have his place under his big cedar tree that used to be his favorite place to sleep. That was a long time ago." George said, wiping a single tear from his cheek. "Can you help me get him into the back of the pickup?"

We loaded Nick and said our good-byes. They were having some difficulty talking right now. They needed to get home and finish this terrible day. Hopefully, Rosie will handle the loss okay.

***

It was several months later, during one of our early October rainstorms, when a young couple came through the door with a very wet Lab.

"We found her alongside the road up by Mountain House," the young woman said.

The dog went right to the treat jar and sat down, staring at the jar, as if to make it open.

Sandy came around the counter to get a better look, opened the jar and handed the wet dog a treat. The treat instantly disappeared.

"She acts like she knows the place," the young man said. Sandy read the rabies tag hanging from the collar.

"It's our tag, so she's been here before," Sandy said as she looked up the number.

"Oh my!" Sandy exclaimed, "This is Rosie."

Rosie stood up and wagged her tail at the mention of her name. "She wasn't lost, she lives about a mile up the creek from where you picked her up," Sandy explained. "But that's not a problem, we will make sure she gets home."

"It's hunting season, and I am sure that Doc will be more than happy to take you home tonight when he's done," Sandy explained to Rosie as she handed her another treat and escorted her back to a kennel.

"If you have time, you need to dry Rosie off a bit," Sandy mentioned to Ruth as she went back to the front desk.

That evening I threw my rifle in the truck and loaded Rosie into the front seat. The drive up the river was a pleasant one. The rain had changed to a light mist. The wind was blowing, and it was brisk along the river. Yellow and orange leaves were flying off the trees, tumbling in the air and floating down the river. Rosie sat up, looking at the road as we sped along. She seemed to know exactly where we were going.

The Dunns were on the porch when I pulled into their driveway. Rosie was standing and wagging her tail. She almost knocked me over as she scrambled to get past me as I was getting out of the truck. "Oh Doc, we have been sick all afternoon looking for Rosie. We thought we had lost her for sure. How did you get her?" Alice asked.

"A couple of kids picked her up down at the highway. They thought she was lost. They said they just opened the door and she crawled into the car. They brought her to the clinic early this afternoon."

"I wish we had a phone, it's terrible that you had to bring her all this way. Can we pay you anything for your trouble?" Alice asked. "No, I'm happy to be able to do it. Besides, I thought I would run up the creek for a few minutes and see if I can get that old buck that George has been feeding all summer."

"That would be great, Doc. Let me grab a coat and come with you. I just happen to know where a little forked horn sleeps," George said.

A couple of miles up the road, we came to the giant Douglas fir tree that had been saved for public view.

"Slow down here and pull off in that pull-out up ahead," George said, speaking in a hushed voice as if the deer could hear us from inside the truck. "Close your door real quiet like, this guy is going to be in that little clearing between the tree and the creek."

I walked around the truck, George placed his hand on my shoulder and pointed to trail through the brush. We made our way toward the creek, not saying a word, but I could hear George's breathing behind me. As we approached the clearing, George grabbed my shoulder to bring me to a stop. He pointed over my right shoulder to the far side of the clearing. There was the little forked horn, unaware of our presence, browsing on a low bush.

Bang! One shot through the heart, the deer lurched forward, maybe a few steps, and fell forward in a pile.

"Good shot, clean kill, just like it should be," George said in a normal voice now. "You bring the truck around to the road toward the creek, and I'll get this guy out to the road."

I pulled the truck around toward the bridge on the side road. George had already dragged the buck out to the road. It didn't take very long to take care of him.

"I never take the heart and liver, Sandy won't cook them," I told George.

"Oh, we like those, and I'll take the kidneys also."

"I'll give you half of this deer, George. I would have never found him," I said.

"All the hunters just go a barreling past this little place, but I don't need half, just a hind leg will do us fine. We have plenty of meat most of the time."

I had a large plastic bag that I used for the heart, liver, and kidneys. We skinned out a hind leg, carefully severed the meat from the pelvic bones, and disarticulated the hip. I removed the lower leg, at the break joint just below the hock, and slipped the whole leg into the bag with the organs.

"You do quite a professional job, Doc. You would be a handy guy to be around hunting camp."

"I've never had the time for a hunting camp. My hunting is just like this, a stolen hour once in a while. Always feel lucky if I get anything."

"Doc, if this happens again with Rosie, you don't have to bring her all the way up here. We'll run down to Cascadia and use the phone at the professor's house. You know, Dr. Hayes. You can also leave a message for us with him."

"Okay, and we can hang onto her for a couple of days for that matter."

"What do you suppose is going on with her, Doc?"

"She was pretty close to Nick, probably just having trouble getting used to his passing. Maybe you guys should get a puppy."

"No way, we are too old to take on a puppy. It wouldn't be fair to the pup. As it is, we might end up being in a race with Rosie to see who goes first.

And so it started, it seemed that Rosie came to the clinic every couple of weeks. Her rabies tag was her ticket. She would sit by the road and people would just figure that she was lost. They could not visualize a dog having a home in this area.

Rosie loved to come to the clinic. She would come through the front door and approach the counter with tail wagging. Then she would sit down in front of the treat jar and stare at the jar, mouth open, panting, and saliva draining from the side of her mouth. The people would figure out quickly that they had given her a ride to her favorite place.

"Rosie, what are you doing here again this week?" Sandy would say as she retrieved a treat from the jar.

With the treat in her mouth, she would continue to the doors to the kennel room. She knew her routine very well. The couple who brought her through the door would just stand there, sort of dumbfounded.

"She obviously knows where she's welcome," the young lady said. "We found her lost beside the road up by Mountain House. We couldn't just leave her there to get hit by a car. We stopped and opened the door, and she just climbed in, like she was expecting us." "We see Rosie every couple of weeks. She lives up by Mountain House. Her folks have a driveway about a mile long. Rosie gets bored since they lost their older dog, so she just goes down and sits by the road. Somebody comes along and picks her up, thinking she's lost or deserted. Most of the time they bring her here. Once she was taken to Redmond. Our rabies tag gets her home every time," Sandy explained.

This went on for five or six months. It almost became part of our routine, and we would see the Dunns frequently when they would come to retrieve Rosie. On occasion, the old professor, Doctor Hayes, would be the one to pick up Rosie.

And then, suddenly, it all came to an end. The end was one of those things you felt was more than what it looked like on the surface.

One day Sandy said, "We haven't seen Rosie in weeks. I wonder if something has happened to her."

It was several weeks following that realization when we bumped into the Dunns at Thriftway. Thriftway was not the biggest grocery store in town, but it was the only one that I would use.

"Hi, Doc," George said as we met at the doorway.

"George, how are things? We've been thinking about you guys at the clinic. We haven't seen Rosie in a long time. Is everything okay with her?"

"You were right, Doc, about the puppy thing. We didn't get a puppy, so Rosie sort of took care of things herself. It was sort of funny, you know how she hated the raccoons who came around. Well, an old sow raccoon with a bunch of babies got hit by a car down on the highway. There were dead raccoons scattered everywhere. Rosie must have heard it, or maybe she was just going down there to catch another ride. Pretty soon, here she came, with a baby raccoon in her mouth. She must have found the only one to survive. Anyway, she adopted the thing. She spends all her time taking care of the little gal."

"Isn't that funny," I said. "I don't really approve of raccoons as pets, it's illegal for one thing, and there are some health factors, like the raccoon roundworm."

"It's no pet, Doc. Rosie takes care of it on the porch. It can come and go as it pleases. It won't have anything to do with us, except to eat the food we provide. But it sleeps with Rosie, she washes the thing with her tongue every night. I don't know what will happen with it as it gets older, but right now, Rosie is happy as can be and back to her old self." ~

The Angry Awn

I glanced up the hill a hundred yards, where my son, Derek, was moving through some high grass. There was a chill in the early morning October air. This was the first weekend that I was free to hunt. We were carefully covering my favorite clearcut on the backside of Buck Mountain.

As I watched, Derek suddenly grabbed his face and buckled to the ground. It took me a couple of minutes to climb the hill to where he was on his knees, with his hand over his eye.

"What's wrong?" I asked as I approached through the chest-high dry grass.

"Aw, I have something in my eye," Derek said.

I pulled his hand away to look at his eye. It was tearing heavily and was mostly closed from the pain, and the pupil was pinpoint.

The culprit was already on his cheek—a grass awn an inch below his left eye.

"You had a grass seed in your eye," I said as wiped the seed off his cheek.

"It really hurts," Derek said.

I was starting to wonder if I was going have to pack him out of here. That would be no easy task. At sixteen, Derek was no longer a boy. He was taller than me and growing by the minute.

And there was a steep hill up to the road where the truck was parked. "I have a first aid kit in the truck, and it has some eye ointment and an eye patch in it," I said. "Do you want me to go get it, or

do you want to try to walk out of here?"

Derek was quiet for a moment. "I think I can walk out of here with a little help," he finally said.

I slung both rifles over my shoulder and helped Derek to his feet. "Keep that eye closed, and it will feel better," I said.

We were some distance from the truck, but Derek did fine once we were moving. We got through the high grass and cut across the clear-cut to the cat road that went up the hill. I had to provide some support on his arm as we climbed the hill to the truck.

I got Derek into the truck and then opened the first aid pack. I carried more of a first aid pack than what you would find on the drug store shelf. I was prepared for lacerations, fractures, and penetrating wounds, but I was a little limited on eye injuries.

I did have a small tube of eye ointment. It was a triple antibiotic ointment, but I figured it should be okay for this situation. After I squeezed it into his eye, the pain was alleviated somewhat.

It was a long drive back to town, not in miles but in time. The logging roads were not highways, and speed was not an option.

We were lucky that Saturday morning when the local optometrist was still in his office, and he accommodated us with an emergency exam.

"There are a couple of tiny little scratches on his cornea," the doctor said. "It should feel fine if we keep it lubricated with some ointment for a day or two."

***

It was just a few days later when Mike came through the door with Bob, who was wagging his tail stub. He always seemed happy in the clinic. Bob was a springer spaniel who lived for the fall bird hunting.

"Good morning, Doc," Mike said. "Bob has a sore eye. I would like you to look at this morning if you have time." I glanced at Bob, and his right eye was half-closed, and the side of his face was wet with tears. Other than the eye, he looked like nothing was wrong. "This eye started bothering him a few days ago," Mike said. "We hunted on Saturday, and everything seemed fine. On Sunday

morning, I noticed he was squinting his eye a little."

"Let's get him up on the exam table where I can get a look at it," I said.

Mike was a big, muscular young guy who cut trees for a living and spent most of his spare time hunting or fishing. Bob was his constant companion on these hunting and fishing trips.

He lifted Bob onto the table for me, and I placed a couple of drops of topical anesthetic into his right eye. I thought that maybe I should put some of this in the first aid kit after Derek's near incapacitation.

"We'll give that a couple of minutes to soak in, and then I will be able to look at this eye a little better," I said. "Where were you guys hunting?"

"We were up Canyon Creek," Mike said. "There is a lot of quail up there. I miss a lot them, but Bob has a grand time. He is not much of a pointer, but he flushes the hell of them. Keeps me in shape just trying to keep up with him."

I spread the eyelids wide on Bob's eye. I could see there was an extensive ulcer on the surface of the cornea. I ran a blunt forceps under the upper and lower eyelids to make sure there was no foreign body. Then I grasped the third eyelid with the forceps and lifted it away from the corner of Bob's eye. There it was, a large grass seed awn stuck under the third eyelid. I grabbed it with the forceps and pulled it out.

"This is the problem," I said as I held the seed up to show Mike. "Now, I need to put a little dye into this eye so we can see how much of the cornea is damaged."

A drop of dye and a blue light from the ophthalmoscope and over half of the cornea's surface glowed green.

"Look at how much the cornea is ulcerated," I said. "What do we need to do now?" Mike asked.

"I need to hang onto Bob for a couple of hours," I said. "We need to suture his third eyelid up over his eye to serve as a patch. We'll send him home on some medication, and things should heal just fine. We will take the sutures out in a week and expect the eye to be healed."

Suturing the third eyelid was an easy procedure. With Bob under brief anesthesia, I placed a couple of mattress sutures through the upper eyelid. I used a small piece of rubber-band to serve as a stint so the sutures would not cut into the eyelid.

When Mike came to pick him up, Bob bounced out of the kennel like a new dog.

"He looks like he is feeling a little better," Mike said.

"I will tell you a little story," I said. "Last Saturday, I was hunting with my son up on Buck Mountain. My son got a grass seed in his eye. By the time I got over to him, the seed was already on his cheek. Now I'm telling you, he was in so much pain, I thought I would have to carry him out. When we got to the doctor, he had a couple of tiny scratches on his cornea. Bob comes in here wagging his tail, and over half of his cornea is ulcerated, and the grass seed is still there."

"What does that say about how tough this dog is?" Mike said. "Most dogs are pretty tough, and maybe people are just pansies,"

I said. "Eye pain might be more intense in people because eyesight is more important to us. I don't know, but there is definitely a big difference." ~

Charlie and Betty's Fish Pond

O ver the next few years, Charlie would call for a post-
breeding infusion on every mare on her second
breeding. I don't think we had a 100% conception rate, but it
was close enough for Charlie and his clients to be pleased. On
one of these visits, Charlie asked me if I wanted to look at his
fish pond. He had dammed up the creek that ran through the
back of his property, dumped in a couple of truckloads of fine
pea gravel to provide for breeding, and planted it with trout.
This pond covered nearly a half-acre, and the water was deep.
The creek had year-round flow. These fish became like his pets.

"I let my brother Lee, the pharmacist, bring his kids up to
catch a fish once in a while," Charlie said as he retrieved a
coffee can full of pelleted fish food from the little shack beside
the pond.

Charlie threw the pellets into the water in front of us. The
water was instantly alive with trout. These were no little trout
one might expect to see at a fish hatchery, these were large fish.
They looked like they were all twenty inches or more. I stood
there amazed, probably had my mouth open.

"I think they have pretty good reproduction with all that
gravel I dumped in up there where the creek comes into the
lake. I haven't planted any fish for a couple of years, and the

157

numbers don't seem to go down any. I think there must be some freshwater shrimp in there because they all have pink meat. That or they eat their fill of all the goldfish that you see along the edges," Charlie said, pointing to a group of twenty to thirty six-inch goldfish hiding in the willows.

"If you want to bring your kids up, they can catch a fish," Charlie said.

"Well, my son, Derek, and our youngest daughter, Dee, would love to catch one of these fish. I'm not too sure about the other two. I wouldn't want to catch more than we could eat anyway," I said. "You bring them up tomorrow evening, I'll honk when I go by your place on my way home."

The next evening Dee and Derek clambered into my truck with their fishing poles. I had set the stage and they were excited.

When we got to Charlie's, he was waiting at the pond. He had a jar of old salmon eggs in his hand. He looked at the poles the kids were carrying.

"I don't know if these will work," Charlie said as he examined the hooks and four-pound test leaders. "These are pretty big fish, but let's give it a try."

Charlie placed a small glob of salmon eggs on Dee's hook. "Just cast it out there a little way, not too far," he says.

The eggs hit the water and begin to sink below the surface. Bam! A large trout rolls as it grabs the eggs. There is a sharp pull on the line, then nothing. When Dee reels it in, everything is gone, hook, line, and sinker.

Charlie says, "I better get my pole," as he heads for the shack. Charlie's pole is an old rusted steel pole with about twelve to fifteen feet of line tied to the end. The line is heavy, it looks like a fifty-pound test line tied to the tip of the pole with a half dozen granny knots. Then a large double hook at the other end of the line, probably a number four hook size. The knot securing the hook to the heavy line was the same series of knots that tied the
line to the tip of the pole.

"Now this ain't no fancy pole, but it catches these fish. We just put a big glob of eggs on this hook like this," Charlie says as he baits the hook.

He walks to the water's edge with the baited hook. "Now I am going to throw this into the water, you need to stand here beside me," he says to Dee.

"When you hook the fish, and it will happen as soon as this bait sinks, you just hold the pole and back up toward the shack there," Charlie explains. "I'll get the fish when you pull him out of the water."

Charlie threw the baited hook into the water. About the time it disappeared under the water, there was a tremendous tug on the line. Dee almost lost her grip but recovered quickly.

"Now, just back up," Charlie reminded her.

Dee backed up, struggling to hold the pole with the fish fighting on the other end of the line. A few more steps and this large trout was floundering on the bank. Charlie scoops him up and pulls a little club from his back pocket and wallops him on the head a couple of times. He holds up the fish, probably twenty-three inches long and close to eight inches deep.

We repeat the process with Derek. At four years of age, he was three years younger than Dee and had a little more of a struggle with the fish, but it didn't take long before the second fish was on the bank. That fish was slightly smaller but still an impressive fish well over twenty inches.

"Any time you get hungry for a fish, just give me a call," Charlie says as I loaded the fish and the kids into the truck.

"Thanks a lot, Charlie, I'll try not to take all your fish," I say as we head the truck down the driveway. ~

Rambo and the Eagle

A t least I'm not in the ditch," I said to Jim as we parted toward our respective balls.

Dr. French had always told me that if you are paying attention to your practice, you will never have the time to be a good golfer. I could see his point. I took Thursday afternoon off to play with the Pineway Men's Club and most of the time with a group or two once on the weekend. But I really felt that athletes are born, not made. Of course, with work and coaching, we could improve and reach our potential, but some guys are just born with a ball in their hands. We all knew them, they were stars in Little League, and they excelled on the basketball court. They are the ones who didn't go out for football until they were seniors, and they made All League. The coach always tries to take the credit, but it is just the way it is.

And my slice was a good illustration. I could beat just about anyone on any one hole. But I could never hold my concentration for the next hole. I got to my ball, it was in the short rough, about a foot from the ditch that ran down the right side of the fairway, a position I knew well. I could reach the green from this position on this short five-par hole. This position actually set me up well with my ball flight. There was a slight dogleg to the left; with my slice, I liked to call it a fade. I

160

could start my ball left of the hole and it would run up the front apron to the green. I just needed to fade the ball, not slice it.

As I addressed the ball, I caught sight of Jack Wright's cart starting down the eighth fairway. Rambo, his little poodle mix, always rode on the back of the seat in Jack's cart. Rambo had already spotted me. I could hear him throwing a fit from two fairways over.

Jack loved it, and here he came in his cart with Rambo barking up a storm over his shoulder—just what I needed to hold my concentration on this shot.

"Good morning, Doc," Jack said over Rambo's constant barking—louder now that they were parked just across the ditch. "How is your game this morning?"

"It has been pretty good so far," I said. "With a little luck, I'll reach this green in two."

"Rambo spotted you and wanted to say hi," Jack said with a laugh. "I think you're the only person he knows on this entire course."

"Yes, I notice that almost every Thursday," I said. "I don't know what the problem is, I've never done anything to him other than his shots and stuff."

Jack chuckled again, "He just wants you to know what he thinks of you."

"Well, I guess it's good to be loved by my patients," I said.

"I'll let you get back to your game, good luck, and fly that ball right at the stick for a change," Jack said as he turned the cart and headed back to his fairway, Rambo on the back of the cart, facing me and barking as loudly as he could.

I addressed the ball again, trying to think what it was that I had done to Rambo to make him dislike me so much. Then trying to brush that thought away, I took a deep breath and started my back swing.

I swung with all my strength and caught the ball perfectly. The ball seemed to hang on the club face briefly, then sprang into a high flight. This was my Ping 5 wood, my favorite club. Probably because I could hit the ball straighter with it than any of my other woods.

The ball started out on a line about ten yards left of the green and then started to fade to the right. Then the fade became a slice and it was struck hard enough that distance was going to be more than usual for this club. I held my breath and leaned to the left, as if to guide the ball a little.

The green ran on a diagonal left to right and the hole was cut in the far back corner. I had hoped to land in the fairway and run the ball up on the green, but this ball was going much more to the right than I had hoped. Then it came down, and stuck on the back edge of the green, maybe ten feet from the hole.

A perfect shot and it surprised everyone, including myself. "Maybe I should talk with Rambo more often," I said to myself as I picked up my bag and started toward the green.

Bruce West was coming down the sixth fairway. He pointed at the ball near the pin and asked, "Whose ball is that?"

Jim pointed at me, "Larsen's, good shot, don't you think?" "If he makes the putt," Bruce replied.

I could still hear Rambo barking as I walked up on the green. He was out of the cart and standing under the trees over the eighth green, only thirty yards away. He pounded his front feet with each bark in a little bounce, just to add emphasis to his distaste.

Jack had loaded him up and headed to the ninth tee box just as I addressed my putt. I was relieved that the barking was fading off in the distance.

One small breath, and I stroked the putt, straight putt, right to the bottom of the hole. "Take that Bruce," I said as I stepped quickly to the hole to retrieve the ball.

I made an eagle that day and no loud objections from a cranky poodle mix were going to keep me from that rare bird. ~

A Market Collapse

T ell me again, Jack," I said. "What are you doing with these gals?"

Jack had called to have his llama herd checked but was not very specific as to what was going on. I did a lot of work for Jack, most of the time, working on his cows. The llama herd was sort of an expensive hobby.

Llamas were expensive animals. I was never able to figure out why. I guess they were sort of a status symbol. There was certainly no viable use for them that supported the prices that were being paid. Female llamas were valued at $20,000 to $40,000 each. I had worked on one llama that the owner had declined an offer to purchase for $80,000. Nobody ate llamas, and their wool was used, but it was not valuable. In South America, it was considered to be peon's wool.

Jack was a smallish man but with rugged features and physique, a long-time fixture in the Lebanon-Sweet Home area. I was not sure of all his trades, but his name fits. He was a "jack-of-all-trades." He had owned both a feed store and a grocery store at different times in Sweet Home, but probably made most of his money in logging. He told me once that he was the first logging company into the Thomas Creek drainage.

"I need to have them preg checked," Jack said. "I'm selling the whole bunch of them in a couple of days."

"The whole herd?" I exclaimed. "You must be planning some major vacation."

"Well, the price is getting high enough, I just think it's time to cash in," Jack said. "I got this herd at a pretty good price almost ten years ago. We've made more off of this bunch of twenty some llamas than we make off the whole cow herd, if you can believe that. I get a little nervous, these twenty females are approaching a half million. And there's no basis for the price. You can sell the males for pack animals and get seven hundred dollars each. The wool is worth pennies, and nobody eats them. How do you justify such a price?"

"I agree, there's just no basis for the price," I said. "I just wish that I could tell you the sex of the baby when I do a preg check. How much do you think it would be worth to know whether the baby was going to be worth seven hundred dollars or twenty thousand dollars if you were buying a new llama."

"That would be great information," Jack said. "Why don't you work on that, Doc?"

"I've thought about it a little," I said. "A guy could probably do an amniocentesis and make the diagnosis. Just too much else to do right now." A pregnancy exam on a llama was a little worrisome for me. Llamas were much smaller than a cow but still large enough to accommodate a rectal exam. Their reproductive tract was different. They had a long vagina, and the non-pregnant uterus was small and easily reached before you were in up to your elbow.

We worked Jack's herd through a regular cattle chute, and the twenty head did not take long to complete.

"Let me know if you need anything else with these girls," I said as I loaded my things into the truck. "And you have a good time on that vacation."

I had a feeling that Jack had made the right decision to sell the herd. I had heard from several other llama owners who were concerned about the continued escalation of the price of a llama. One breeder was continually trying to get me into the business.

"I can almost guarantee you will own one or two female llamas, free and clear, after two years," he would say. "And it doesn't matter what you pay. If you're lucky, all the babies will be females."

The next spring, when I visited Jack's ranch to look at a cow, I noticed he had a new bunch of llamas.

"Aw, you must have missed the llamas," I said as Jack approached me at the barn.

"My accountant made me go out and buy another herd," Jack said. "He said I would lose too much in taxes. So what's a guy going to do? You lose money one way or the other."

I did my routine work for Jack for the rest of that year. We always had some cow work to do, and there were a couple of sick llamas also.

Come spring, there were rumors that the price of a llama was falling. The stories soon became fact, the price had dropped almost overnight. Wealthy llama owners were taking catastrophic losses.

It was hard to put a dollar figure on their losses because nobody wanted to talk about it in exact terms.

Jack called shortly after the collapse, he had sold his llamas and needed them preg checked.

We were working his herd through the chute when Jack was explaining the loss to me.

"This gal you're checking right now, I bought for twenty-seven thousand dollars last spring," Jack said. "Tomorrow, I'm selling her for eleven hundred and fifty. I guess that will make my accountant happy." ~

The Bite of the Chigger

I came to the end of the gravel on this side road off of Pleasant Valley Road. There was just a dirt path in front of me. I say "path" because it would probably not meet any criteria to qualify as a road. I took a deep breath and continued on, finally breaking out into a pasture whittled out of the young forest.

On the far corner were several ramshackle travel trailers that served as the family living quarters. I pulled up to these trailers. Kids and chickens were running everywhere. Finally, Annie stepped out of the far trailer.

"I am glad you found us," Annie said. "We're moving back to Missouri, and we have this little heifer that needs a health certificate to make the trip."

"You're sort of hidden back in these trees," I said. "It must have taken a little work to clear this pasture."

"It was done before we came," Annie said. "We've lived here a couple of years but can't make a go of it. Time to go home, I guess." "Let's look at this heifer," I said. "I have to give her a brucellosis vaccine and a quick exam. The rest is just paperwork. Do you want any other vaccines for her?"

"No, we just want that piece of paper," Annie said.

Annie and her family group left Sweet Home not long after that visit. They faded into my memory like so many others. And it was several years later that events reawakened my memory of that day. Marilyn had Tiger in the clinic for a routine exam. Marilyn had quite a group of cats, indoor-only cats and outdoor cats, and then a small group of cats that were allowed to come in and out of the house. Tiger belonged to this last group, moving about as he pleased. Marilyn lived on another road system, but her home was not far up the hill from Annie's settlement.

As I worked through the exam, I noticed a row of little white bugs attached to Tiger's ear margins. I looked closely at these bugs and scraped a couple of them onto a microscope slide.

"I've noticed those every spring for the last couple of years," Marilyn said. "They only seem to be on the outdoor cats, and they don't seem to cause much of a problem."

"Maybe we should send them to the lab and find out what they are," I suggested.

"I don't think so," Marilyn said. "They'll be gone in a few weeks, and they don't seem to cause much of a problem. I'd rather not spend the money on the lab."

Over the next couple of years, I would see other cats with these bugs on their ear margins. They all seemed to come from the Pleasant Valley area.

Finally, Susan came in with Rudy, a large black cat. The white bugs on his ear margins really stood out against his black hair.

"Doc, I've noticed these things on his ears for several years," Susan said. "This year, there are a lot of them, and they're bothering him." "I can put some ear mite ointment on them," I said. "That will take care of the problem for now. But I have seen several cats from your area with this same problem. Maybe we should send some of these little guys to the lab and find out what we're dealing with." "Yes, that would be good," Susan said. "Even if we can't do anything with them other than treat them, it would be good to know what they are."

I scraped most of the bugs off one ear into a blood vial to send to the lab. Then I applied some ear mite lotion to the ear flaps. Rudy's ear margins were a little eroded, but with the bugs gone, that should resolve in short order.

The diagnostic lab called when they received my sample. "We are going to send these critters over to Oregon State's Entomology Department for identification," the secretary said. "It is hard to say how long it will be before you have any results."

"That's fine," I said. "There is no urgent situation here." Surprisingly, it was just two days later that I got a call from Randy, a graduate student in the Entomology Department. " Doctor Larsen, I'm looking at the sample you sent to the Diagnostic Lab a couple of days ago," Randy said. "This is exciting stuff. Can you give me any background on Rudy, the cat that you collected these from."

"Not much, Rudy is a pretty typical cat, indoors and outdoors, at his choosing," I said. "I see these bugs on the ear margin of outdoor cats, most of them from the Pleasant Valley area, every spring for the last few years."

"These bugs, as you call them, are larval chiggers," Randy said. "What's interesting here is that chiggers of this species are rarely reported in Oregon. I'd like to write up this case for publication if that's okay with you. I could give you credit in the paper."

"That's fine with me," I said. "I really have no need for any credits, I won't be doing any research in my career. You're free to use any information on the lab request. And if you need more information, just call."

The fact that I was just now seeing chiggers and in an area associated with Annie's settlement, makes one wonder if they were a Missouri import, for Missouri is known as a hotbed for chiggers. ~

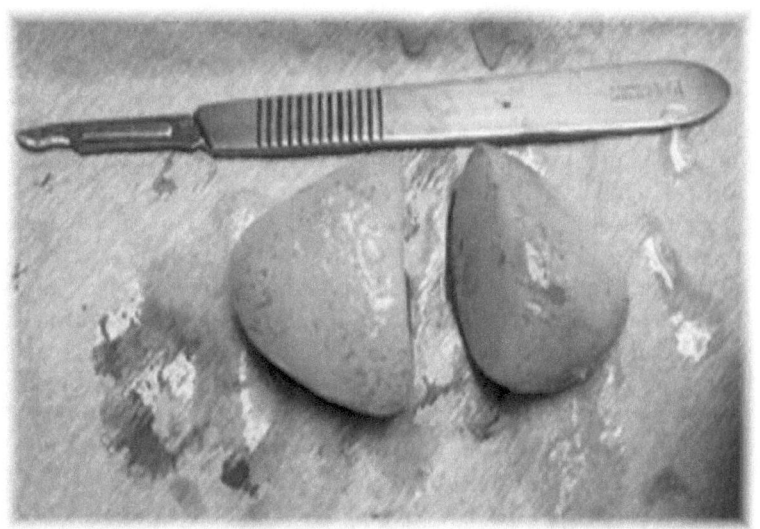

The Stone's Story

Raymond came through the door with little Sophie cradled in the crook of his arm. Sophie was a very small Chihuahua, and Raymond, her owner, was a large man. It was one of the things that I always found a little curious, that some of the largest men were attached to these tiny dogs.

After he stretched a towel out on the exam table, Raymond placed Sophie in the middle of the towel. Sophie, at four and a half pounds, was overweight. Her spindly legs looked undersized for her round body.

"She has blood in her urine, Doc," Raymond said. "And she pees a little puddle every five or ten minutes. The wife is getting upset with all the cleaning up after her."

I looked at Sophie, her gray muzzle told she was past middle age. She should probably weigh two and a half pounds, not four and a half. Her membranes were normal, with normal capillary refill time. Heavy tartar on her teeth and some chronic periodontal disease suggested that she was a good candidate for a heart murmur. That was confirmed when I placed the stethoscope on her chest.

Chronic periodontal disease leaks bacteria into the bloodstream. These circulating bacteria take up residence on the heart valves, in the kidneys, and the liver. Poor dental hygiene, most common in small dogs on pampered diets, leads to all sorts of significant health complications.

She was heavy enough that it was difficult to palpate her abdomen accurately. But when my fingers reached the posterior abdomen, I bumped a hard firm bladder. Sophie immediately squatted and peed a small puddle of bloody urine onto the towel.

"Raymond, we're going to have to pick up the towel so I can get some urine off the tabletop," I said as I lifted Sophie up so Raymond could remove the towel.

I set Sophie down and felt her bladder again, more carefully this time. There was a large stone in the bladder. I could feel some movement in the stone, probably a couple of stones. They were large, making the bladder feel full, but there was little room for urine. Sophie squatted again, depositing a small puddle of bloody urine on the exam table.

I drew the urine into a syringe and placed a small drop on a microscope slide. A quick look at the slide under the microscope showed the blood but also many bacteria and struvite crystals.

Struvite stones were the most common type of bladder stones in a dog at that time. Struvite stones in a dog are caused by a urinary tract infection that leads to acidity changes in the urine, crystal formation, and then the development of stones. These stones grow with time. In male dogs, they often cause urinary tract obstruction as the small stones try to pass down the urethra. That seldom happens in the female.

Today there are diets that can dissolve struvite stones in the bladder. That was not the case in the 1970s and '80s. Stones as large as Sophie's are best removed by surgery, even today.

"Raymond, Sophie has a large stone, or more likely two or three large stones in her bladder," I said. "These are caused by an infection in the urinary tract. She has a lot of bacteria in her urine. We need to do several things. We need to do a culture on her urine, and while we're waiting for the culture results, we'll get her started on a good broad-spectrum antibiotic. We need to get an x-ray, so we can see how many stones we're dealing with, if there are stones in the kidneys, or a bunch of little stones, also. We need to do some blood work to make sure

Sophie's kidney function is normal. These stones are going to have to be removed with surgery."

"Doc, you sound like you're talking about a lot of money," Raymond said. "I don't have a lot of money. Are there some short cuts we can take?"

"We can shortcut some of the things if that's what you want to do," I said. "You need to understand, shortcuts are great if everything works out fine. But if things don't go just right, we end up spending more money than we would have doing things right in the first place."

"What kind of things are you talking about, Doc?" Raymond asked.

"Looking at her urine, her kidney function is probably okay," I said. But if it isn't, and a random urine sample is not the best indicator of kidney function, we might be delayed in finding that out, and we could lose her. If she happens to have an infection that requires a particular antibiotic, we might not know that without a culture. If we have a bunch of little stones along with the big ones I can feel, we could leave a stone behind and have to do a second surgery."

"She's sort of long in the tooth, Doc," Raymond said. "Let's put her on some antibiotics and do the surgery. If things don't work out, at least we tried."

"That's fine, just as long as you remember this conversation," I said as I shook Raymond's hand.

"Will I be able to take her home tonight?" Raymond asked. "We're early enough that she should be able to go home tonight,"

I said. "We'll have her on CD diet for a time. That will be important, nothing else."

"You're going to ruin her life and make mine miserable," Raymond said.

"You know you're killing her slowly with kindness, don't you?" I said.

"What do you mean, Doc?" Raymond asked.

"Look at her, Raymond," I said. "She weighs twice what she should, her teeth are a mess. She should have those cleaned, and there will be many teeth that are not savable. The infection in that mouth could have been what started this bladder thing, and her heart valves are leaking a little. She needs to be eating dog food, period. But we can work on those things after we get this bladder thing fixed."

I gave Sophie an injection of amoxicillin and Gentocin. I planned to send her home on Clavamox. We gave her 80 ccs of fluids by subcutaneous injection and placed her in a kennel while we got the surgery room ready. Sophie was unhappy in the kennel. How dare we treat her like a dog!

After anesthesia was induced and the abdomen was prepped for the last time, I draped the incision site, first with towels and then a surgery drape. I made a short incision over the bulge in the posterior abdomen caused by the large stones in the bladder. I was able to squeeze the bladder out of the incision. It was the size of a full bladder but hard as a rock.

I placed a couple of stay sutures to hold the bladder in position when I incised it to remove the stones. Then I made an incision into the bladder. The bladder wall was thickened from the chronic infection and the mechanical damage from the stones.

I popped out the first stone, then the next—amazingly large stones for such a small dog. The bladder lining was burgundy red and almost bubbly from the chronic inflammation. I flushed the urethra in both directions and carefully explored the bladder to make sure no small stones were hiding.

Then I closed the bladder in two layers with Maxon and returned it to normal position. I was careful to remove a couple of drops of urine from the incision and flushed the area liberally. Then the abdomen was closed with a standard three-layer closure.

Sophie recovered quickly and was probably more comfortable than she had been in months. Raymond was pleased with how lively she was when he picked her up.

"I want to see her in a couple of days, just to check the incision and feel her bladder," I said. "If you get a chance, try to get a look at her urine in the morning. Mainly to see if the blood is cleared up. And Raymond, you have to be strong—CD diet only for three weeks. No bacon off the breakfast table. You understand, we have come this far, don't ruin it by being weak when she begs."

"I'll do my very best, Doc," Raymond said.

"I can guarantee you that, Doc," Sue, Raymond's wife, said. "He just spent our summer trip to the coast, and he'll finish the job if he knows what's good for him." ~

The Last Cow in the Chute

I stepped through the small gate into the crowding alley behind the chute. Ag swung the tailgate open and I grabbed the tail of this large Charolais cross heifer with my right hand. I worked my gloved left hand into her rectum. There was enough squeeze on her that she could not bounce around too much.

I had been doing this for most of the day. We took some time for a lunch of a special soup Ag had made. Homemade bread and a hearty soup would make the afternoon go faster. The most significant advantage of the lunch break was that my left arm got a rest.

In the big cattle country, a cow doctor might have herds of four hundred cattle to check every day for a couple of weeks. Their arms became accustomed to the workload. For me, it was one or two herds a week, and most of those herds were less than a hundred cows. My arm was in shape enough to do over a hundred cows, but I had to rest it every chance I could.

I was skilled at rectal palpation. Using my left hand, I would first attempt to retract the uterus. This would bring the uterus into the pelvic canal where I could feel along the entire length. I would first try to feel the membranes slip between my fingers when I pinched the body of the uterus near the bifurcation. If present, this slip was a positive sign of pregnancy. Then I would explore down each horn of the uterus to find an amnionic sac or a fetus. Based on the size of the amnion sac or the fetal head, I could age the pregnancy to plus or minus three days.

A uterus with pregnancy over ninety days duration could seldom be retracted. One could usually find a fetal head by sweeping a hand along the length of the pregnant uterine horn. After a hundred and twenty days of pregnancy, the fetus was generally out of reach until very late in pregnancy. Aging a pregnancy after a hundred and twenty days was difficult and getting between plus or minus fifteen days was considered the best one could do. Inexperienced veterinarians could miss the age by months.

The obvious benefit of pregnancy exams in a commercial herd was to enable ranchers to cull the cows that were not pregnant. In that way, ranchers would avoid the expense of winter feed for those cows. On rare occasions, I would detect a problem in the breeding program by finding a high number of open cows. Most of those problems could be seen by adequate observation during the breeding season.

The primary goal was to have cows fall into a forty-two-to eighty-four-day pregnancy window. Cows outside that window would be culled. This would select productive breeders, cows who would become pregnant on the first cycle she was exposed to the bulls. Then those cows not pregnant on the first cycle would have a second chance at pregnancy. By culling cows who could not breed back with two cycles, we condensed the calving season to a shorter time. This would allow ranchers to concentrate their observation of the calving efficiently.

For the plan to be successful, that cow that doesn't fit in the pregnancy window must be culled. Fertility is highly heritable. If you fail to cull that favorite cow who doesn't get pregnant within two cycles, you will end up with two calving seasons. The first calving season for the main herd and then some weeks or months later, the following season for that favorite cow and all of her descendants.

It obviously would take several years of work to arrive at the desired calving window. With Ag's herd, we probably had over seventy percent of the herd calving in the first twenty-one days of the calving season. This was ideal, and it allowed for some elective culling.

Elective culling would allow you to cull individuals based on other factors than fertility. Cows with better milk production would wean calves with a higher weaning weight. Cows with poor udder conformation might cause a lot of extra work at calving and could be susceptible to mastitis. In any herd, there are cows with behavior issues, culling them would reduce stress on the rancher and on the herd.

I always told my clients to cull the last cow in the chute. If you have a hundred cows in the corral to work through the chute, there will always be the last cow. She is seldom last by chance.

Ag never listened to me on this point. She had a large Brahman cross cow that was almost impossible to get into the chute. So difficult, in fact, that I had only checked her one time. We would try and try to get her in the chute.

"Let's just forget her," Ag would say. "She's always pregnant. She's too mean to not be pregnant."

"I am telling you, Ag, you need to get rid of that cow," I would always say.

And true to form, after five years, there was the old mama cow and then three of her daughters, all trying to be the last one in the chute. ~

Charlie and Betty, All Bad News

I t was not long after the fishing expedition that we got the
sad news. Charlie's brother, Lee, called me at the clinic
one afternoon. "I have some bad news," Lee said, his voice
almost breaking. "Charlie has prostate cancer. It is very
advanced and has already metastasized. I am afraid he doesn't
have much time." Not much time. Everybody wants to know
how much time they have when they get a cancer diagnosis for
themselves or for their pets. I have never understood how
doctors could be so blatant about the figures they hand out. Be
it one year, six months, or three weeks, people always think
they really know. As I veterinarian, I can read the book too, but
the times are the best guess, at best, and complete BS, at worse.
Charlie's time went fast. In less than two weeks, he was on his
death bed, and he was gone a few days later. Probably better
that it went quickly, the end was pretty painful for him.

Sandy and I closed the office and went to his funeral. We
had lost Sandy's mother a couple of months earlier, and we
were starting to realize we had entered that age group where
funerals seemed to be more common than weddings. Charlie's
service was small, mostly family. The preacher did an excellent
job for having met Charlie on his death bed. Although we knew
we were welcome, we almost felt like we were intruding. We

both shed more than a few tears. Walking back to the clinic, we both decided, almost at the same time, that we should not be attending funerals for clients. We held that as a policy for many years until we started losing some good friends who just happened to be clients, like Charlie.

***

The week following Charlie's funeral, Betty came to the clinic with her little dog, Taco. Taco was a little Chihuahua crossed with a dachshund, black, short hair coat except with long hair on his ears. Betty put Taco on the exam table and looked at me with great concern. "He can't pee," she says with tears in her eyes. "What am

I going to do? I can't lose him, too, I just can't."

"Let's look first before we start worrying about something that maybe doesn't exist," I said.

I began an exam when his distended bladder jumped out at me. He can't pee for sure, but there are a couple of drops on the exam table.

Betty pointed to urine on the table. "That's what he does everywhere, never more than a couple of drops."

I put an exam glove on and lubed my left index finger. This would be a tight fit but should be no real problem. Dixie came in and held Taco as I inserted my finger into his rectum. There are a lot of reasons for urinary obstruction, and some are quite simple to deal with. I reached the level of his prostate, and my heart sank. Taco had been neutered for many years, and his prostate should have been small and smooth on palpation.

Taco's prostate is grossly enlarged, solid, and hard, with extensions of this hard tissue in all directions. Both vas deferens are four times their normal diameter and hard and bumpy. This extends as far down each vas as I could reach. This was unlike anything I have ever palpated. Old intact male dogs often suffer from an infected prostate. Their prostate may reach a massive size, maybe the size of a grapefruit in a large dog. Those cases resolve quickly with antibiotics and neutering. But this was not an infected prostate. Prostatic cancer is now number one on my list, and there is no way I can say those words to Betty at this point in time.

"Betty, he has a problem for sure," I explain. "We need to get him under an anesthetic, pass a catheter, and drain his bladder. That is number one, then we can do some lab work and get some x-rays. We'll also do a pneumocystogram, which is an x-ray where we fill the bladder with air. That allows us to see the lining of the bladder and the pelvic urethra. We should be able to get this done this morning. So if you set up an afternoon appointment, we can go over our findings."

After anesthesia, I passed a catheter quickly. I took x-rays, plain film, and then a pneumocystogram. The prostate was large, and the urethra that passed through it is was eroded and large, with tissue hanging into the lumen. This urethral abnormality extends down the pelvic urethra for some distance. The neck of the bladder was also involved with an abnormal lining that extends into the prostate. This has to be prostatic cancer. Something I have not seen in a dog. Time to hit the books.

It turns out that prostate cancer in the dog is rare. I know that already. It also seems to occur more commonly in neutered dogs. This is not well understood because prostate cancer is thought to be testosterone dependent. It could just be a numbers game. Veterinarians see many more old, neutered male dogs than they see old intact male dogs. The pictures are disturbing, they look exactly like what I am feeling in Taco.

At this time, there are few specialists to send Betty and Taco. She would not go anyway; she thinks I can do anything. The truth is, Taco is on borrowed time, just like Charlie was. My guess is we have very few options. Attempting to remove this prostate will be at the very edge of the ability of this clinic. And even with surgery, we probably will only buy a few weeks at best.

Betty returned in the afternoon, and I reluctantly went over everything with her, the x-rays, the lab work, and the book findings. The diagnosis was prostate cancer, the only thing lacking to confirm that diagnosis was a tissue biopsy. The prognosis was grave, meaning I didn't expect Taco to survive this cancer.

"How can this be happening?" Betty says with tears in her eyes.

I can hardly talk. "We can find a specialist to send you to if you would like."

"No, no, Charlie would never allow that. If anything is going to be done, you are the one we want to do it."

"There is not much I can do, Betty. This surgery is at the very edge of my skill and equipment. And even if he comes through surgery, I may buy him only a short time, maybe a couple of weeks, maybe less."

"We have to try because it could be maybe more. I have seen some of the things you do. We have to try," Betty says. "When do you want to do this?"

"We'll make time this afternoon," I said.

We had Taco under anesthesia and prepped for surgery, on a slow IV drip of Ringers Lactate, and we had passed an eight-inch urinary catheter into the bladder. His prepuce is reflected to the left side of his abdomen and clamped in place with a towel forceps. Then a posterior ventral abdominal incision was made, passing on the right side of the prepuce, ligating preputial vessels as they are encountered, the linea alba exposed all the way to the pelvic brim. When opened carefully, the bladder and prostate are exposed.

It looks far worse than it felt.

The entire prostate is involved with cancer, and it extends down both vas, beyond my vision. I grasped each vas deferens and pulled them free of any attachment. Then I threaded a length of OB tape around the pelvic urethra and secured it approximately one centimeter distal to the abnormal tissue. I severed the pelvic urethra and tilted the prostate and bladder up to allow me to pull the tip of the catheter out of the prostate. Next, I severed the prostate from any bladder attachment. Now I removed the entire prostate with both vas deferens attached. I ligated any bleeding vessels, examined the cut edge of the bladder carefully. I trimmed away any tissue that looked suspicious. Then, after reinserting the catheter into the bladder, and using 3-0 Maxon, I sutured the bladder to the pelvic urethra. We filled the bladder with saline and put it under pressure to check for any leakage. Everything was good.

With a neutered male, we didn't have to worry about sexual function, but I had to trim enough of the bladder that I was sure that Taco would leak urine. It probably wouldn't bother Betty at this point, she will just have to find a diaper that fits.

The closure was routine and recovery uneventful. Taco went home the next day. Betty was pleased, even though she knew that time was short. This would at least give her a short time to come to grips with the recent events of her life.

Taco did live a couple of weeks longer than I had expected. Betty was sad but buried him out by the pond, near where Foster was buried. The horses were gone now, and the ranch was for sale. Betty planned to move east of the mountains to live with her sister. I am not sure what happened to Charlie's fish.

I could always deal with the death of a pet without a lot of emotion. I guess that is the farm boy in me. I still remember the calf that was born without a rectum. It was a perfectly healthy little calf but had no rectum. It did well for a few days, but it obviously had no future. I was in the seventh grade, and when I got off the bus on the calf's third day, Dad said, "I want you to go get the rifle and take that calf without a rectum up on the hill and shoot her." Simple task, I got the rifle, an old Model 94 Winchester 25-35, pulled the calf out of the pen, tied a twine around her neck, and led her up on the hill for a couple of hundred yards. I sat down on a log with her at my feet. Her big brown jersey eyes looking at me, we talked a little about her problem. I must have sat there ten minutes with her before I gathered enough strength to stand up, shoot her in the head, and, after ensuring that she was dead, returned to the barn to do my evening chores.

Pets and animals die at times, and they die sooner than people in the best of times. I could handle that in my mind. When we started to lose clients, often clients who were also friends, that became difficult, and that was something I was never really able to deal with satisfactorily. They weren't family and they weren't part of our own circle of friends. They were in that special place in our lives—business clients, yes, but clients who trusted us to share the most intimate parts of their lives with us, and this made those special friendships. The loss of these special people was just hard to deal with in our minds. ~

Table Manners for the Old Dog

Frank pushed through the door with Harley. Harley was an old yellow Lab, very overweight, and suffering from arthritis due to all the extra weight.

"I need to see Doc, right away if possible!" he said abruptly. "Old Harley, he is not eating much since Kara passed. I'm not eating much either, for that matter."

Frank and Kara had been very close and worked together on their small farm out at Liberty. Harley was always happy to see me when I would make a farm call, but in the office, he knew he was the one to get the shot, not the cows. Today he sort of looked confused, like he was not sure what was going to happen next.

"Let's get a weight on him, and then I'll get Dave to get him up on the table," Sandy said as she started for the scale at the end of the hall.

"Harley, you have not lost any weight, you still weigh a hundred and eight pounds," Sandy said, patting Harley on the head as she ushered them into the exam room. "I'll get Dave, it will just be a minute."

I came into the exam room and swooped Harley up with both arms under his chest and belly and landed him on the exam table. "One of these days, you won't be able to do that, Doc!"

Frank said. "What brings you and Harley in to see me today?" I asked Frank with some concern in my voice. I knew things must be hard for

them without Kara. She was the world to both of them.

"Well, I'm telling you Doc, old Harley here is not eating. I tell you that, and Sandy tells me he is not losing any weight. Now, how can that be, Doc?" Frank asks.

"He must be eating something. Maybe he is cleaning up the grain after the cows," I said.

"No! He doesn't eat a bite of his dog food. The only thing he eats is what he begs from me at the table. Maybe I give him more than I figure," Frank says.

I did a full exam on Harley, something I do with every patient. Start at the nose and end at the tip of the tail.

"Everything looks fine, he just needs to lose some weight, like ten pounds for a starter," I said as I lift Harley off the table. He is happy now, no shot, and he knows a treat is coming. He snatches the treat out of my hand, and it is gone in a second.

"One thing I never understand about dogs," I said, "that treat touches his tongue of a tenth of a second, but he thinks it is the best-tasting thing in the world right now."

"One thing I never understand about you vets," Frank says, "You tell me he needs to lose weight, and then you feed him. Now, don't you go and try to sell me some of that damn expensive dog food you have. He won't eat a bite."

"I won't sell you any dog food. You just have to stop feeding him from the table. And I give him a treat so he will like coming back here. You know I have some patients who don't think well of me." "Okay, Doc, I'll quit feeding him from the table. But you know, Kara has been gone for over a year now. There's not a lot of joy in our house, for Harley or for me. Feeding him from the table is something we both enjoy."

"I know you guys have gone through a lot in the last year or more, but you want this guy to be around for a while. Don't kill him with kindness. You eat your dinner, don't look at him, or put him outside. Then you go outside and throw the ball for him a little. Don't get so vigorous that he tears out a knee, just a little exercise. Then you sit on the front porch with him while he eats his dinner." I explain.

Dave Larsen

"You think that will really work, Doc?" Frank asks.

"It might take a few days or a week or so. If the ball isn't his thing, go for a little walk with him. What you do is not important, just spend a few minutes with him. It might even make you feel better." I reply. "Now you do that, and then you come back in a few months, and we'll talk again while Sandy gets a new weight on Harley. It doesn't have to be an office visit."

As is often the case, it was over a full year before I heard anything from Frank. He had called, wanting me to look at a cow that was not coming into heat. Frank had a small place and maybe a dozen cows. He usually borrowed a bull from one of his neighbors. Not the best practice, but they were all small farms, and most of the herds were very stable. So there was not a significant risk of introducing a reproductive disease. It also meant that he needed to get his cows all bred within two cycles, three cycles at the most. He had not seen this cow in heat since he picked up the bull almost two months ago. If she didn't cycle soon, she would miss her chance to get pregnant, and Frank would have to send her down the road to the sale barn.

When I turned into the driveway, I could see Frank and Harley down by the barn. It looked like they had the cow in the small corral. Frank did not have a squeeze chute, so we would have to rope her and tie her head. That would make the job a little more difficult.

Frank's farm was neat as a pin. This reflected his German roots. There was nothing out of place, any manure in the corral would be quickly picked up and placed in the manure pile at the back corner of the barn. When Kara was alive, I would have to be watchful when I was working on a cow. She would be picking up manure as it fell, I would have to dodge the pitchfork as best I could. The house was close to the road, a small house with a large front porch, painted off-white with new black shingles on the roof. The yard was large, both front and back, and unlike the majority of farmhouses around here and where I grew up, the front door was used as the main entry. Today I noticed a new car, a little blue Ford, parked outside the garage behind the house.

Frank and Harley were quick to greet me when I pulled up to the corral. I opened the back of my truck and pulled out the rope. "How are things, Frank?" I asked. "It looks like you and Harley
a little brighter than when I last saw you at the clinic. Harley is trimmer, too."

"Yes, things have been going pretty good lately. Old Harley expects me to throw the ball a little every night, just like you suggested, Doc. I think it's has helped us both," Frank said.

"Let's get this cow looked at," I say as I crawl over the fence with my rope in hand. I toss the lasso at the cow as she turns to the left to avoid the throw. The rope neatly falls over her head. I pull it tight and throw the free end over the fence to Frank.

"Take a wrap around the post there and take up the slack as I pull her into the fence," I say as I start to pull the cow toward the fence. She probably has a name, I think to myself. She is tame, almost seems halter broke, and getting her snubbed up the post is not a problem.

"Give me some slack, Frank, and I'll get a loop around her nose so she doesn't choke herself," I said.

Frank let out some slack, and I pulled a loop of the rope through the lasso and looped it over her nose. This essentially makes a halter and prevents the noose from tightening around her neck and choking her.

"Okay, Frank, if you could grab that other rope in the back of the truck, I'll sideline her so I can do a rectal exam without chasing her rear end."

Frank handed me the rope, and I threaded it around her neck and between her front legs, so when I closed the loop with the quick release latch, it includes her right front leg. This is also to prevent her from being choked if she struggles. I strung the rope down her right side and took a wrap around the next fence post. When I pulled it tight, it held her left side against the fence. This will allow me to do a thorough rectal exam with my left arm. I am right-handed, but we were trained to use the left hand for rectal exams, so your right hand would be free to make notes or whatever is necessary.

"What's her name?" I ask Frank.

"Kara called her Flossy. She was a favorite of Kara's. That's one reason I am anxious to get her pregnant. Well, in reality, it probably doesn't matter Doc, I wouldn't sell her anyway," Frank explained. I pulled the fingers off a plastic OB sleeve and pulled it on my left arm. Then I put a latex exam glove on my left hand and pulled the fingers off another OB sleeve and pulled that on. This will give me full digital sensitivity and protect my hand and arm from manure. After applying ample lube to my gloved hand, I grasped Flossy's tail with my right hand and eased my left hand into her rectum. I removed several handfuls of manure from her distal colon. Then I inserted my hand and arm up to my elbow. I swept my hand over the brim of the pelvis. This was going to be an easy exam. The uterus was full. Flossy is pregnant, judging from the size of the cotyledons, those 'buttons' where the bovine placenta attaches to the uterus, I would say she was four months pregnant. I removed my arm and pulled off the sleeves, being careful to turn them

inside out as I removed them. "That was quick," Frank says.

"What is the most common reason a cow doesn't cycle?" I ask Frank.

"How the hell do I know, that's why I hired you," he replies.

"Flossy is pregnant, probably four months along," I say. "Impossible, there hasn't been a bull on the place since last year,"

Frank says emphatically.

"There's no question about the pregnancy, and time will confirm that. Just have to wait about five months. So there had to be a bull here somehow. Are you sure a neighbor's bull didn't jump the fence?" I asked.

"No way, there's nothing here except the cows and a couple of steers. They are getting near market weight," Frank replies.

"How were the steers castrated?" I ask.

"I banded them when they little, they're about two years old now," Frank replied, a little defensive now.

"You must have missed a testicle on one of them. That's a common error. You think you have both testicles in the scrotum, then when you release the rubber band, one testicle slips through the band above the scrotum. The majority of retained testicles will not be fertile, but in reproduction, 100% certainty is difficult to obtain," I explain.

"That's sort of academic now. Flossy is pregnant, and you might find you have one or two of the other cows calving early this year. The steers will be at market soon, so that issue is fixed. Next spring, give me a call and I'll show how to castrate young calves with a knife. That solves this problem as long as you can count to two. Plus, you end up with some nice mountain oysters to fry up," I say. "I don't know about mountain oysters. We have enough problems with regular stuff around here anymore. Peg has been doing

the cooking lately," Frank says. "Peg?" I ask.

"Margaret McFadden, we call her Peg, me and old Harley," Frank replies.

"Yes, I know Margaret. She and Hank used to come into the clinic. I think Hank died a few years ago," I said.

"My neighbor talked me into going to the Senior Center downtown. You know, a man can't walk into that place alone without being jumped on by half the old women in the place," Frank says as he explains their meeting. "Anyway, Peg was sort of quiet, like me. We hit it off pretty well. She has been coming out here and trying to get things straightened out."

"So that must explain that new little car up at the house," I say.

Peg was a short woman, thin but rather striking for an older gal. Her gray hair still had streaks of black in it, giving a hint to her jet black hair that she was younger. Her facial features were almost stern until she smiled. If she had a defect, it was the prominent mole on the right side of her jaw. I often found myself looking at it rather than at her eyes. I am sure it bothered her some because she would usually cover it with her hand when she was talking. I often wondered why she didn't have it removed.

"Yes, that's Peg's car. She doesn't like to ride in my old farm truck. She's sort of a city girl, you know," Frank says. "For the most part, we get along fine, been talking about getting married, or at least living in the same house. But you know what they say, a skinny woman probably doesn't like to cook. You go into a restaurant operated by a skinny woman, and you get good salads," Frank said.

"You might have to do the cooking, Frank," I said

Frank replied, "Well, taking a line from Red Skelton on that subject, 'Now, I'm not saying anything about her cooking, but she sure cured old Harley from begging at the table,' ". ~

Yuri Andropov (you're a drop-off), with Puppies on Board

"What do you think, Doc?" Bert asked.

"They are just drop-offs," Jan added. "We don't want to spend a lot of money, but my gosh, we have to do something for the poor little things."

"How do you get so lucky to have two of them dropped off?" I said. "Even for dachshunds, they look pretty thin." I lifted the skin on the back of the smaller one's neck. It held that position for several seconds before slowly returning to normal.

"She's dehydrated, not breathing well, her abdomen feels empty, and she's skin and bones. I don't know; she may have a diaphragmatic hernia. That would be my guess, but we'll need to get an x-ray to confirm that suspicion," I explained.

"I don't know," Jan said, looking at Bert for a clue as to what he was thinking. "Can we do something simple, just to get some meat on their bones? There's really no need to take an x-ray because we aren't going to fix anything on a stray dog."

"Okay, let us hang on to them for a couple of hours. We will check a fecal exam and do a good exam. It could be a little deworming medication, some good groceries, and some TLC help. If not, we can decide on another course of action in a couple of weeks. What do you call them, by the way, just for the record?"

"I don't know; we've only had them overnight," Jan replied. "We will think about that over the next couple of hours."

The fecal exam showed a massive infection of both roundworms and hookworms. Roundworms were almost always present in young dogs around Sweet Home, but it was unusual to see hookworms. "A good dewormer and some canned food might do these pups a world of good," I said to Dixie. "Give them a couple of weeks, and they will look like new dogs."

The larger of the two pups had a normal exam, plus a thirty-day pregnancy. That will add to the stress of recovery.

Palpation of the abdomen of the smaller of the two revealed almost no content in the anterior abdomen, and the empty abdomen allowed for the easy detection of a similar thirty-day pregnancy. My guess was she had a diaphragmatic hernia—the wall between her chest and abdomen was ruptured. Dogs can live with this injury for a time if they survive the initial insult. Sooner or later, it will require surgical repair if the patient is going to survive. This growing pregnancy was going to be a problem for her respiration. Bert and Jan returned to retrieve the pups in the late afternoon.

"We have decided on Anna and Maria for names," Jan said. "Any preference on which name goes with which pup?" I asked.

Jan looked at the two little dogs watching her closely from the kennel.

"Let's call the small one, Maria," she said.

"Anna checks out pretty good. They're both skinny and have a heavy burden of intestinal worms. We gave them some medication for the worms, and some good groceries will help put some meat on their bones."

"That's good," Jan said. "We're just going to do the basics for them. As far as we know, they could be gone tomorrow."

"But that is only the half of it," I said. "They're also pregnant. You guys really hit the jackpot."

"And how does Maria check out?" Bert asked.

"Her problem is she very likely has a large diaphragmatic hernia. My guess is her liver, stomach, and a lot of intestines are in her chest. Sooner or later, this will become life-threatening. And as this pregnancy gets closer to term, her respiration may become an issue."

"Do you think she can survive the pregnancy?" Bert asked.

"I don't know. I think the best recommendation would be to spay her and repair the diaphragmatic hernia now."

"She's just going to have to make do," Jan said, glancing at Bert with a bit of a frown. "We've decided that we're just going to do the basics for now."

"I understand that completely and they're probably lucky they found your house," I said. "Make her a bed so she can sleep with her head and chest elevated. That will help with her breathing."

"That's just the way it's going have to be," Jan said.

"I know, but these little dogs grow on you after a while. Your thinking might change in the future."

With that, the visit was over. Anna and Maria slipped into the recesses of my memory for the time being.

A full six months later, Jan had Maria on the exam table waiting for my evaluation. Maria was a completely different dog; no longer skin and bones, she almost looked like a typical dachshund.

"You can't imagine how many dogs we had running around with all those puppies," Jan said. "But they're all adopted, and that was a chore in itself. Anna has even found a home. But Maria has her chest problem. She had to sleep in a box with her nose held in the air when she was pregnant. We've decided we need to repair her chest."

"We know this hernia is at least six months duration, maybe longer," I said. "Maria might have some permanent lung damage."

"So, what are our options?" Jan asked.

"Not many options," I said. "Fix her or not is just about it. If we repair the diaphragm and get the lungs to expand, we're probably home free. I have to hedge a little because her lungs have been collapsed for a long time, and we may have difficulty expanding them. If everything goes well, we can spay her at the same time." I looked at Jan with a curious eye. She was really attached to Maria now. I remembered warning her that these little dogs would grow on her.

"When do you want to do the surgery?" Jan asked.

"I think my surgery schedule is petty open right now," I said. "We can schedule her any morning at your convenience, but the sooner, the better. We can monitor her all day. She'll need a chest tube after surgery, maybe for the afternoon, maybe for several days. I don't like to send them home with a chest tube."

"Let's take her back and snap a couple of pictures of her chest," I said as I handed her off to Dixie. "It will only take a minute, and we'll have them for you to look at in the morning."

"You warned me that I would get attached to her. I didn't really believe you at the time. But she is so sweet, I think she's part of our family now."

"No breakfast in the morning and have her here at eight."

With the x-rays taken, Jan took a deep breath and gathered Maria up in her arms, kissing the top of her head. She looked at me with some concern on her face. "This is a serious surgery, isn't it," Jan said. "Yes, it is a serious surgery," I replied. "It would have been more serious had we done it when Maria was first dropped off. Her condition at that time would have made it very risky. I can do this surgery, Jan. It's not something that I do every week, but I can do this. She's in good hands."

"Doctor Larsen, I'm not questioning your skill. I just feel so guilty," Jan said.

"You should always question a surgeon's skill, for your dogs and for yourself," I said. "You have no guilt here. If there's any guilt, it's for the people who dumped her at your driveway."

The x-ray showed Maria's chest's left side was filled entirely with abdominal content, liver, stomach, spleen, and intestines. No wonder the abdomen was mostly empty on palpation. The chest's right side was intact, but there was some compression from the left side content. This was going to be a challenging repair.

Jan was prompt in the morning, coming through the door a few minutes before eight in the morning. We were ready for her. I usually did not start surgery until ten leaving some time for early morning appointments and emergencies. But with this surgery, I wanted to get through it as quickly as possible so we would have the whole day to observe Maria's recovery.

We were brief at the check-in. I went over the x-rays with Jan. They were dramatic films, even for a novice. Then we had Jan sign a release for surgery and say her goodbyes.

"If we get exceedingly lucky and can pull her chest tube this evening, I'll probably send her home," I said. "I wouldn't plan on that, but it's possible. You should check by in the late afternoon. I'll give you a call when I'm out of surgery to let you know how things are going. This is a major operation, and there's a possibility we could lose Maria. I wouldn't expect that, but there are some pitfalls we have to get across."

"We know you'll do your best. That's all we can ask for," Jan said with tears welling up in her eyes. "I'll see you late this afternoon." We went right to the surgery with Maria. I placed an IV catheter in her right front leg and started IV fluids at a slow drip. It only took a couple of minutes to get her under anesthesia and on the gas machine. I double-checked the seal on the endotracheal tube. When we opened her abdomen, we would have her on positive pressure breathing. Due to her small size, we had her on a non-rebreathing circuit. We would have to breathe for her using the bag in the circuit.

When she was prepped and draped, I made a long incision on the ventral abdomen. I needed an incision that would allow me the repair the diaphragm in the anterior abdomen and one that would also allow for the removal of the uterus.

I would repair the hernia first, and if all went well, we could do the spay. If there were problems, the spay could easily wait for another day.

Almost all the entire abdominal contents were in the chest, passing through a large rent in the diaphragm's left side. Maria had most likely been hit by a car. At her small size, she was lucky to have survived the severe blow that would have been required to cause this size of a diaphragmatic hernia.

I started carefully pulling the contents back into the abdomen. The intestines were easy. The spleen and stomach proved a little bit of a challenge. The liver took some careful manipulations to pull it out of the chest without injury. After all the content was back in the abdomen, I packed off the large rent in the diaphragm with some lap sponges.

Now we needed a little luck to expand the left lung lobes that have been collapsed for over six months. Using the bag, we put slow, steady pressure in the circuit to expand the lungs. Much to my surprise, these lung lobes expanded quickly, turning from a dense reddish-brown color to a fluffy pink in no time at all. There were just a couple of small areas along the edges of the diaphragmatic lobes that failed to expand. My guess was they would return to normal after a few weeks of normal respiration.

With the lungs expanded to fill the chest, my concerns about a chest tube being needed for several days were probably unfounded. I placed a chest tube and attached a Heimlich valve.

That done, I just needed to close the tear in the diaphragm, evacuate the air from the chest to form a good vacuum, and we would be done with plenty of time to do the spay.

I routinely closed the abdomen. It was a long incision. I was reminded of Dr. Annes' comment from school, "Incisions heal from side to side, not end to end. Always make your incision long enough to get the job done".

Maria recovered quickly. I think she felt so much better with a fully functional chest that there was little post-surgical pain to control. I called Jan with a report on a successful surgery, and the news was warmly received.

By the middle of the afternoon, we were able to remove the chest tube. Maria was dancing a jig around Jan as they started out the door. One happy dog with a new lease on life and one happy client.

"We thank you, Doctor Larsen, and now Maria will be well enough to be adopted. That will be hard, but I have a special young boy in mind who can use a pet." ~

Snake Bit in Sweet Home

I always told folks that if they wanted to get a veterinarian to treat salmon disease in the dog, don't go to Kansas. Likewise, if you're going to get a veterinarian to treat a snake bite, don't come to Sweet Home, although I have treated one local snake bite, and it was on a horse.

That call came in the early afternoon on a hot August day of 1977. "Doc, I have a horse with a large swelling on his chest," Bob said. "I was wondering if you could come up and get a look at him." Bob was a young man, maybe a few years older than I. He was well built, and his skin was deeply tanned. I suspect it was a farmer's tan. He wore a wide brim hat with a snakeskin band on it. "Sure, Bob, I can get up this afternoon," I said. "I'll need directions, and maybe a hint as to what you think might have happened."

"I live on a small place upon the top of Fern Ridge," Bob said. "It's on the right side of the road, has a large white house and an old barn, you can't miss it."

"And do you have any idea what happened to the horse?" I asked again.

Bob pointed to the band on his hat. "We have a few of these critters around up there. We see them more this time of the year.

They tell me there is an old rock quarry over the hill from us a little way."

A little later, I pulled onto Bob's place. He had the horse tied to the fence a short distance up the hill from the barn. I surmised that what Bob was seeing was a large abscess if it was a snake bite. I was not confident that a snake could strike a horse in the chest, however.

Looking at the horse, a large grey gelding named Joe, everything was fine except for the sizable fluctuant swelling on the right side of his chest, over his pectoral muscles.

I shaved the swelling. There in the middle of the swelling were two deep, red fang marks.

"It must be a snake bite, alright," I said. "I don't see how a snake could strike this high."

"I have this road that runs up the hill, and there's a steep bank on one side," Bob said. "It could easily happen if the snake was on that bank."

"How many snakes do you see around the place?" I asked. "Not many, this one," Bob says as he points to his hatband. "And the one that bit the horse. That's enough for me. Folks say this is about the only area where they're found around Sweet Home." "How did you find that one?" I said, pointing to the hatband.

"I walked into the barn one afternoon, the cat was standing in a corner with a mouse in his mouth. This snake has him cornered in a standoff," Bob says, pointing to his hatband again. "I ran back to the house and got my twenty-two pistol and decided the argument in favor of the cat."

"Some story, that might make a person a little worried about doing anything under the barn," I said.

"For sure," Bob said. "What do you think about this bite on the horse?"

"I think this happened a few days ago, maybe more," I said. "Just a big abscess right now. I'll open that, drain the pus and flush the wound. Then give antibiotics and tetanus vaccination, and that should do it. You'll need to keep the area clean and sprayed for flies. I'll come back in a few days and remove the drain. It should be a piece of cake. If he was a racehorse, I would be a little worried about whether that muscle under this abscess was damaged, but it shouldn't be a problem. And if it was damaged, there isn't anything we could do about it."

So that was about that. I scrubbed up the area. I injected a little Lidocaine before making a sizable hole in the abscess. The pus that drained was really rank smelling, not typical at all. After flushing the wound with hydrogen peroxide and followed with Betadine, I sutured a Penrose drain in the opening and gave a hefty dose of long-acting penicillin and a tetanus booster.

After spraying the whole area for flies, Joe was fine until the fly spray but settled right down when it was over. I tossed the can of spray to Bob. "Twice a day, the more, the better. I'll be back on the third day and check things over and get the drain out. I would expect things to heal fine."

That was close to the extent of my snake bite experiences in Sweet Home until one evening when a guy comes through the door right at closing time. He has his wife and five kids and a hound dog with him.

"We just moved into town a few minutes ago," Jim says. "We moved from Susanville, California. This hound was snake bit a couple of days before we moved, I was hoping you could get a look at him. He's really swollen."

So the bite was at least three days ago. This was probably going to be a replay of the bite wound on Joe.

Jim lifted Burno onto the exam table. Burno was a large bluetick hound. He had more black on him than many blueticks but some black ticking on white on his legs and front shoulders. His exam showed an elevated temperature and a submandibular abscess.

"I was afraid the swelling was going the shut off his airway," Jim said.

"It's pretty loose. Shouldn't be a problem just yet," I said as I opened Burno's mouth and used my finger to explore the back of his mouth and upper airways.

"How do you do that without getting bit?" Jim asked.

"I keep my thumb on the roof of his mouth with quite a bit of pressure," I said. "That keeps his mouth open, that and then you have to be quick. His airway is fine. This is just a large abscess at this point in time. I'll drain it with local anesthesia, flush it, and place a drain for a few days. That and antibiotics should be all he needs." Burno's treatment was identical to Joe's except for the tetanus vaccine. Dogs are pretty resistant to tetanus and are not routinely vaccinated.

I have talked to veterinarians in other areas about how they handled snake bites, and there is a wide variety of opinions.

Antivenom is expensive, but so many veterinary patients survive without it.

So now, having treated two cases of snake bites, both multiple days old, I could almost call myself a novice. ~

A Cat's Breakfast

I could see Bill and the hired man bringing the cow down from the upper pasture as I pulled up to the squeeze chute. This cow had a dead calf this morning. Bill was unsure what went on, but he was just starting into the calving season and wanted to make sure he didn't have a problem.

"She looks like she is in good shape," I said, as they ran the cow down to the squeeze chute. "Do you have any idea when she was due?"

"I told Mary Jane that you were going to chew me out for not having had the herd preg checked this year," Bill said. "The calf looks pretty good size. I would guess she was near full term."

"I'm going to take the tractor back up there and get the calf," the hired man said as he started up the tractor.

"We just want to make sure we don't have a problem that's going to go through the herd," Bill said.

"I'll draw some blood for this cow and from her dead calf if I can. And I'll get a sample of her afterbirth from a cotyledon and samples from the calf. The lab will be able to give us a pretty accurate diagnosis if it's something important. But, a lot of the time, maybe I should say most of the time, they won't have an answer." "Mary Jane wants you to get us on your schedule to do some pregnancy exams this fall," Bill said as I was finishing up with the sample collection from the cow.

"That will be good, I have a sheet of recommendations on breeding times and when we should do the exams," I say. "It is good to try to get your calving season down forty days or less. It takes a few years to get there for most herds, but you'll enjoy life better once we make it."

"I wonder what is taking Don so long to get that calf?" Bill said. "It's only halfway up the field. He should have been back here a long time ago."

Bill had no more than uttered the words when the tractor came into view. He had the calf in the front end loader.

"I got up there, and the calf was gone," Don said. "I looked all over and finally found it up at the top of the field, on the other side of the fence. And you need to take a look at this."

Don pulled the calf out of the loader and stretched it out on its back. This calf had a half dozen large chomps along the margin of the rib cage that opened the abdomen. The entire liver was gone. "What the heck do you suppose did that to this calf?" Bill said. "A cougar did this," I said. "Look at the size of these chomps along the ribs." I placed my fingertips along the width of the bite marks, spreading them wide enough to cover each bite mark. "This was a large cat, look at the size of these bites."

"Yes, large enough to pick this calf up and haul it over a hundred yards up the hill and carry it across the fence," Don said.

"It's eleven in the morning and that field is right beside the county road," Bill said. "This cat situation is getting a little scary." "When I first came to Sweet Home, I seldom heard a story of a cougar," I said. "Now I hear stories almost every week. When they stopped hunting them with dogs, it changed the cats' behavior. Even the hound guys tell me that their behavior has changed. Their dogs get tore up by cougars if they corner them. When they were hunting them, they would run to a tree. The cats have lost any fear of man and most fear of dogs.

"They see cougars downtown all the time nowadays," Don said. "Several things have happened," I said. "The environmentalists will say we are invading the cats' territory, but with all the land use laws, things have not expanded around most towns in western Oregon. What has happened is the National Forest has stopped most timber harvest. So now there are few clear cuts in the high country. Clear cuts are where all the production happens. All the logging has moved to private lands, most of those lands are located closer to towns. The deer and elk need a lot of browse and they don't get it in the timber, so they move to where the clear cuts are located. The cats follow the primary food sources. With not much hunting, the cat population expands, and they tend to end up in town once in a while. They find hunting cats and dogs pretty easy living. Encounters are only going to get more frequent as time goes on."

"What can a person do to change things?" Bill asked.

"Probably not much, a lot of people are champions for the cat," I said. "Hunting without dogs does very little to control their population. They can be right beside you in the brush and you'll never see them. Don was probably lucky this cat didn't want to argue over who owned this calf."

"I never thought about that," Don said. "He probably wasn't far away when I took it."

"I had a client tell me a story not long ago," I said. "His dog was very mean—one of those dogs that I see only to get a rabies shot into every three years. This dog was so mean that he bit the owner more than once in a while. This guy was telling me he was walking along a cat road through some small timber with his dog on a leash. The dog started throwing a fit, enough that the guy thought he was going to get bit. He turned the dog loose, it jumps in the brush, right beside them, and kicks out a cougar."

"The state is quick to use dogs if there's a problem cat somewhere," Don said.

"Nothing will change until a cat drags some kid out of a schoolyard someday," Bill said.

"I better get some samples from this calf. The liver is a pretty important sample that the lab asks for. They probably won't believe me when I tell them that a cat beat me to it." ~

DR. LARSEN AND ASSISTANTS PERFORMING
A MANICURE JOB ON PING-LI

The Battle of Ping-Li

It was the end of a busy afternoon when I leaned into the reception desk to check on what remained of the day.

"I'm beat. How close to being done are we?" I asked.

"You poor man," Sandy replied. She seldom gave me any sympathy. "Your last appointment is in the exam room. It's just a nail trim on a cat, you should be able to handle it okay."

I stepped into the exam room and met Al and Vivian. They were new clients, but I had met Al when I was on a farm call out on Upper Berlin Road some weeks before. Al was a short guy, stocky, and with white hair and mustache. Vivian was taller than Al by several inches.

Vivian was in immediate command of the conversation. Al would add a quip every now and then. They were parents of a long-time client and had just moved to the area from San Francisco. Al had retired from a machine shop some years earlier but continued with his passion as a western cartoonist and illustrator.

"Ping-Li is in the carrier," Vivian said. "We just need his toenails clipped. I'm on this blood thinner, and he doesn't seem to understand that I can't be his scratching post anymore."

"And, Doc, he doesn't really like to have his feet messed with," Al said. "That is why we're here. We didn't get one nail clipped last night."

"Well, let's get him up on the table and see what he thinks of us," I said as I started to pick up the rather large carrier sitting on the floor.

I was surprised at the weight of the carrier. I leaned over and looked into the carrier as I set it on the exam table.

Ping-Li was a large cat, well over twenty pounds and not fat at all. Ping-Li made his feelings known from the start with a loud hiss at my face.

"I am not sure he wants to be friends," Al said as Ping-Li hissed and jumped at the cage door.

"I think we'll get some reinforcements before we get him out of the kennel," I said. "You guys might want to wait out front."

"He is pretty much a baby at home, but it's just the two of us most of the time," Vivian said. "If anybody comes over, he generally hides. I am hoping this won't be too traumatic for him."

"Once we get a hand on him, we should be able to handle him okay," I said. "I have a couple of gals here to help who are real cat ladies."

"I don't think I want to have him sedated for this," Vivian said. "If it comes to that, we will rethink things."

"He is one of the larger cats that we deal with around here," I said. "But I think we can get him under control without sedating him." With that, Marilyn, Joleen, and I closed ourselves into the exam room with Ping-Li. The first task was to get him out of the kennel. He made it very clear that nobody was going to reach in and grab him. We opened the kennel door, and Joleen and I tipped it up to dump him onto the exam table. Good idea, but Ping-Li had himself braced against the sides of the kennel with all four feet. We shook the kennel several times before finally getting Ping-Li onto the exam table.

I attempted some soft talk and petting to calm him down. He hissed and swatted at the air close to my chest. Joleen made a quick grab for the back of his neck, and that got him a little under control. Using the extra-large cat sack, it took all three of us to get him stuffed inside and zipped up. He was almost too large.

Once secured, I did a quick once over. Everything looked okay. Every time I came close to his head, I was greeted with a hiss. Using the scale on the tabletop, Ping-Li weighed in at just under twenty-five pounds. I looked at a couple of cats that weighed a couple of pounds more than that, but they were very obese. Not Ping-Li.

Once we had him in the sack, clipping his nails was no problem. We would just unzip a bottom opening by each foot, fight with Ping-Li to get the foot out of the sack, clip the nails and move to the next foot. By the time we were done, the hiss had become a loud growl.

Marilyn checked with Al and Vivian to make sure there was nothing else. They came back to see Ping-Li in his sack before we returned him to the kennel. Vivian wanted to pet him to calm him down a little, but her efforts were met with hisses and growls.

We pointed Ping-Li into his kennel and started unzipping the cat sack. He was squirming out of it before it was half undone. He hit the back of the kennel, turned and hissed.

"Oh, I think he's mad," Vivian said

"It will probably be more difficult next time," Al said. "He's a pretty smart cat, and he'll remember you, Doctor."

Ping-Li became a regular visitor to the clinic. On most of the visits, he was much more manageable than he was on this first visit. But he continued to hate having his nails clipped, and it almost always required a cat sack to get the job done.

I liked to think most cats became our friends, or they came to tolerate our invasion of their space. Ping-Li probably came to tolerate that invasion to a degree, but he never became our friend.

Some months after that battle with Ping-Li, Al came by with the cartoon at the top of this story. It still hangs in my study. ~

It's Her Job

I stepped out of the crowding alley quickly as Ervin released the cow that I had just checked. The next cow was charging down the alley with Ella right on her heels.

Ella was a middle-aged border collie. She had been on the farm enough years to know her job well. When one cow left the chute, Ella had another one heading down the alley. The cows also knew Ella. If they failed to follow her instructions, they would have her biting at their heels.

"You trained her well," I said, as Ervin caught the next cow in the headgate.

"Wasn't any training involved," Ervin said. "She watched my old dog a couple times when she was a pup. The rest was just instinct. She loves these days or the days when we change pastures. The rest of the time, she's is just waiting for me to head for the pickup.

She likes to go to town in the back of that thing—bouncing from side to side as we go down the road and then guarding the truck with her life when I go into the store. It's only different when I pull into your parking lot. She knows that place, and she doesn't like it much."

"I see a lot of working dogs," I said. "Most of them live to work. And most of them are pretty good at what they do. But

Ella has to be one of the best. I think she has the cows trained. They just know what she wants them to do."

I had been to Ervin's place many times before, but usually just for one or two cows. This was the first time that we were working through the entire herd, checking for pregnancy status. At most places, it was a job to keep the crowding alley full and have the next cow ready to go into the chute. Not so with Ella here. She was in total command of the herd, and she worked hard at her job.

Ervin was one of the older ranchers in my practice. He was tall and thin and always looked like he shaved about four days ago. His face was long and accented by a somewhat pointed nose. The few tufts of gray hair on his head were covered with an old beat-up cowboy hat, and he always wore cowboy boots. That told of his roots coming from Montana. He was probably the only true cowboy in my client base.

We worked through Ervin's herd in about three hours. Ella was resting at the back of my truck as I was cleaning up and putting things away. Her tongue was hanging out, and she was panting a lot, but I think she was hoping that there was something else to be done.

Two days later, Ervin pushed through the clinic doors with Ella following with very guarded steps. Ella stood close to Ervin's leg as he waited at the counter. She was a little hunched up in her stance.

"What's going on with Ella this morning?" I asked as I opened the door to the back.

"I don't know, Doc," Ervin said. "She was a little slow yesterday, and I just figured she was tired from working those cows. She is getting a little older, you know. But this morning, she doesn't want to move. And she wouldn't jump into the bed of the pickup. I loaded her into the cab for the trip into town. I figure she must be close to death for her to want to ride in the cab."

Ella tensed when I started to pick her up to put her on the exam table.

"Do you think she could have been kicked the other day?" I asked. "That's what I was thinking," Ervin said. "But if she did, I didn't see or hear it happen."

I ran my hands down her back and along the muscles of her back and hind legs. There was no indication of any pain. Then I palpated her belly. She tensed at my initial touch. When I palpated her abdomen, I immediately detected a large tumor in the middle of her gut. This tumor was the size of a cantaloupe. That is a massive mass for a dog of Ella's size.

"Ervin, she has a large tumor in her abdomen," I said. "We need to get some x-rays and see if we can determine what it is and to check the status of her lungs."

"Can you do anything to help her, Doc?" Ervin asked.

"It all depends on what it is," I said. "We might not really know until we get in there and look. And then with a tumor of this size, if it is malignant, we might not buy Ella much time."

"Okay, I want to try to give her a chance," Ervin said. "I don't want to sell the farm, but let's see what we can do."

We took a set of x-rays of Ella's chest and abdomen and drew some blood if we were going to be doing some surgery. When the films were developed, I put them on the viewer for Ervin to see.

"The good thing here is the lungs look clear," I said. "But look at the size of this mass in the middle of her belly. This could be just about anything. I think the only thing to do is to go in and look. If we can get it out of there, we will do that. If we can't get it out, then you have to decide if you want to wake her up or not."

"When can you do this, Doc?" Ervin asked.

"We can do her the first thing in the morning," I said. "You can leave her overnight if you like."

"Oh no," Ervin said. "You give her something to make her a little more comfortable, and I'll take her home. If this is her last night, she'll be on the farm and beside the fire in the house tonight." "I am amazed at her grit," I said. "She worked those cows the other day just like nothing was wrong."

"Well, Doc, that's her job," Ervin said. "It's just like the old farmer out in the field hoeing his corn. A fancy city slicker comes up and asks him what he would do if he was told he was going to die tomorrow. The old farmer thinks for a minute and looks around at his cornfield. Well, he says, I guess I would hurry up and get my hoeing done. No different with Ella, she just figured it's her job." I was amazed at the size of the tumor when Ella's abdomen was opened the following morning. With exploration, it was determined to be the right kidney. Her left kidney appeared normal,

and her kidney numbers were normal in her preoperative blood. I carefully isolated the renal artery and triple ligated it first.

Then with careful dissection and ligation, I removed this mass. It was a full ten inches in diameter.

Ella recovered well and bounced out of the kennel when Ervin came to pick her up. She is an excellent example of why the closure of the incision is so vital in these dogs. I doubt that she is going to restrict herself much.

"What do you think, Doc?" Ervin asked.

"Surgery went well, and the rest of her abdomen looked good," I said. "We'll just have to wait on the report from the pathologist on what type of tumor this is and what kind of a prognosis we can expect."

"I guess it doesn't really matter," Ervin said. "We are not going to put her through any of the stuff that they put you and me through. That stuff probably doesn't buy much time anyway."

A couple of weeks later, Ervin and Ella bounded through the door. "Doc, I want to thank you," Ervin said with a broad smile on his face. "That tumor must have been bothering Ella for a long time. She has been like a puppy ever since the surgery."

"I would bet that if you or I walked around with a mass the size of a small watermelon in our gut, we would be slowed down a little," I said. "Let's get Ella up on the table and get those stitches out, and then I will go over the pathology report with you."

Ella's incision was well healed. It has always amazed me how well dogs, cats, and cows tolerated abdominal incisions. When I had an appendectomy, I didn't walk straight up for a month. Ella has probably been running around the barn and the pastures for over a week now.

"The pathologist says Ella's tumor was an embryonal nephroma," I explain. "This is a rare kidney tumor in the dog.

But for the most part, it's considered benign. So maybe we've dodged the bullet. Let's hope so, at least."

"That good, Doc," Ervin said. "But you know, at my age, and Ella's age, we just take what the world throws at us when we get up in the morning."

And in Ella's case, the world did throw her a curveball. She was fine for the next six months. She worked and enjoyed life right to the very end. Then one morning, as if that final straw was thrown onto the camel's back, Ella could hardly catch her breath.

Ervin rushed her to the clinic, and we took a set of x-rays of her lungs. Those lungs were full of cancer.

I didn't have to tell Ervin a thing when I went out front to discuss the films with him.

"I guess that pathologist didn't know what he was talking about," Ervin said.

"That's right, but we probably can't blame him much," I said. "He has probably seen about as many of these things as I have. And that is only in Ella. He was just reading out of some book for us." "I don't want her to suffer no more than she has already," Ervin said. "I think it is about time for her to buy that last lotto ticket. I have a place next to the corral that will be perfect for her." ~

The Taint That Ain't

It was 12:30 on Thursday afternoon, and we were mostly closed. Thursday afternoon was reserved for golf. But the phone kept ringing, Sandy had stepped into the back, and I was tempted to not answer. But duty calls.

"Good afternoon, this is Doctor Larsen," I said as I picked up the receiver.

"Oh, Doctor Larsen, I am so happy I caught you," the woman said. "I know you close early on Thursday."

I recognized the voice. It was one of the sisters who lived on a small farm not far out of Sweet Home. They were older, maybe spinsters, but I did not know much about them. They were Edith and Elsie, it was almost impossible to tell them apart in person. On the phone, I had no chance of knowing which sister I was talking to. Most of the time, their emergencies were minor problems or no problem at all.

"Yes, we're closed, I was just about to switch the phone over to the answering service," I said. "Is there something I could help you with briefly?"

"This is Edith, I know that you probably have a golf game scheduled this afternoon," Edith said. "But we were feeding our pig just now and noticed that he has some large swellings on his rear end. He doesn't act sick, but if he has a large abscess, I would hate to have to leave it for another day."

"Tell me about this pig," I said. "How old and how big is he?" "He's young, I think we got him in February as a weaner pig,"

Edith said. "He's growing fast, getting big enough that we are going to have him slaughtered sometime in October."

"Has he been castrated?" I asked.

"Castrated, well, I guess. Don't they usually do that to weaner pigs?" Edith said.

"Just where on the rear end are these swellings?" I asked. I was convinced now that they had just noticed the testicles on this pig. "They are just below his butt, they are just bulging out," Edith said. "They can't be normal, Doctor. We would really like you to check them."

"It sounds to me like you are looking at his testicles," I said.

There was a long pause on the phone. Then I could hear the sisters talking to each other.

"He thinks they are testicles," Edith says.

"Testicles?" Elsie says. "I don't think they could possibly be testicles. They are way too large."

Now I remembered, Edith always did the phone calls and most of the talking. Elsie just seemed to disagree with everything that was said.

"Doctor, we don't think they could be testicles," Edith says into the phone. "These swellings are larger than a grapefruit. Each one of them."

This discussion was going nowhere fast. And it was not going to be resolved over the phone.

"I'll tell you what," I said. "I'll be going right by your place on my way to the golf course. I'll stop and just get a look at this pig. If it looks like something that won't wait until tomorrow, I'll stop by on my way home and take care of it tonight."

"Thank you, Doctor," Edith says. "We were hoping you could get a look at him."

"You be ready, I'm leaving here shortly, and I won't have much time," I said. "I'm just going to glance at him for now."

"We'll be waiting for you," Edith said. "He's in a small pen, so it won't be any problem looking at him."

* * *

I pulled into the driveway, and both sisters were waiting for me. It was just a short walk to the pigpen out beside the small barn. The thought occurred to me that I might not be acceptable on the golf course if I got splattered with pig manure, but I didn't have time to put on coveralls and boots just to glance over the fence.

I could see the pig through the slats in the fence of the pigpen as we approached. This was a good-looking young pig, probably over two hundred pounds. He had a long body and black and white in color.

I approached the pen so I could get a good look at the rear end of this pig. One glance and I stepped away.

"Those swellings are testicles," I said.

"But Doctor, they are so large," Elsie said. "Are you certain? I mean, I have seen lots of testicles but nothing like these."

"I didn't make the design, that's just way pigs are put together," I said. "I'm certain, and I have seen a few testicles also. Now you probably have a couple of choices to make with this guy."

"What do you mean by choices?" Edith said.

"When pigs are not castrated, their testicles will produce products that can flavor the meat when they reach sexual maturity. This guy is close to market weight but has obviously gone through puberty. You may be okay if you slaughter him now rather than waiting until fall. Otherwise, castrating him now would be a good idea." "What do you mean when you say flavor the meat?" Elsie asked. "It's called boar taint," I said. "It's in the fat, and in bad cases, it will run you out of the house when you put sausage in the frying pan. Some people say it tastes like piss. It probably occurs in twenty to thirty percent of boars slaughtered. The larger he gets, the greater the chances that his meat will be tainted."

"We were hoping to get him bigger," Edith said. "I mean, he's growing so well."

"It might be a good idea to talk with the place you're going to have him slaughtered," I said. "Some of those places won't even consider hanging a boar in their cooler."

"A boar, I have been told you can't eat a boar," Elsie asked. "When do you start calling him a boar?"

213

"I would say about when those testicles start hanging there, so they are noticed. That's why I would suggest you either slaughter him now or have him castrated."

"And I suppose that castrating him is going to cost some money," Edith said. "That will sort of change the economics of this whole project."

"At this age, if I castrate him, it will require anesthesia," I said. "And yes, it will cost a little money. Actually, there will be more expenses than just the surgery and anesthesia. The procedure always comes with some risks, and he will lose some of his growth. That's why it's so much easier to do it when they're a few days old."

"We'll give it some thought," Elsie said. "But I think we'll go ahead and slaughter him on our original schedule. The odds are in our favor."

It was sometime in November when Edith stopped by the clinic to let me know that I was probably correct.

"Elsie still is determined to eat that pork, but I make her cook it outside on the barbecue," Edith said. "It's just like you said it would be when it hits the frying pan, it runs me out of the house. I won't touch the stuff, but Elsie isn't going to admit that she was wrong in her decision. She says it ain't too bad." ~

A Stone for His Mantel

Today was a late spring day with mostly blue sky but some heavy dark clouds. Walt was waiting when Ruth and I pulled into his barnyard. Ruth was short with dark hair. She had worked for me for a couple of years and although not a farm girl, she really enjoyed the farms we visited. Walt's farm had offered a variety we didn't often see with draft horses along with the cattle.

Walt greeted us with his beaming smile and an outstretched hand. His handshake was firm and sincere. I knew these men judged the men they met by their handshake, something I didn't learn in school, but I had learned long ago growing up around men who earned their living working with their hands.

The little steer calf was standing in the loafing shed twitching his tail and stomping his hind feet. When I moved a little closer, he pressed against his mother's hind leg. Mamma shook her head at me and moved into the corner of the loafing shed.

"He's pretty uncomfortable," I said to Walt. "How did you recognize him out in the pasture?"

Walt was a tall, thin man with a broad smile on his face most of the time. Lean does not mean that he was not strong. Slim, wiry, and tough as nails, Walt could work most men into the ground. Walt had a team of draft horses, Belgians that he used to put up his hay in the field that was next to the highway. I'm sure that many people would observe him and fail to realize how rare the spectacle was today. I always enjoyed watching the horses work and would often take the back road so I could stop and watch for a time.

"The little guy was not moving around at all," Walt said, showing his obvious concern with a fading smile. "I noticed him and his mamma standing over in the corner of the pasture, all by themselves. With all this stomping and tail twitching, I figured something must be wrong."

"He is pretty young for a urinary stone, but this is what they act like early on in the course of things," I said. "We don't see this much around here, but it was common in Colorado where I went to school."

Urinary stones in beef cattle in the Willamette Valley were uncommon, meaning that I would see a case once or maybe twice a year at the most, often going several years between patients.

It was surprising that Walt would recognize the stomping and tail twitching as enough of an issue to call me early. It demonstrated how some of these old farmers were so in touch with their animals that they knew when there was a significant problem.

"It's early yet, and he's uncomfortable because of his distended bladder. In a little while, one of two things will happen: Either his bladder breaks or his urethra breaks. When that happens, the pain goes away, but the problem becomes much more difficult to fix. It's a good thing that you called early."

The calf was easy to catch, and we tied his head and then ran the mamma cow outside. I was sure of my diagnosis but completed a quick exam. His temperature was normal, and his chest was normal. On the rectal exam, I laid my fingertip on his pelvic urethra.

It was continually pulsating. This guy had a stone blocking his urethra for sure.

I took a second rope and tied a loop in the middle of the bight of the rope. I slipped this loop over his neck with the knot lying between his front legs. The rope ends crossed in the middle of his back, ran down his sides, and came out between his hind legs. This was called a "flying W" and is a standard method to throw a cow. It was generally not used on a small calf, but we would have to tie him down for surgery.

I grabbed the two ends of the rope and pulled. The calf stiffened and fell on his side. We rolled him up on his back, flexed his hind legs, and tied each leg with the ropes in a manner that when he kicked, it would put more pressure on his back and add more restraint.

Once restrained, with me on my knees, I could palpate the length of his penis. Stones generally lodge at the point of the attachment of the retractor penis muscle in the sigmoid flexure of the penis. I grasped this portion of the penis with my left hand to stabilize it. With my right hand, I could easily palpate the stone.

"This is going to be easy," I said to Walt. He was watching closely. Most of these guys had not watched a calf thrown so easily before.

"So far, you make it look easy," Walt said.

We clipped and prepped the surgery site, and Ruth opened the surgery pack while I put on gloves. This was barnyard surgery at its best. There was fresh straw down, but the ground's softness under my knees told me we were on top of a foot or more of straw and manure.

The surgery was brief, as I had promised. I injected the area with Lidocaine for local anesthesia, grasped the penis to stabilize it, palpated the stone, and made about a two-inch incision over the stone. I bluntly divided the tissues with a pair of forceps to expose the urethra with the bulge where the stone was located.

Once this was exposed, I elevated the penis. I drove a scissors under the penis and out the other side to maintain the exposure and stable urethra and free up my left hand. I palpated the stone again, then carefully incised the urethra, feeling the stone's grit as the scalpel pulled across it. I grabbed the stone and pulled it out of the urethra with forceps. I placed it on the surgery pack. I took a urinary catheter and ran it up the urethra toward the bladder. It was just long enough to reach the bladder. We relaxed as urine drained out of the catheter.

I could imagine that the calf was feeling some relief at this point. When the urine stopped, I removed the catheter. I then ran it the other direction to ensure the rest of the urethra was open.

Now we had a decision to make, to close or not to close the incisions. I had the option of leaving the incisions open and favored this option because there may be more stones in the bladder, and they would have the chance of passing out the incision if it is left open.

Barnyard surgery is not the best in the world, and closing the incision always gave the possibility of infection. And closing the urethra on such a small calf could lead to a narrow spot that could cause problems later. The only problem with leaving the incisions open was that urine would flow out of the incision for a week or so until there was enough healing to allow normal flow.

I was getting ready to discuss all this with Walt when the calf kicked. He got one hind leg free from the restraint. He kicked again, and the surgery pack went flying. The decision was made by the calf. I grabbed the scissors, releasing the penis to return to its normal position. Ruth started gathering instruments that were scattered through the straw.

Walt was crawling across the straw on his hands and knees, concentrating on one spot. He ran his hand across the straw a couple of times. Then with a beaming smile raised his hand, he had found the stone.

"This is going on my mantel," he said, still smiling.

We let the calf up, sprayed for flies, and explained the urine flow issue to Walt.

Things turned out okay, and I will never know how Walt could keep track of that stone in all the commotion. ~

Over-sized and Pocket-sized, A Spay is a Spay

I pushed my left arm deeper into the birth canal of the young heifer, sweeping my hand left to right, trying to decide as to what was wrong here.

Then I encountered intestines, this was not good. They were too large to be from the calf. This uterus was ruptured. I shoved my arm up to my shoulder. Finally, there was the calf. The calf was in a breech position. I stuck my finger into its rectum. A contraction, this calf was still alive.

I pulled my arm out and washed. "Sue, someone must have tried to pull this calf," I said.

"Yes, my son, Joe, was here a bit ago, and he tried to work on it but said that he couldn't get anywhere."

"This heifer has a ruptured uterus. The calf is still alive. If we do a C-section, I can save the calf. I don't know if I can fix the uterus or not."

"Okay, do what you can," Sue said. "This is Sam's favorite heifer. She is kind of small, but he treats her like a pet. I hope you can save her also."

The heifer was lying on her left side. This was probably good. A right flank incision might give me the best access to repair the uterus.

For me, C-sections on cows were a chore. But most of the work was closing things up. This one would depend on what kind of damage had been done to this uterus.

We clipped and prepped the right flank, and I did an inverted L block with Lidocaine. It did not take long, and we had the calf out, and she was shaking her head as she looked around at her surroundings in this small barn.

The uterus was mostly torn off the cervix. It was held by a narrow strip of tissue. There was no way to repair this.

"Sue, this uterus is almost completely amputated from the cervix.

I don't think that I can repair it," I said.

"You spay dogs and cats all the time. Can you just remove it?" Sue asked.

The question stunned me for a moment. I looked at the torn mass of uterus and pondered the situation.

The largest dog has a uterus with a diameter less than my index finger. By comparison, this was a massive uterus. But it was worth a try. Otherwise, we shoot the heifer. If the surgery doesn't work, at least we tried before shooting the heifer.

"I hadn't given that any thought, Sue," I said. "I guess it's worth a try."

I had difficulty reaching the left ovary but with that problem solved, I placed a transfixed ligature on each ovarian pedicle. After severing the pedicles above the ovaries, I hung the uterus out of the incision. Severing the remaining attachment at the cervix was no problem. I placed a couple of stay sutures in the cervix to keep it close to the incision when I removed the uterus.

With a good twenty pounds of uterus lying in the straw, now all I needed was to close the cervix and ligate a couple of bleeding vessels. Then it was a standard closure of the external incisions. This probably all took less time than a typical C-section.

After giving the heifer some antibiotics and a Dexamethasone dose, I let her up to tend the calf.

"What do you think?" Sue asked.

"Ask me in the morning," I said. "If she survives the night, I would guess we are good to go. But don't expect her to have a calf next year."

"Is she going to be able to raise this calf?" Sue asked.

"That should be no problem. The uterus and the ovaries are not necessary for milk production."

***

"Mom and calf are doing well." Sue said when she called the following morning.

When I was out to take the sutures out of the heifer, the incision had healed well. The calf was bouncing around, happy to be in this land of the living.

"When you sell her, make sure you are honest," I said. "Some poor guy will go nuts trying to get her pregnant."

"My guess is Sam will make a pet out of her. She'll probably never leave the farm."

***

It was not long after this event when Pat called. Pat was the elementary teacher with a bunch of classroom pets. It had not been too long ago that I had repaired a fracture on a hamster's leg for one of her pets.

"It's Sally, Doc," Pat said. "She has to be days overdue for delivering babies. And now she's not feeling well. The kids think she has a problem."

"Tell me more about Sally," I said.

"Sally is a mouse. They have a gestation for something like twenty days," Pat said. "We've been watching for babies for over a week now. I am certain that she has to be four to five days overdue. I can get away for a few minutes shortly, can I drop her off for you to look over?"

"Does she bite," I asked?

"Sally is the sweetest little mouse," Pat said. "She loves to be petted and handled, and all the kids love her. That's why everyone is so upset."

Sally was just as Pat described, sweet as could be. I rolled her onto her back and rubbed her belly in a manner that became palpation. Sure enough, Sally was pregnant with what felt like eight babies. They were hard as marbles with no feeling of fluid in the uterus. These babies were dead.

I called and talked with Pat.

"Pat, her babies are dead, and there is a bunch of them," I said. "What can we do?" Pat asked.

"If we don't get them out of there, Sally is going to die," I said. "She's already dehydrated. I think I should try to do a spay on her. If, by chance, there are any live babies, we could save them. But I don't think there is anything alive in her uterus."

"You do what you think is best. The kids and I trust your skills," Pat said.

We gave Sally a dose of ketamine for anesthesia and some subcutaneous fluids for her dehydration. I used a razor to shave her belly, and with a surgical prep completed, she was ready for surgery.

With her fur gone from her belly, you could see the lumps in the uterus through the belly wall.

"I think I am going to need some magnification," I said as I put on my loupes. "Things are going to be pretty small in there."

I opened the abdomen and externalized the uterus, two horns of the uterus, one on each side, with four hard nodules in each horn, each about peanut size. The babies were long dead, and all the fluid had been resorbed from the uterus.

The anatomy was the same as a dog or cat, just a lot smaller. I ligated the ovarian vessels and the uterine body and removed the uterus with the dead babies.

Closing the abdomen required only a couple of sutures. Sally recovered slowly from the ketamine, but she was up and eating when I checked her in the morning.

Pat and her class were happy with the results, and we were paid with twenty-some pages of hand-drawn pictures with thank you notes.

The entire class brought Sally in for suture removal. Typical of classrooms that visited the clinic, some students struggled to be as close to the action as possible. Then some sought the comfort of the reception area.

Sally enjoyed the attention. And she managed to live a year or two longer than a mouse in the wild. ~

A Veterinarian's Legacy

Mrs. Dannele stood at the front counter with Dixie in her arms. Well over six feet tall and muscular, Mrs. Dannele was a large and very proper lady. My guess is she was descended from some good pioneer stock.

Dixie was a black and white Boston terrier, excited and squirming in Mrs. Dannele's arm. But Mrs. Dannele had her locked in the crook of her left elbow, and she didn't even notice Dixie's struggles as she filled out the new client sheet with one hand.

"We were Dr. Campbell's patients before he died," Mrs. Dannele explained to Sandy.

I did not get a chance to meet Dr. Campbell before his recent sudden death, but I had heard stories of him. He was well-liked and well known, even to my clients in Sweet Home. Veterinarians who die while they are in practice always seem to walk on water for many years following their deaths. I knew that from the stories about Dr. Story, who practiced in Lebanon and had died several years before I arrived.

I did have dinner with the young veterinarian who assumed Dr. Campbell's practice. At least more youthful than me, he was young, well educated, brash, and felt that he knew everything. In the dinner at a local veterinarian association event, I learned everything I needed to know about the guy. And none of what I learned impressed me. On the way home that evening, I had told Sandy that he would have trouble filling Dr. Campbell's shoes.

"Dixie is having some chronic diarrhea, and the new doctor who took over for Dr. Campbell hasn't been able to solve the problem," Mrs. Dannele said. "We have heard good things about Dr. Larsen and would like him to look at her."

"We were sorry to hear of Dr. Campbell's death," Sandy said. "We never had a chance to meet him, but we have heard nothing but good things about him."

"Yes, he was a super veterinarian and a good man," Mrs. Dannele said. "Dixie loved him, and so did we."

"Let's get you into an exam room, and Dr. Larsen can get a look at Dixie."

When I entered the exam room, Mrs. Dannele was quick to take command of the conversation.

"Good morning, Dr. Larsen, I am Mrs. Dannele, and this is Dixie. Our daughter gave us Dixie because she thought I needed some companionship when I was away from home on business. That was a good thought, but she might be more than I want to deal with away from the house."

"I understand that Dixie is having some diarrhea problems," I said as I laid my hand on Dixie's head and rubbed it a little.

Dixie was wiggling all over the table. And trying to jump up to lick my face.

"We were Dr. Campbell's clients, and we loved him. This young doctor who took over his practice is a world apart from Dr. Campbell. We just don't know what our options are at this point."

"You don't have any commitment to the new doctor," I said. "You are free to go where you would like."

"That makes me feel better," Mrs. Dannele said. "We almost felt like we were sneaking behind his back when we came here today." "There are many factors that go into a selection of a veterinarian, or any professional, for that matter. Actually, location, or proximity, is the number one factor. But it is important for you to feel comfortable with the relationship. And you should not feel guilty about making a change. People do that all the time.

"But let's get a look at Dixie," I said. "Is she eating okay?" "Yes, everything is fine except for her nasty diarrhea, and I doesn't go away. We have changed diets, and he has given us a lot of different medications. And now he wants to do some testing to check her pancreas."

"Well, the pancreas is sometimes a problem, but that is pretty rare," I said. "I was always taught that when you're out around a barn and you hear hoofbeats, you should look for a horse, not a zebra." I worked through a clinical exam and found nothing out of order except for diarrhea. There was a large drop of loose stool on the thermometer when it was removed from Dixie's rectum. I placed that on a microscope slide.

"I am going to get a real quick look at this under the microscope," I said. "And then we can talk about what we can do for Dixie."

Taking the slide to the microscope, I placed a couple of drops of flotation solution on the small sample. I mixed it a little before dropping a coverslip on the liquid.

When I focused the microscope on the sample, the field of view was covered with roundworm eggs. I would expect to see a few, maybe, but nothing like these numbers on a simple smear. Dixie had a massive roundworm infestation.

"Mrs. Dannele, when was Dixie dewormed last," I asked?

"I don't know for sure, probably when she got her puppy shots."

"She has a massive roundworm infestation. If we deworm her, it will undoubtedly solve her diarrhea problem."

"Now, why didn't he find that? It only took you a couple of minutes," Mrs. Dannele said.

"That is the difference between looking for a horse instead of a zebra."

"What do we do now?"

"We will send you home with some liquid worm medicine," I said. "You will see Dixie pass a surprising number of roundworms. It will gross you out, I am sure. It might cause her a little distress, but it will be for a short duration. I would expect her to have a normal stool in a day or two. When her stool is back to normal, we should check a sample to make sure she doesn't have some other parasite. The medicine we give her will take care of roundworms and hookworms, but there are other worms and parasites, and we need to check to make sure she doesn't have those."

"Is she going to take this medicine at home?" Mrs. Dannele asked. "Maybe you should give it here."

"This stuff most dogs will lick off the spoon," I said. "The deal is, Dixie has a massive number of roundworms. On that microscope slide of a tiny sample, there must be a hundred roundworm eggs. That type of sample is generally not a good way to make a diagnosis. I might expect to see an egg or two in a puppy with a heavy infestation. I am afraid that if we give Dixie medication here, you might have her passing worms before you get home. There is a possibility that she will vomit worms also. You don't want that going on in the car."

"We will take the medicine home and give it there," Mrs. Dannele said. "We will give you a call in a couple of days. I expect Dixie to have a normal stool by then, and we will ask you to bring a sample in to have it checked."

When Sandy called, Dixie was back to normal. Mrs. Dannele was already on her way with a sample.

"We are so pleased, and Dixie is pleased also," Mrs. Dannele said. "Now, we would like to know what we have to do to move Dixie to your clinic."

"From our view, it is done. You may want to call the other clinic and have them send her records. There is nothing more you have to do."

"I think something should be said to the new doctor," Mrs. Dannele said. "He needs to know that he missed a simple diagnosis." "You could make a statement to the receptionist when you ask for the records to be sent. The doctor would get the message." "Do you think that would be enough or appropriate?" Mrs Dannele asked.

"It is appropriate, but to be honest with you, I have met this young doctor, and he is well educated. His problem is he thinks he knows all there is to know. I doubt there is anything you or I could say that would teach him anything."

"Thank you for your honesty. We will just leave it at that. We are going to be far happier here." ~

My Calf Needs a Little Repair

"Doc, I think I have a calf that needs a little repair," Larry said into the phone.

"What's the problem, Larry?" I asked.

"One of the hind legs isn't working quite right. I think it's broken. The cow was having a problem getting it out. She got out into the oak grove up here and was twisting around and slammed it into one of those big oak trees. Is that fixable?"

"That depends, Larry. Where's the break located?" "I think it's the thigh bone," Larry said.

"Tell me about this calf, Larry. Sometimes the best medical decision is not necessarily the best financial decision."

"He is a nice looking bull calf, a half Simmental, but just a market animal," Larry said.

"The thigh bone isn't very amenable to a splint like we used on the front leg of that heifer of yours a couple of years ago. That leaves a surgical repair. My guess is the vet school in Corvallis would love to repair it, but you'll have to sell him and several of his friends to cover the expense."

"Do you think you could fix him?" Larry asked.

"Well, bring him down to the clinic, and I will get a look at him. If we cut a few corners and get lucky, I might be able to fix him. I need to know if this kind of a repair is a viable option at this clinic anyway. At least we can try. I could maybe split the profits with you."

The calf was a healthy newborn that was over a hundred pounds. He was a bit of a handful, but with several sets of hands, we could get him under anesthesia with a mask.

After he was under anesthesia, I could do a good exam. His left femur had a mid-shaft fracture.

"Larry, this feels like a clean break, but without taking x-rays, it will depend on what we find in there. I'm planning to place a couple of pins in this bone, and if we're lucky, this guy will walk out of here."

"Do your best. That's all I can expect," Larry said.

"Plan on picking him up a little after noon. This surgery won't take long, and he will recover pretty quickly," I said.

We prepped the leg and draped it for surgery. I made a lateral approach to the femur with no problem.

"I am planning to use both of those large quarter-inch intramedullary pins," I explained to Ruth.

"Wow! Why two pins?" she asked.

"This guy isn't going to lie around for a few weeks. He's going to be up following Mom and gaining weight daily. We'll try to get Larry to keep her in the barn for the first few days, but that's a bit of a two-edged sword. It will reduce his activity, but the incision will be kept cleaner out in the pasture. This repair has to be strong enough to support that activity. By stacking two

pins side by side, we provide enough strength to hold the weight, and they will control any rotation at the fracture site."

Once exposed, the fracture was a simple transverse fracture with no splintering of the bone. I placed both IM pins retrograde in the upper fragment, pushing them out through the top of the bone at the hip.

With the two pins in position and ready to be pushed into the distal fragment, I brought the fractured ends together and drove the first pin into place. When I finished seating the second pin, I was pleasantly surprised at how stable the fracture site was when I manipulated the leg.

"I think this is going to work pretty well," I said to Ruth. "Now I just need to close this up and wake this guy up."

The closure went well, and we recovered the calf in the large dog kennel.

"He is going be a lot bigger when we take those pins out in six weeks," Ruth said.

"My guess is that there's not going to be any taking those pins out. This guy will grow so much, those pins will be buried in the bone. That's probably a good thing because anesthesia is a much bigger problem in an older calf than in a newborn."

"Why is that?" Ruth asked.

"In six weeks, this guy will have a rumen that is starting to function. He will have to be starved out for twenty-four or forty-eight hours before anesthesia. Then we'll need to use an endotracheal tube rather than just a mask. Not to speak of the fact that he will be much larger and harder to get on that table."

The calf was on his feet when Larry returned to pick him up. "He looks pretty good, Doc. Better than I expected," Larry said.

"If we can keep him restricted for a few days, that would be ideal. But if he can't be in a clean stall, a small pasture would be better." "Yeah, I think I can put him and his mom in the small orchard behind the house for a time. That way, I can watch him better, and they won't have to deal with the rest of the calves."

"The other thing, Larry, those pins we put in this bone are going to stay there. When it comes time to slaughter this guy, you need to remember to tell the butcher that those pins are there. Otherwise, he is going to be pretty pissed when he runs his band saw into them."

The calf did exceptionally well. I stopped by a couple weeks later and took the sutures out, and you couldn't tell anything had happened to the leg except for the incision.

"I think you can turn them out with the herd and treat him like any other calf," I said.

Dave Larsen

The calf grew normally and became a fine market steer. He was close to eleven hundred pounds when he went to slaughter. And Larry brought the femur in to show me. The butcher had boned it out and carefully cut around it in the middle to expose the pins. Larry probably still has that bone and pins. ~

Fang

B ite wounds have always been part of the hazards in
veterinary medicine. Cat bites are the most serious
because of infection, and dog bites are less infectious but more
damaging.

Large dogs usually would tell you what they were thinking.
If they were going to tear your hand off, they would make sure
you knew it was coming. Small lap dogs would often bite
without warning. And then there was the Chihuahua.

"You have Fang coming in this morning," Sandy said as we
organized the morning workload.

"Oh great," I said. "Make sure you leave some extra time
for us to deal with him."

"With a name like that, you would think he was an ornery
German Shepard," Joleen said. "And I would take one of those
over Fang any day."

"He is just coming in for his vaccinations," Sandy said.
"Are you sure you need extra time for him?"

"Yes, once I get a hold of him, which isn't easy, it takes me
five minutes just to let go," Joleen said.

It wasn't long, and there was Bobbi seated in the reception
room with Fang sitting on her lap. Bobbi stroked Fang's head
with trembling hands. Fang's muzzle was wrinkled, and his lips

were tensed to show his teeth. He knew where he was, and he didn't like it one bit.

"What are we doing with Fang this morning?" I asked Bobbi as I came into the exam room.

"He needs his rabies vaccination," Bobbi said. "I wished he would reach an age when he didn't need those anymore."

"It would be nice," I said. "Especially when the vaccine probably protects Fang from the public health folks more than the disease these days."

"What do you mean, Doctor?" Bobbi asked.

"If Fang would be in the house with a rabid bat, the public health people would require that he either be euthanatized or quarantined for 6 months," I said. "It's a lot easier to make sure he is vaccinated."

"I see," Bobbi said. "I wish it wasn't such a chore with the little rascal."

"We do, too," Joleen said. "The vaccine is not the problem. The problem is getting a hold of him and then letting go."

"I brought his chew toy today," Bobbi said. "It might make it a little easier for you. Let him bite on it, maybe even play tug of war with him, and it might help."

"I don't know if Fang will want to play with us in this place," I said.

"Give it a try," Bobbi said. "You might be surprised."

Bobbi gave the braided toy to Fang and placed him on the exam table.

"I'll step out and leave you to do whatever is necessary," Bobbi said.

Bobbi stepped out of the room and closed the door behind her. I grabbed the toy dangling from Fang's mouth. For a second, he didn't know if he should attack my hand or fight for the toy. I gave it a pull, and he pulled back. Joleen grabbed him by his neck with both hands.

"That worked pretty easy," I said.

I gave Fang a quick once over and popped him with his rabies vaccine. Then I noticed the scars on each side of his chest.

"I haven't noticed those before," I said. "Probably because it was such a struggle to handle him before. I wonder what happened to him."

"I still have to let go of him," Joleen said as she continued her grip on his neck.

I grabbed the toy again and pulled. Fang instantly growled and shook his head, fighting for control of the toy.

Joleen released her grip and opened the exam room door. Bobbi swooped in and gathered Fang into her arms.

"This worked like a charm this time," I said. "Maybe we learned something today."

"I'm glad it made things easier," Bobbi said. "He embarrasses me when he is so combative."

"I hadn't noticed those scars on his chest before," I said. "What happened to him to get those."

"That was an awful event," Bobbi said. "It happened when we lived in California. Fang and I were walking back to the house after doing chores in the barn. This big chicken hawk came down and grabbed Fang right in front of me. It happened so fast I couldn't do a thing. The hawk started flapping his wings to take off, and Fang bent around and grabbed him by the leg. The hawk lifted off the ground with Fang chewing on his leg. They were about ten feet off the ground when the hawk let go. There was Fang still hanging from his grip on the hawk's leg. Fang finally let go and bounced when he hit the ground. The hawk took off, never to be seen again."

"Maybe that is where Fang got his personality," Joleen said.

"No, he was this way from day one," Bobbi said. "I have given up trying to change his ways."

"Well, at least we have figured out how to handle him here at the clinic," I said. "You might think about bringing him by once in a while just for us to play tug of war. He might even learn to look forward to his visits."

"I think you are dreaming, Doctor Larsen," Bobbi said.

.

A Puppy from Alabama

Rosalie was waiting in the exam room with her Boston terrier, Daisy. Dixie had just finished getting them ready for me and was waiting at the treatment room door to speak with me before I went into the exam room.

"Rosalie is in the exam room," Dixie said. "She is a new client, but she is unhappy about something. I thought I would just give you a heads-up."

When I entered the room, Rosalie stood at the exam table, holding Daisy in her arms. The expression on her face approached a frown. Rosalie was a large woman, and she was not obese, but she towered over me. She was well over six feet tall.

"Hi, I'm Doctor Larsen," I said. "What can we do for Daisy today?"

Rosalie sat Daisy on the exam table. "Daisy has had constant diarrhea for the last two weeks, and we can't get it under control," Rosalie said in a stern voice. "We have gone to Dr. Clark for years and loved the dear man. But he up and died on us."

"Yes, I never had the opportunity to meet Dr. Clark, but he enjoyed a fine reputation in the profession," I said. "I'm sure his sudden death shocked many of his clients."

"We never dreamed we would have to look for a new veterinarian," Rosalie said. "But we are unhappy with the new young man who took over for Dr. Clark."

"There are a lot of factors that go into a client's selection of a veterinarian," I said. "But, all the studies say that the number one factor is location. Driving to Corvallis with a stinky dog in the car is not the most pleasant experience."

"We live in Brownsville," Rosalie said. "So we are used to driving for many of the things we do."

"I will look Daisy over, and you can tell me all the things that the new veterinarian in Dr. Clark's office has done for her," I said as I turned my attention to Daisy. The now squirming little Boston on the exam table.

"That won't take long," Rosalie said. "As near as we can tell, he hasn't done a thing for her. We have had her over there three times in the last week, and nothing has helped."

"How long have you had Daisy?" I asked.

"My sister got her for us," Rosalie said. "She picked her up about four weeks ago, just before she came to visit."

"So Daisy is not from around here?" I asked.

"No, my sister lives in Alabama," Rosalie said.

"So, has Daisy been wormed?" I asked.

"Wormed, I don't think so," Rosalie said. "No, wait a moment. My sister said the breeder had wormed her before she picked her up."

"But, in Corvallis, did they worm her or at least check her stool?" I asked.

"No, he said he was going to submit a sample for culture if things didn't improve," Rosalie said.

"We have a puppy from Alabama, and parasites should be number one on the list," I said.

"Doctor Larsen, I don't think he knew that Daisy was from Alabama," Rosalie said. "He just did a quick exam and sent us on our way each visit. There was no conversation or discussion involved."

"Well, I know Daisy is from Alabama," I said. "And I also know that dogs who grow up in the Southeast have real parasite problems. I'm going to just collect a drop of stool material off the thermometer and get it under the microscope before we go any further."

I reinserted the thermometer into Daisy's rectum, and it came out with a drop of brown liquid suspended from its tip. I carefully transferred that drop to a microscope slide.

"This is only going to take me a second to look at this," I said as I started out the exam room door.

At the lab counter, I added another drop of floatation fluid to the slide. I mixed the sample with a wooden applicator stick. Then I put the slide on the microscope stage and adjusted the scope.

To a veterinarian who had been educated in Colorado and practicing in Oregon, this was a remarkable slide. We were accustomed to taking a stool sample the size of a peanut and putting it through a process that would concentrate and collect the eggs onto a microscope slide. If we saw a dozen eggs in a field of view, we would consider that patient heavily parasitized. I was looking at a mere drop of stool from Daisy, and the entire field of view on the microscope was covered with worm eggs, latterly, hundreds of eggs in one view. Most of the eggs were roundworm eggs, but some hookworm eggs and whipworm eggs were evident.

"Dixie, you want to make sure you look at that microscope slide," I said as I stood up. "We won't see another sample like this one, probably ever."

"Rosalie, I suspect that you will be amazed at the results of today's treatment," I said when I returned to the exam room. "Daisy is loaded with parasites. Mostly roundworms, but also hookworms and whipworms. I will give her some deworming medication. By this evening, you will see her pass an unbelievable number of worms in her stool. And the good thing is, this will probably take care of her diarrhea overnight."

"Is that all you're going to do?" Rosalie asked.

"For now, that is all we are going to do," I said. "There will be a lot of follow-up for Daisy. We should see her next week just to recheck and repeat the deworming. The life cycles of these parasites are a little complex. The medications we have today will only remove the parasites in the gut. Many others are migrating in her body or are encysted in her tissues. We will need to treat her like an Alabama dog for the rest of her life. That is a bit of history that her veterinarians need to know."

"Okay, we will see how things go," Rosalie said.

"Now remember, Daisy is going to pass a wad of worms tonight," I said. "There will be so many, it will be alarming to you, and it could cause her some momentary distress."

***

The following week, Daisy was a different puppy when she came bounding through the door into the clinic. I stepped out to the reception room to greet her and Rosalie. Daisy was squirming all over the place, trying to contain her enthusiasm. She bounced around my feet and jumped up on my leg.

"She looks like she feels better," I said.

"Oh, yes," Rosalie said. "She was well the next day, just like you said. And were you ever correct about the worms she passed. But she is a different puppy, and we are so pleased."

Dixie came out and scooped up Daisy to take her to the exam room. She had to turn her face away to keep from being licked.

"Do you think she knows we helped her?" Dixie asked.

"I doubt it. We are seldom given any credit from our patients," I said. "I think she feels so much better that she has a lot of being a puppy to get caught up on now."

"Today, we will repeat the deworming, and I will send you home with some deworming liquid to give her every two weeks for the next couple of months," I said. "By then, we should be into a situation where we can manage her parasite problem with a treatment a couple of times a year."

"Doctor, how can you make that diagnosis so quickly when the Corvallis vet couldn't find it in three visits?" Rosalie asked.

"Having all the information makes the diagnosis easy," I said. "Knowing that Daisy was a puppy from Alabama made the diagnosis before I even looked at the slide. But, for parasites not to be on the list of possible problems in any puppy with diarrhea is a serious mistake. But veterinarians are like anybody else. If your mind starts down the wrong path, sometimes it is difficult to change your thinking. It was just an oversight on his part."

"We would like to change to this clinic," Rosalie said. "What do we have to do to accomplish that change?"

"There is no process," I said. "In our view, it is done. Having Dr. Clark's office send us your records would be a plus, but if Daisy is your only pet now, that is very optional."

"How should I deal with that new veterinarian in that office?" Rosalie asked. "We are certainly not happy with his services."

"Talking with his office or sending a note to let him know the diagnosis would probably be appropriate," I said. "But if you're mad, it will probably roll off like water on a duck's back. Be informative; we are all in this business to learn. Sometimes we learn from our mistakes or oversights. That's why they call this a practice."

***

Rosalie and Daisy were regular visitors to our clinic for many years. In those years, we suffered with Rosalie's grief over the loss of her husband and then the unexpected loss of a daughter. Through all those hard times, Daisy remained a bright spot in Rosalie's life, and her visits to the clinic were always punctuated by her bouncing joy. She was one of those rare patients who truly loved to come to the clinic.

George

Jim waited patiently in the reception area with George lying at his feet. He tried to busy himself, looking at his hand, then out the window. I hurried to the next exam room so we could work George into the busy schedule.

"Dixie, get Jim into the surgery room, and I will look at George as soon as I am done here," I said to Dixie as we passed each other between the exam rooms.

George was a farm dog, and he sure wasn't much to look at, but he was a constant companion for Jim.

Jim and Joyce had a small farm out on the Calapooia River. They had a few cows, a few sheep, a lot of cats, and George.

Dixie had George up on the surgery table when I stepped into the room. George was lying with his head stretched out on the table.

"I'm sorry to be such a bother," Jim said. "I guess I never realized how sick George was. He hasn't eaten for several days, and I noticed he vomited some water in the yard this morning. Then this afternoon, I saw him take a crap, and it was like brown water."

I ran my hands over George. I could feel his ribs with no fat covering them, and I noticed a few swollen lymph nodes.

"Don't worry about the bother, Jim," I said. "We are happy to work you in when it is something that needs attention. It feels like George has lost some weight."

"Yes, I noticed that when I picked him up to put him in the pickup this afternoon," Jim said. "You can't see that looking at him with all that hair."

I lifted a pinch of skin up on the back of George's neck, and it was slow to return to normal when I released it. Opening his mouth, his tongue was shrunken and wrinkled, and his tonsils were swollen and red.

"What do suppose is wrong with him, Doc?" Jim asked.

"George is vomiting and has diarrhea, his lymph nodes and tonsils are swollen, and he is dehydrated and losing weight," I said. "In my mind, George has salmon disease until I prove otherwise. We can confirm that when we have time to do some lab work."

"Doc, I think a lot of George, but the facts are we have limited funds to spend on him," Jim said. "I don't know how he could have salmon disease, but I don't think that sounds good."

"Jim, you live on the river," I said. "There would be ample opportunity for George to get a bite of dead fish or fish guts, and I would be making the same statement if you lived in the middle of Portland."

"So, what do we need to be doing for him?" Jim asked.

"We need to keep him for a few days and treat him with IV fluids and antibiotics," I said. "He is in the advanced stages of this disease. Over ninety percent of dogs with salmon disease die within ten days of becoming ill if they are not treated. Hopefully, we can turn things around for George."

"I trust your diagnosis," Jim said. "Let's put our money into treatment rather than a lot of lab work."

"Okay, I will be able to confirm the diagnosis with just a fecal smear at this stage of the game," I said. "George will need a lot of fluids if he is going to survive."

"I need you to keep a running tab for us," Jim said. "I would guess that we will reach a point where we will have to draw a line."

"If you have a few minutes, I can give you a pretty accurate figure for the first two days," I said. "But the problem, Jim, is George will not be well in two days."

Jim looked at the estimate I handed him and shook his head.

"Doc, we will give him two days, but there will be nothing beyond this estimate," Jim said. "Do your best, but if he is going to die, I will take him home to die, where he will know his surroundings."

We hospitalized George and placed him on IV fluids and doxycycline. His fecal smear showed large numbers of fluke eggs, confirming the diagnosis.

* * *

George somewhat stabilized with treatment, but when Jim came to check on him, he was still quite ill.

"The thing I don't understand, Doc, is how come they can feed salmon to dogs in Alaska with no problem, but it kills dogs here?" Jim asked.

"It is a complex life cycle, Jim," I said. "The distribution of the disease extends from northern California to the Puget Sound. Maybe a little further on both ends; I don't have the latitudes on the top of my head. It also occurs on a similar range of latitudes on the east coast of Siberia. That range is controlled by the presence of a snail involved in the life cycle."

Jim gathered George up in his arms to carry him out of the clinic. George's eyes were bloodshot and had mucus in their corners. I doubt if he weighed thirty pounds.

I patted George on the head as I handed Jim a bottle of antibiotics and wished him luck. I was sure it was the last time I was going to see George.

* * *

It was probably two months later when Jim called for me to come by and pregnancy check their little blind heifer.

I pulled into the driveway and stopped at the house before going to the barn. To my complete surprise, George came bounding off the porch to greet me. He was back to his old self. Joyce stepped out of the house.

"Jim will be out in a moment," Joyce said. "We have the heifer in the barn."

"George was a complete surprise to me," I said. "I figured he had zero chance to survive."

"It looked that way for several days," Joyce said. "After Jim brought him home, he laid around here looking like death warmed over. One evening Jim was telling me that he would take George out behind the barn in the morning and shoot him. I don't know if George heard his comments or not, but that next morning George was at the front door, wagging his tail and looking for food. It was just like that, and he was instantly well."

George followed Jim and me to the barn, and I checked the heifer. She was two months pregnant.

This heifer had been born with tiny eyeballs in her eye sockets. Microphthalmia was a rare condition and could have been genetic.

"It will be interesting to see if she has a calf with normal vision," I said.

"Yes, it will be interesting," Jim said. "But it doesn't matter. We will keep it either way. Beth here gets along fine in her pastures."

George escorted me to the truck, and I patted his head before I left.

New Job, New Equipment

I stood at the corral fence and pondered my dilemma. I had just tried to uncoil my new lariat, and it was so stiff it was all but unusable.

"Doc, it looks like you need to drag that behind your truck for a couple laps around the pasture," Jim said. "That will take that newness out of it and make it so you can throw a loop with it. You're lucky today. This old girl is so tame you can just walk up to her and drop a loop over her head."

Jim was right on both counts. The lariat needed some work, and the cow was a real pet. She nuzzled my arm as I fashioned a halter with the rope and tied her to a post.

"How long has she been in labor?" I asked.

"I found her almost three hours ago," Jim said. "I had Dean come over and check her. He said her head was turned back. He tried to fix it, but he couldn't get it. He is the one who said to call you. Otherwise, he said I would be waiting all day to get somebody out of Albany."

I tied her tail to a twine that I tied around her neck to keep her tail out of the way. After scrubbing her vulva, I ran my left arm into her birth canal.

The head was turned back to the calf's right side. That always seemed to be the direction that a retained head took. I don't know why, or even if that was a valid observation. There was not enough room for me to reach the head.

"Are you going to be able to get it?" Jim asked.

"Yes, I think so," I said. "I am going to have to turn one leg back, so I have more room in the birth canal, but I should be able to reach the head then."

I attached an OB strap to the right front leg of the calf and pushed it back and down out of the birth canal. With the extra room now, I pushed my left into the birth canal up to my shoulder. I grasped the calf's head by its eye sockets and pulled it forward.

Then I cupped the calf's muzzle and popped the head into the birth canal. As I pulled my arm out of the cow, I paused and stuck my finger into the calf's mouth. The calf sucked on the finger. It was still alive. With a bit of traction on the OB strap, I quickly pulled the right front leg of the calf back to a delivery position.

"This is going to be a tight fit, Jim," I said. "This is a big calf for this cow. That is probably why the head got turned back."

"I'm still pretty stout. The two of us should be able to pull it out," Jim said.

"The problem, Jim, is that once we start, that calf has to come quick," I said. "When the calf is this large, there will be some significant compression on its chest. This calf has been being pushed on for several hours. If the chest compression lasts for any period of time, the calf will die."

"So, what's the plan, Doc?" Jim asked.

"I'll grab my calf puller, and I will be able to pop this calf out in a short minute."

I attached an OB strap to both front legs and then washed my arms before going to the truck to retrieve my calf puller.

This would be the first time I used this calf puller in Sweet Home. It is brand new and looked it. When I was in Enumclaw, all my equipment was hand-me-down stuff. I was always worried that it didn't provide a favorable professional impression. But now, this equipment made me look like I had just come out of school.

I pulled all the pieces of the case and carried them back to the corral. I threw it all over the fence. Hoping it would get a little dirty and scratched up in the process.

"Doc, this thing looks brand new," Jim said. "Are you sure you know how to use it?"

"Ha! I have to admit that this is the first time I have used this one," I said. "But, I can assure you, I have used these things many times."

"I guess everything you have is brand new if you are just getting started in a new practice," Jim said.

"Yes, I sort of feel like a kid with a new shotgun," I said. "Afraid to use it until I finally walk through the brush and put a scratch on it."

"Sort like when your wife puts a dent in the new car," Jim said. "You are just happy that she did it before you."

I hooked up the OB straps on the calf to the calf puller, and with everything positioned correctly, I started jacking the calf out of the birth canal.

When the calf's chest and abdomen were pulled into the birth canal, a large volume of mucus came out of the nose and mouth. Most of this probably came from the stomach, but I quickened my pace.

The calf's hips hung up on the cow's pelvis briefly. I lowered the rod on the calf puller, changing the direction of the pull and elevating the hips higher in the cow's pelvis.

The cow strained at the added pull. She stiffened and pulled against the rope tying her to the post. She fell, stiff-legged, in a flop onto her left side.

The calf plopped out on the ground. My brand new stainless steel bucket squirted away from the cow's impact and laid, severely bent, in the straw some ten feet away.

The calf raised his head and shook some more mucus from his nose. I unhooked the OB strap and cleared some more mucus from his mouth.

Jim retrieved my bucket and pressed the edges of the bent top, sort of straightening it out a little.

"Sort of like that scratch on the shotgun," Jim said with a broad smile as he handed me the bucket.

I wiped the mucus from my forehead with the back of my hand and chuckled with Jim.

"It's good steel. It will still serve its purpose," I said.

One Large Wart

"D oc, I have a heifer that is going to fair at the end of the summer," Bruce said as he leaned on the front counter. "They tell me that they won't let her into the fair with a wart."

"That's right, Bruce," I said. "Warts are caused by a virus, and it is considered a contagious disease. They will send her home."

"Is there anything that we can do to get rid of it?" Bruce asked.

"There is a vaccine," I said. "It works, but I always try to crush a few off at the same time I give the vaccine. I guess I probably have more confidence in the crush than in the vaccine. But that is just my impression. I don't have any data, one way or the other."

"What do you mean by crushing a few off?" Bruce asked.

"If there are a few small ones, I just crush them off with a needle nose pliers," I said. "Not very surgical, but it works. You see, the virus that causes warts is intracellular. So it is slow to get exposed to the blood supply to allow the animal to develop an immunity. By crushing the base of the wart, you expose that virus to the blood supply."

"What if the wart is too big for doing that crush thing?" Bruce asked.

"Just what size of a wart are we talking about?" I asked. "Maybe I should be getting a look at this wart if you want to take this heifer to the fair."

"It is about the size of a large orange," Bruce said. "Well, it might be the size of a large grapefruit. It just hangs on her neck, just below her jaw."

"Are there any smaller ones around it?" I asked.

"I haven't really looked at it close, Doc," Bruce said. "The daughter came home in tears from the last 4-H meeting, and I had never heard about it before."

"I would suggest I look at this wart. The sooner, the better," I said. "I would also suggest your daughter come up with another animal to be on standby, just in case we don't get rid of this wart before fair time."

"We have her tied outside the barn now," Bruce said. "Sara is teaching her to lead, and they tell us that keeping her tied for a few days helps in the process. You could come by anytime."

"When is your daughter home?" I asked. "I like to have the kids around when I work on their 4-H animals, and they need to learn as much about the health care of their animals as they can."

"She is home any afternoon," Bruce said. "Are you thinking about coming today?"

"Yes, I have some time, and it will take some time to get rid of a large wart," I said.

"So, what happens to the wart?" Bruce asked. "I mean, does it just fall off?"

"Pretty much, it just falls off," I said. "When the animal develops some immunity, the normal tissue under the wart sort of cuts the blood supply to the wart, and it just falls off. Sometimes after a few weeks, you can just pull them off. There is no bleeding at the point, and the spot heals pretty fast. Sometimes, it might be more of a process on large warts. And it might take more time."

"How large do they get?" Bruce asked.

"I have seen some pretty large warts," I said. "One Holstein cow had a wart, or a mass of warts, that was on and around her udder. There was more wart than there was udder. I have seen some animals with masses of warts on their necks. So they can get pretty large."

"Okay, I will tell Sara to watch for you," Bruce said.

***

Sara was out with her heifer by the side of the barn with I pulled into the driveway. Sara looked like she was twelve or thirteen, and she was a petite girl with long dark hair that hung over her shoulders.

"This is Bessie," Sara said. "She is a Shorthorn

I petted Bessie and stepped back to look at this wart hanging from the ventral midline of her upper neck. Bruce was pretty accurate when he said it was the size of a grapefruit. The good thing, it was hanging from a relatively narrow stalk of tissue. The first thing that came to mind was that it could be cut off without too much trouble.

"That's a pretty large wart," I said. "How long has it been there?"

"It has been there several months," Sara said. "It has been growing slowly, but there are some smaller ones now, sort of around it."

I felt the wart and tugged on it a bit. Sometimes an animal will already have developed some natural immunity, and these warts will just pop off. No such luck with this one. I ran my hand over the skin around the wart. There were a half dozen small warts present. They were about the size of a pea and would be just the right size to crush.

"I think we can get this thing to fall off before fair," I said. "But one thing you should think about, Sara, is if it doesn't fall off in time, you should have another heifer ready to go in Bessie's place."

"That's what dad said," Sara said. "I don't want to do that. If Bessie can't go, I won't go."

"Okay, I can understand that. But you are putting a lot of pressure on me to make sure I get the job done," I said. "So let me explain what I am going to do. First, I am going to give her a vaccine. And we will give her a booster to that vaccine in three weeks. I am also going to crush these small warts off of her neck. That won't hurt too much, but it will make them bleed. I don't want you to clean up that blood until tomorrow. Tomorrow you can shampoo the blood out of her hair coat and comb it if necessary. If it bleeds when you do that tomorrow, just let that happen, and don't clean up the new blood until the next day. It is important that the blood supply is exposed to where I crush those small warts."

With the explanation out of the way, I gave Bessie a subcutaneous injection of wart vaccine behind her elbow where any lump would be unnoticed. Then, I crushed each of the small warts surrounding the large wart with my needle-nose pliers. Bessie shook her head a little when I crushed the warts, but that was her only reaction. She was dripping blood from the area when I was finished.

"I will be back in three weeks," I said. "If we are lucky, this big wart might be ready to fall off by then. If not, I will give Bessie another dose of vaccine, and we will wait another few weeks."

"What is it going to look like when it falls off?" Sara asked. "I mean, is she going to have a big scar?"

"I think it will heal up and have hair covering any scar by fair," I said.

***

Three weeks passed in no time. Bruce was out with Sara this time when I arrived.

"Doc, I think this thing is just about ready to fall off," Bruce said.

"That's a good thing," I said. "Let me get a look at it."

All the small warts were gone. This large wart was half detached, and it would probably be ready to fall off by next week. Pulling it off now would cause some bleeding, and we had plenty of time to resolve things before the fair.

"I am confident that this big wart will fall off in the next week or so," I said. "All the little ones are gone. I am going to give Bessie another dose of vaccine, and I will stop by next week sometime and check her."

"That crack around the side of that thing looks a little nasty," Bruce said. "What if the flies start bothering it?"

"You can use some fly spray around it, and you can put some ointment on it," I said.

"I have some gentian violet. Will that work?" Bruce asked.

"It will work, and it will make one hell of a mess out of her," I said. "That stuff is terrible to work with, and she will still have a purple neck when fair rolls around. Let me give you a little bit of ointment to use. You won't need much."

***

Nobody was around when I stopped by the next week, but Bessie was still tied at the corner of the barn. The wart was gone, and the spot looked like it was healing well. Bessie would be ready for the fair.

Sudden Death in a Calf

The ground was frozen solid, and I stumbled as I traveled over the uneven mud headed to the small barn. I was carrying my medical bag and a bucket of warm water, and I hoped I wouldn't splash out most of the water before making it to the barn.

Jan was leading the way with a flashlight that cast a dim beam. I hoped the batteries would last till we got to the barn and I could get my lantern out of my bag.

Inside the barn, it was just as cold as the outside, and there were no lights. The little calf was laid out in a thick bed of straw. I dropped to my knees and opened my bag. Turning on the lantern helped light up this corner of the barn.

The calf's muzzle was cold, and I stuck a finger in his mouth, and he had only a weak suck reflex.

"You said this calf was normal this morning?" I asked.

"Yes, he was bouncing around like all the other calves," Jan said. "I was surprised when I came out this evening and found him stretched out like he was dead. I'm sorry I called so late, but we were gone this afternoon, and I didn't get out to check on things until after dark. I could have missed him altogether if I hadn't almost tripped over him."

"You should convince Frank that you should put lights out here," I said. "Even a battery-operated lantern like this one would help."

"What do you think about the calf?" Jan asked.

"He has some diarrhea, but for that to cause this kind of collapse in twelve hours would be unusual," I said. "He would have been dead in the morning if you hadn't found him, and I'm not sure we can save him. This weather is pretty rough. Do you have any place you could put him where it would be warmer?"

"The garage is just as cold as the barn," Jan said. "I don't think enough of him to bring him into the house. He is going to have to make it here. This bed of straw is the best I can do. I guess we could see if we have an extension cord long enough so we could hang a heat lamp for him."

"I am going give him some oral fluids that will put a warm spot in his belly," I said. "And I will give him a big dose of IV antibiotics. If he is dead in the morning, we should send some samples to the lab. If you have a hot bug on the place, we need to know about it. We don't want any others to show up like this one."

* * *

"Jan is on the phone," Sandy said. "That calf you treated last night is dead this morning."

"You need to free some time up for me to run out this morning to do a necropsy on that calf," I said.

"She was hoping she could bring it into the clinic," Sandy said. "Just to avoid paying for another farm call."

"Tell her I will run out there for no farm call charge," I said. "If there is a hot E. coli in that calf, we don't need to contaminate the clinic."

I checked to ensure I had everything I might need in the truck. I thought I would need several samples from the calf, to include fresh samples for culture and samples in formalin. When everything was loaded, I headed out to meet with Jan.

"I don't know when he died," Jan said. "He was cold and stiff this morning."

"That doesn't surprise me," I said. "I think he was pretty close to being gone when we treated him last night."

"I know you are worried that there was something important that caused his sudden death," Jan said. "But we are a little concerned about the expense of a lot of lab work."

"I can understand that," I said. "And it is a valid concern if we send samples to the lab with a blank check. But we can hold them to some specific tests. But let me get a look first, and there might be an easy explanation."

I opened his abdomen from his chest to his pelvis with the calf on his back.

"What the heck is this?" I said, more to myself than to Jan. "His small intestine is ruptured."

There was intestinal content all through his abdomen. There would have been no saving this fellow. I searched through the intestines until I found the transected loop of the bowel.

"What could have caused that to happen?" Jan asked as she watched over my shoulder.

"That's a good question," I said as I continued to explore the abdomen. "It looks like it was strangulated. I guess I better check his belly button."

When I looked at his umbilicus, there was a large hernia present, and there was no content in the hernia.

"It looks like he had a large umbilical hernia," I said. "Apparently, a loop of bowel got in there and strangulated. The bowel must have returned to the abdomen when it ruptured, so it wasn't obvious when I treated him last night. Not that it would have made any difference, there was no saving him, probably not even with a heroic surgery."

"So, are you still going to need to send stuff to the lab?" Jan asked.

"No, this was just one of those things, sort of the luck of the draw," I said. "The interesting thing is we usually don't worry about umbilical hernias in the calf. But, obviously, they can be a problem if they are large enough."

"Are these hernias genetic?" Jan asked.

"I don't know for sure," I said. "I think they are considered genetic, but probably they don't have a simple inheritance factor. I never see enough of them to worry much about them.

When I was in Enumclaw, another veterinarian in the practice bought a bunch of heifer calves to raise. We repaired several hernias in that bunch. After we did that, those calves seemed to do a lot better. We wondered after that event if we should be putting more emphasis on repairing umbilical hernias in calves. This guy would support that opinion also."

The Check is in the Mail

I was wet as I loaded my equipment back into my truck during a brief but heavy April shower. I had just finished pulling a calf in Crawfordsville, and now I had to hurry to the clinic before I was too far behind on my morning appointments.

Dr. Craig had warned me that the cattle practice in Linn County was sort of a feast or famine situation.

"You will be so busy in the spring and fall you can hardly keep up the pace," Roy had said. "Then, in the summer and winter, you will think all your clients have deserted you."

Roy had been spot-on with that bit of information. I was up a six this morning to get out for this calf, and I am sure the appointment book at the clinic is full for the day by now. Once I get behind schedule, nobody is happy. The clients are upset and complaining, and the girls behind the desk are helpless if I don't keep pace.

I pushed a little harder on the gas pedal. By speeding, I would only gain a few minutes, but a few minutes might allow me to gain a step in the appointment book.

Dixie noticed when I pulled up in front of the clinic and came out to help me carry things in so we could clean everything up for the next call.

"We are in good shape," Dixie said. "Anita was the only early appointment, and she had some shopping to do at Safeway. She left the dogs, and they are only due for vaccines. Judy and I have them all ready for you. The only problem is Judy is on the phone right now, and it sounds like another calving problem."

Dixie and I were in the back cleaning up the calf puller and the other equipment when Judy came back and leaned against the wall.

"That was Darwin on the phone," Judy said. "He has a cow having some problems calving. He doesn't think it is too bad, but he would like you to look at her."

"What is his account status?" I asked. Darwin was one of our chronic slow payers. He always called with an emergency when he was short of cash, and then he would take months to pay the bill.

"He has two outstanding bills," Judy said. "The one is from almost four months ago. We have him marked to be turned over for collection when we do statements next week. I didn't promise him anything. I told him when you had a few minutes, you would give him a call."

"He is going to say he will have money next week," I said.

"Any time we call him on the account, he is always going to send a check, but it never comes," Judy said.

"That's okay, let's get Anita's dogs done, and I will give him a call," I said. "You might need to try to reserve a little time later in the morning in case I have to run out there."

When we were caught up, I settled into my office chair to call Darwin. The phone rang four or five times before he answered.

"Good morning, Doc," Darwin said. "Thanks for returning my call."

"What do you have going on, Darwin?" I asked.

"I have this old cow with a couple of feet out for the last hour," Darwin said. "I just thought if you had some time, you might be able to come by and help her out a little."

"Darwin, are the soles of those feet pointed up or down?" I asked.

"I never thought about it, but I think they are pointed up," Darwin said. "What does that mean?"

"That means they are the back feet," I said. "That is a common cause of dystocia in an older cow. Most of the time, we need to pull those calves."

"Can you come out and do that for me, Doc?" Darwin asked.

"Darwin, Judy tells me you have a couple of long past due bills," I said.

"Yes, I know that, Doc," Darwin said. "I can put a check in the mail to you in the morning."

"Judy also tells me that your checks never seem to arrive when you put them in the mail," I said.

"I know, Doc, but times are rough," Darwin said.

"Yes, I know, times are rough," I said. "But, Darwin, I have to make a living, plus I have to pay wages, keep my supply shelves stocked, and pay my monthly expenses. If I don't do that, I am out of business, and you are back to waiting two or three days before an Albany veterinarian can get out here to help you out."

"I'm telling you, Doc, I will put a check in the mail in the morning," Darwin said.

I recalled a story Dr. Craig had told me at one of our dinner outings. At the time, I thought it was pretty severe, but I decided to use it with Darwin.

"Darwin, your check story might get the girls in the office off your back for a few days," I said. "But it doesn't work in this situation. I will come out and take care of your cow, but when I get there, if you are not standing out at the end of your driveway with four hundred dollar bills in your hand, I will drive right on by."

"Doc, you are just like all those other vets. You are just after the money," Darwin said.

"Don't pull that crap, Darwin," I said. "I already explained why I need to be paid. I am more than happy to provide you with veterinary services. But if you aren't going to pay your bill, you can go find another veterinarian who can afford to work for free."

"Okay, Doc, my wife has some money stashed for just this kind of a thing," Darwin said. "You come ahead, and I will meet you at the driveway with the money."

"I have a couple of things to do here, so I will be half an hour before I am at your place," I said. "I will see you there. I trust that you have the cow caught."

"She is in the pasture," Darwin said. "But I can get her in before you get here."

"Okay, you get her in, and you get your money, and then give me a buzz on the phone," I said. "Once the vet arrives, those tame old cows get pretty wild if they are still in the pasture."

It wasn't long, and Dixie and I were on our way out to Darwin's small farm.

"Do you think he is going to have the money?" Dixie asked. "And if he doesn't, are you really going to drive on by?"

"I think that is a yes on both counts," I said. "This guy probably has more money than I will ever have. These guys skip out on their bills either out of habit or they think they will earn a little more interest if they wait. We haven't added a late charge to our billing, so it costs them little to wait until Judy sends them a collection notice. I think we will have to correct that in the near future."

When we came around the corner to Darwin's place, he was at the end of the driveway, and he waved a handful of bills.

"My wife put a little extra in there," Darwin said as he handed me the money. "She thought we needed to carry a credit balance for a while."

"Thank you, Darwin," I said. "Where do you have the cow?"

"She is in a small pen in the barn," Darwin said. "The barn is over the little hill from the house. It's about a half mile from here."

"Good, you will get some exercise today also," I said with a smile. Darwin sort of frowned. "I was kidding. Go ahead and crowd in, and we will let you give directions."

Darwin's barn was an older one, and it had seen better days. The cow was chewing on a bit of hay. She was oblivious to her difficulty.

261

I tied her to a corner of the pen while Dixie was getting things out of the truck. I tied her tail out of the way with a length of twine tied around her neck. Then I lifted the bucket of warm water from Dixie over the fence.

After washing her up, I did a quick vaginal exam. Sticking a finger into the calf's butt, there was a slight response.

"This calf is alive, Darwin," I said. "But, I would guess she has been in labor for some time. Often, the cow will be slow to start labor with the calf is backward. Hopefully, this calf will be okay, but another hour or two and he will be dead."

"How can you tell all that with your hand in her for a few seconds?" Darwin asked.

"I almost see with these fingers," I said, holding up my left hand. "But in this case, I stuck a finger in this calf's butt. He had a pretty weak response to that finger. A vigorous calf would pinch down hard on that finger."

I hooked the calf puller up and started cranking the calf out.

"This won't take long," I said. "I have to be fast because this calf still has his head inside mamma when his umbilical cord is pinched during delivery."

I cranked faster, the old cow had delivered many calves, and she stood the entire time. The calf came out in a flop and landed on the straw. I quickly picked him up by his hind feet and swung him a bit. A large amount of thick fluid drained from his nostrils. This fluid was probably more from his gut than his lungs, but it made me feel better to have it out of the way.

The calf shook his head when I laid him back on the straw.

"It looks like he will be okay," I said as I squirted some iodine into his navel. "We have to run to get back to the clinic. We sort of worked you into the schedule. Dixie will leave you a dose of BoSe to give his guy under the skin. You will need to make sure he is up and nursing in an hour or two. If he isn't, you need to milk this cow a little and give it to him in a bottle. Doing a little of that now might be a good idea."

We loaded up and headed back to the clinic.

"Do you think his wife was a little embarrassed?" Dixie asked. "Otherwise, she wouldn't have put extra money in the pot."

"She probably wasn't even aware of the situation with his account," I said. "Hard to say, she maybe has been giving him money to pay the bill, and he spends it elsewhere. It will be interesting to see if things are different with his account in the future."

The Porter Creek Incident

The kids were finishing up getting settled in the crowded car. Brenda, our oldest, had taken her seat on the front bench seat between Sandy's folks, Pap and Grandma. Amy, Dee, and Derek struggled to get comfortable with cousins Dustin and Darin in the back seat.

"You guys are going to have your hands full this next week with this bunch," I said as I gently pushed the rear door closed.

"We will be busy," Pap said. "But it will be a fun busy."

His first grandson, Russ, gave Pap his name fifteen years earlier. Russ called him Papas, but the name was shortened to Pap over the years. Pap was a retired longshoreman. in his sixties, he was starting to show his age.

Pap was old school. His voice was gruff, and he only said things once. His sons knew that he was not to be argued with, me not so much. He tolerated the grandkids pretty well.

Sandy and I stood and watched as the car pulled out of our driveway in Sweet Home. We were looking forward to a week by ourselves.

"Those kids are going to be tired of bumping into each other by the time they get to Myrtle Point," Sandy said as she gave a final wave. "I hope Dad can keep his cool all the way."

"They will do okay," I said. They are excited to have the whole bunch.

***

As they approached Roseburg, almost two hours into the drive, Brenda leaned against Grandma as the ruckus in the backseat was intensifying.

"Are we going to stop for lunch?" Brenda asked.

"Yes," Grandma said. "We will stop at Porter Creek. It's not far past Roseburg and Pap's favorite."

With that statement, there was a minor groan in the backseat.

"The food at Porter Creek is awful," Darin whispered to Derek.

Derek was our picky eater. That was the worse thing the Darin could say to him. Feeding Derek at home usually resulted with his mother fixing him something special every night, much to the discus of his sisters.

At a restaurant, it was a real struggle. Usually, we would end up with a plain hamburger, and I would usually have to explain to the waitress just what Derek meant by a plain hamburger.

"When he says a plain hamburger, he means plain, bread, hamburger and bread," I would explain. "That means no butter on the bun, no mayonnaise, no mustard, no lettuce, nothing! Just meat and bun."

After Pap and Grandma got the kids all seated at a couple of tables, they placed their orders. Pap took the order from the kids and relayed it to the waitress. Pap always had difficulty with the four younger kids, all their names started with "D', Dee, Dustin, Darin, and Derek. He usually had to say the whole list before finding the correct name.

Derek ordered a plain hamburger. There were no special instructions for the waitress.

265

True to form in a small country restaurant, the food came slow, and keeping the kids entertained was difficult for the grandparents. Pap's patience was wearing thin by the time everyone had their food..

Derek looked at his hamburger. It had lettuce, tomato, onion slice and pickle on the side, but the bun was loaded with mayonnaise, mustard and some kind of special sauce. There was no way he was going to eat this burger. He folded his arms and sat back in his chair.

"What's the matter, Derek?" Grandma asked.

"I ordered a plain burger," Derek said. "This has a bunch of stuff on it."

Grandma walked around the table. "We can just scrape this stuff off, and it will be fine," she said.

"I ordered a plain burger," Derek repeated. "I won't eat this."

Now Pap realized what was going on.

"Listen up, Derek," Pap said. "I paid for that thing, and you will eat it!"

Derek sat there, arms folded and a frown on his face. He didn't say anything.

Everyone finished their meals. Derek sat there frowning. He never took a bite.

Pap motioned to Grandma, pointing to Derek's burger.

"Norma, you wrap up that burger, and he can eat it when we get home or for dinner tonight," Pap said.

Derek didn't say a word as Grandma carefully wrapped the burger in several napkins. His frown deepened as he realized another battle was pending.

Everyone loaded in the car again, assuming their previous positions. Nobody dared to say anything about Derek's burger. They all knew that Pap had a temper when provoked.

The ride to Myrtle Point was less than an hour from The Porter Creek Cafe. However, Oregon's Highway 42 was notorious for its curves.

When they arrived, Grandma carefully put Derek's burger into the refrigerator.

"I will warm it up for dinner," she said to Derek. "Do you want a bite of something to tide you over until dinner?"

Pap overheard that exchange.

"If he wants something to tide him over till dinner, he can take a bite or two of that burger," Pap said, in a gruff voice.

"I'm not eating the burger," Derek replied.

"You will go to bed hungry then," Pap said.

Grandma tried to hush Pap. She could see that there was a test of wells brewing,

"Derek, you run along and play with the others outside," Grandma said as she ushered him out the door. Then she turned to Pap. "Brenda says that Sandy usually cooks something special for him at home."

"Will, this is my house," Pap said. "I paid almost two dollars for that hamburger, and he damn well better eat it."

Nothing more was said. At dinner, Pap retrieved the hamburger from the refrigerator. Norma intercepted him and stuck it in the microwave. But it eventually ended up in front of Derek.

Derek just folded his arms and sat there.

"That's your dinner tonight," Pap said. "If you don't want to eat it, you can go to bed hungry."

"I am not going to eat it," Derek replied. He sat through the meal.

When everyone got up to run outside to catch the waning hours of sunlight, Grandma caught Derek as he passed through the kitchen. She handed him a toasted cheese sandwich, and, without saying a word, pointed to the table on the back porch.

Derek sat and ate his sandwich. Grandma went in and talked with Pap to keep him distracted.

In the years following, whenever Pap's memory comes up, the discussion always seems to include the Porter Creek Incident.

Acknowledgements

How does one acknowledge the multitude of people upon whose shoulders he stands?

The many professors and clinicians at Colorado State University College of Veterinary Medicine who spent years ensuring I was prepared for practice. There were times in my years of practice when I had shortcomings, but there was never a time that I could fault my education for those shortcomings.

Possibly by accident, the US Army provided me the maturity to continue and complete my education. And Don Miller, the friend who never had the opportunity to return home, provided me the inspiration to do the same.

Many clients and their animals, both large and small, provided me the stage to practice my profession and enjoy, first hand, the stories laid out in this memoir.

The friends and family who offered encouragement for me to write. And to continue to write, even when my stories were the mere scribbles of an amateur.

Linn-Benton Community College instructor Linda Smith provided some structure to my prose. Sharon Waldman's memoir writing class planted the seeds of this book with her instruction. Classmates in Sharon's class, Julia Plante, Steve Yellan, Sharon Nixon, and Releta Brandon, showed genuine enjoyment in reading my stories.

Scott Swanson, owner and editor of The New Era, Sweet Home's weekly newspaper, has provided editorial assistance, advice, and column space in his paper, allowing me to share some of these stories with the community.

Eva Long, for her editorial coaching, designing, and shepherding this venture to completion—something that may not have happened without her expertise.

And a special thanks to Joan Scofield, for bringing her excellent proof-reading skills to this work and bringing me a little closer to being a real writer.

Photo Credits

The Needle in the Brier Patch: Dids/Pexels

Ernie's Pig: Mali Maeder/Pexels

A Saturday Afternoon Outbreak: Kat Jayne/Pexels

A Summer Evening on Strychnine: Tanino/Pexels

Dinner with Roy: Hanxiao/Unsplash

Ageless Ida and Kitty: Belén Rubio/Pexels

Gus and the Manure Pile: Pitsch/Pixabay

Charlie and Betty Land, Breeding Mares: Thibault Carron/Unsplash

Fetotomy on Whiskey Butte: Dids/Pexels

Block and Tackle C-Section: Oskar Malm/Unsplash

My First Ellwood: Nithish Narasimman/Unsplash

Gus and Blackie: Mel Elías/Unsplash

Pat's Menagerie: Alexandra-Alexas_Fotos/Pixabay

Two Down at Once: Frano Duvnjak/Unsplash

A Little Bit of Magic Helps Sometimes: Taras Kasich/Unsplash

Harry's Place: Deshawnda Dye Carver, with permission

A Few Precious Hours: Roman Klimenko/Unsplash

Blackjack and Newt: David Bartus & Mustafa ezz/Pexels

The Wicked Witch of the West: Trina/Pexels

Egor: Jozef Fehér /Pexels

Charlie and Betty, At the Track: Mathew Schwartz /Unsplash

Don't Give That Injection: Cole Wyland/Unsplash

Bill and Mary Jane: William Moreland/Unsplash

A Kitten's Tale: Pixabay/Pexels

Saved by Daisy: Dominic Buccilli/Pexels

Charlie and Betty and Foster: Ave Calvar /Unsplash

There's Gold in Them Hills: Csaba Nagy/Pixabay

The Birds and the Bees and Basset Puppies: Ben Michel/Unsplash

Dave Larsen

The Salamander's Tale: Dyann McCollum
The Painful Quill: Dušan Veverkolog/Unsplash
Rosie: Ben Sweet/Unsplash
The Angry Awn: Chris Barbalis /Unsplash
Charlie and Betty's Fish Pond: Dan Gold/Unsplash
Rambo and the Eagle: Markus Spiske/Pexels
A Market Collapse: Monika Kubala /Unsplash
The Bite of the Chigger: Lisa Fotios/Pexels
The Stone's Story: David E. Larsen
The Last Cow in the Chute: Jorge Zapata/Unsplash
Charlie and Betty, All Bad News: Mylene2401 from Pixabay
Table Manners for the Old Dog: superloop on Unsplash
Yuri Andropov...: Dayvison de Oliveira Silva/ Pexels
Snake Bit in Sweet Home: Alexis Chateau from Pexels
A Cat's Breakfast: Pixabay from Pexels
The Battle of Ping-Li: Al Martin Napoletanohas
It's Her Job: Aloïs Moubax from Pexels
The Taint That Ain't: Leah Kelley from Pexels
A Stone for His Mantel: Matt Seymour on Unsplash
Over-sized and Pocket-sized...: Colin Davis on Unsplash
A Veterinarian's Legacy: Erik Mclean from Pexels
My Calf Needs a Little Repair: Photos by Larry Coulter
Fang: James Homans/Unsplash
A Puppy from Alabama: Melissa Jansen Van Rensburg/Pexels
George: Bojan Popovic/Pexel
It's Only a Bump, Doc: Anil Sharma/Pexels
New Job, New Equipment: D. E. Larsen, DVM,
     (Same bucket, forty-some y ears later)
One Large Wart Julissa Helmuth/Pexels
Sudden Death in a Calf: Diego F. Parra/Pexels
The Check is in the Mail: Karolina Grabowska/Pexels
The Wolf Hybrid: Steve/Pexels
The Porter Creek Incident: Mart LMJ/Pexels

About the Author

D r. David Larsen grew up on a farm in the Coquille River Valley of Southwestern Oregon. Animals and their care have been a part of life from the very beginning.

Veterinary medicine was always on his radar, but it took four years in the Army to provide the maturity for him to complete his education.

First graduating from Oregon State University with a degree in zoology, he then attended Colorado State University, receiving a Doctor of Veterinary Medicine degree in 1975 at the age of thirty.

With a growing family, he moved first to Enumclaw, Washington, where he practiced for a year and a half. Then he moved to Sweet Home, Oregon, where he started Sweet Home Veterinary Clinic. He was in practice for over forty years.

Today he spends his time with his family, writing, and doing a little fishing. He and Sandy travel when they can. There is much yet to see in Oregon and the rest of this country.

www.ingramcontent.com/pod-product-compliance
Lightning Source LLC
Chambersburg PA
CBHW030912120626
46554CB00001B/122